To Ingrid,

Matt

with much
love

All the Wyldes.

"For depth of scholarship, ranging over Africa, Latin America, Asia and other regions, and acute, lively analysis of highly contemporary issues such as globalisation, the New Partnership for Africa's Development, and sovereignty versus interventionism, Dr Greg Mills' *Poverty to Prosperity* is in a league of its own."

STANLEY UYS, former political editor, *The Sunday Times*

"Greg Mills' study of the African condition has much to recommend it. The book is a genuinely comparative study of the variety of solutions attempted to resolve acute social and economic problems in Asia, Latin America and Africa. As such, the work effectively challenges the conventional Afro-pessimism. Its findings will provoke healthy debate among scholars and practitioners alike."

PROF. JACK SPENCE, *King's College, London*

"A welcome tour through the minefield of clichés and accepted wisdom about African development."

JONATHAN KATZENELLENBOGEN,
International Affairs Editor: *Business Day*

"The world is awash with observations about how African countries must learn to benefit from globalisation but few go beyond simple rhetoric. Greg Mills' new book recognises the benefits and drawbacks of globalisation and gives critically important advice to countries on how to engage with the world economy. This is an important book that should be widely read in order to understand Africa's future."

PROF. JEFFREY HERBST, *Princeton University*

"An indispensable piece of work for all those who are championing the course of Africa's economic recovery and good governance in this competitive era of globalisation."

DR PANDELANI MATHOMA, Chief Director:
South African Department of Foreign Affairs

Greg Mills

POVERTY TO PROSPERITY

Globalisation, Good Governance and
African Recovery

TAFELBERG

with

The South African Institute of International Affairs

assisted by the

Sir Ernest Oppenheimer Memorial Trust

Published jointly by
The South African Institute of International Affairs
Jan Smuts House, Johannesburg and
Tafelberg Publishers
28 Wale Street, Cape Town 8001
with the assistance of the Sir Ernest Oppenheimer Memorial Trust

Cover design and typography by Nazli Jacobs
Cover photograph © Eric Miller /iAfrika Photos
Author photograph Russell Roberts
Set in 10 on 12 pt Plantin

Printed and bound by Creda Communications, Cape Town

First edition, first impression 2002

ISBN 0 624 04179 4

Intellectuals analyse the operations of international systems; statesmen build them. And there is a vast difference between the perspective of an analyst and that of a statesman. The analyst can choose which problem he wishes to study, whereas the statesman's problems are imposed on him. The analyst can allot whatever time is necessary to come to a clear conclusion; the overwhelming challenge to the statesman is the pressure of time. The analyst runs no risk; if his conclusions prove wrong, he can write another treatise. The statesman is permitted only one guess; his mistakes are irretrievable. The analyst has available to him all the facts; he will be judged on his intellectual power. The statesman must act on assessments that cannot be proved at the time that he is making them; he will be judged by history on the basis of how wisely he managed the inevitable change and, above all, by how well he preserves the peace. That is why examining the problem of world order – what worked or failed and why – is not the end of understanding contemporary diplomacy, though it may be its beginning.

HENRY KISSINGER, *The New World Order*

It is easy to dismiss Africa, its people, its problems, its literature. It is easy to patronise Africa – all it takes is having a fairly good education and needing someone to feel superior to in order to feel good. It is easy to profess to like Africa – for the wrong reasons. It is easy to have liberal views about Africa. And it is easy to condemn, to bash, to wound, and to insult Africa – all that it takes is ignorance and meanness of spirit and the desire to provoke, to get a reaction, to get some attention.

But it is difficult first of all to see Africa. To look at it, in its variety, its complexity, its simplicity, to see its peoples, and to see individuals, human beings. It is difficult to see its contributions, to see its literature, to hear its laughter, to behold its cruelties, to witness its spirituality, to withstand its suffering, and to sense its ancient philosophy. Africa is difficult to see because it is gun-shaped and heart-shaped. It takes heart to see her. It takes some cultural and racial over-coming.

BEN OKRI, *Ex Africa Semper Aliquid Novi*

CONTENTS

PREFACE & ACKNOWLEDGEMENTS

In the two years since I wrote *The Wired Model: South Africa, Foreign Policy and Globalisation*,[1] more than noticing how correct I might have been about some issues, I have realised how many things have not gone as predicted and how I would now write some things differently. This, as the quotation from Henry Kissinger at the start of this book suggests, is the great luxury of the academic over the policy maker. But the stakes in Africa remain high, not only for those whom Kissinger terms "statesmen", but for citizens and scholars alike. In my job I have had the great privilege of frequent travel and a great deal of exposure to Africa and other developing countries. The more I am witness to the challenges of African development and of other emerging markets, the more I am convinced of the value of exploring their parallels, lessons and shared opportunities. Although the notion of "African solutions to African problems" has obtained a certain currency at the start of the 21st century – and there are many areas in which the continent faces unique challenges, at least in quantity and compounds – the opposite is also true. Globalisation has, paradoxically, stressed both the differences between states and systems and, more importantly, the commonality of the challenges and solutions.

It is, put simply, the desire both to find solutions to the multitude and magnitude of African problems and the related need to derive relevant lessons from the experiences – both good and bad – of states elsewhere that have prompted this study.

★ ★ ★

Only when carrying out a project of this sort does one realise how many friends around the world one has come to rely on for advice, insights, hospitality and constructive criticism. Many helped me along the way, but in particular I would like to single out:

- Miguel Angel Cortes, Manolo Duran, Juan Lopez-Herrera and Ambassador Miguel A. Fdez. de Mazarambroz of the Spanish Foreign Ministry for facilitating a research stay under the auspices of the Fundación Carolina in Madrid during February-March 2002.

---

1 Greg Mills, *The Wired Model: South Africa, Foreign Policy and Globalisation*. Cape Town: Tafelberg, 2000.

When in Madrid, Sara de la Lastra Becker and Cristina García kindly assisted with my itinerary; and Luisa Molinero not only patiently coaxed my halting Spanish, but provided a source of new ideas.

- Professor John McKay of Monash University's Asia Institute, Melbourne, for his and Zita's hospitality and helpful insights on Asia.
- Datuk Baharuddin bin Abdul Kadir, Dato Mustapha Khalil bin Ismail and Dato Abdullah bin Mohamed, all former Lancaster classmates, for their special kindness in Kuala Lumpur. The family meals were a welcome taste of homeliness for the long-distance traveller.
- Jennifer Oppenheimer who alerted me to the possibility of obtaining funding from the Sir Ernest Oppenheimer Memorial Trust, which generously sponsored the research behind this study.
- Tim Hughes, Garth Shelton, Dianna Games and Séan Cleary, whose commentaries on various drafts were both incisive and sympathetic. The faults, however, remain mine alone.
- Professors Jeffrey Herbst of Princeton University and Christopher Clapham of Lancaster University, who have collaborated closely on a joint project with the SAIIA on dysfunctional states on which this study draws.
- Baroness Lynda Chalker of Wallasey, an African expert *primus inter pares*, for kindly writing the foreword and commenting on the draft text.
- Jonathan Oppenheimer, whose enthusiasm for a better Africa is infectious and who kindly facilitated two research visits to Malawi.
- Elizabeth Sidiropoulos, SAIIA's Director of Studies, a very able deputy and good friend, and other SAIIA staff members who so often have held the fort in my absence.
- Lyal White, SAIIA Latin American Researcher, for digging out material on subjects ranging from Argentina to Zimbabwe, from sanctions to debt relief, and for his assistance in compiling the index.
- Mark Venning and Ambassadors Boris Yopo and Jorge Heine, for their assistance and hospitality in Chile; and Gladys Lechini at the University of Rosario in Argentina for her analytical input to the Latin American comparisons.
- Ambassadors Timothy Maseko and Mlungisi Mandawa of South Africa, based in Santiago and Buenos Aires respectively, High Commissioner Fanus Schoeman and Betsie Smith of the SA High Commission in Singapore, and Roberto Read of the Argentine Embassy in Pretoria, for their assistance in setting up meetings in those capi-

tals. David Hallett of the Australian High Commission in Pretoria also kindly assisted in arranging my itinerary in Canberra.

- The Institute of International Relations at National Chengchi University in Taipei, and the Taipei Liaison Office in Johannesburg which together arranged a research visit to Taiwan in April-May 2001. Particular thanks are expressed to Ambassador Du Ling, and Mr YC Chen and Mr John Lee.
- Erika Oosthuysen of Tafelberg Publishers, who together with Pippa Lange expedited the publishing and editing process.
- Janet, for those many morale-boosting faxes and e-mails received in distant, sometimes lonely locations, and for the constant encouragement to put pen to paper.

Finally, this book is dedicated to Percy – friend, companion and unforgettable character – and Amelia, who has brought much joy in a short space of time.

* * *

The second US president, James Adams, expressed the failings of political science thus: "While all other sciences have advanced, government is little better practised now than three or four thousand years ago." Politics has always been less of a noble and more of a cynical, even callous profession. In an age when individuals are exposed to more information daily than their antecedents were annually a century ago, the business of contemporary politics – so-called "joined-up government" – has become obsessed with presentation and spin-doctoring. It is correspondingly hypersensitive to the role of outside commentators and analysts. Remembering Henry Kissinger, I am cognisant of the pressures of time and resources on them, and the importance of their decisions. Although governments prefer, often, to present their situation and cause as unique, I am also aware of the importance of learning from past mistakes and failures and from the experiences of others, particularly in a world of globalisation.

GREG MILLS
SAIIA, Johannesburg
September 2002

FOREWORD

In 2002, United Nations Secretary-General Kofi Annan likened our planet to "a small boat, driven by a fierce gale through dark and uncharted waters, with more and more people crowded on board, hoping desperately to survive. None of us . . . can afford to ignore the condition of our fellow passengers. If they are sick, all of us risk infection. And, if they are angry, all of us can easily get hurt".

This statement of global interdependence was nowhere more vividly illustrated than in New York City on September 11 2001.

No place more starkly illustrates the effects of global marginalisation than Africa, a continent of 850 million people and 54 states, where rates of return on investment can be the highest worldwide, yet attract only 4% of the private global capital flows; where 70% of inward capital flows are accounted for by public development assistance; where 40% of private wealth is located outside the continent; and where the skills shortage is desperate, yet 30% of its professional expertise has emigrated to developed economies.

It is perhaps the greatest irony that the gap created by this loss has been filled by some 100,000 expatriates, a greater number than at independence, and at an annual cost of some US$4 billion.

In this thoughtful book, *Poverty to Prosperity*, Greg Mills has drawn together a myriad of elements – public, private, national, regional and multinational. It is urgently necessary today that these elements should work together to bring about concrete and successful development and to provide a practical outline of actions which need to be taken. Without ignoring the need to re-examine many of the assumptions which underlie major international institutions, Mills argues for change from within and for a commitment by all states to certain universal values and standards, seeking, as he puts it, an "equitable global order that . . . accommodates clashing nationalistic tendencies and varying developmental needs and circumstances".

As Africa embarks upon a major continental initiative – the New Partnership for Africa's Development – which holds out a promise and expectation but which needs partnership between North and South and between business, government and civil society, this book is a timely reminder of the practical difficulties which need – and *must* – be overcome if Africa is to take its rightful place in the world economy.

LYNDA, BARONESS CHALKER OF WALLASEY
UK Minister for Africa and the Commonwealth (1986-97) and International Development (1989-97); Chairman, Africa Matters Ltd

POINTS OF DEPARTURE
Developing Cameos

> Since September 11, there has been a strong sense of global solidarity that the world's poor need better health, good quality education, and more promising lives not only as a moral principle but also because these are the ingredients for a more stable, secure world. As we now see, this global solidarity has a price. It may look intimidating in total, but it may prove to be one of the most profoundly transforming investments the world community ever makes.
>
> JAMES WOLFENSOHN, *President: The World Bank*
> 21 February 2002[2]

> We have to build the pool of potential partners and reduce the pool of potential terrorists. Most important, in our hearts, we must make the world a home for all its children.
>
> BILL CLINTON, *Harvard University,*
> 19 November 2001[3]

Ten personal experiences provide an idea both of the development situation in which African and other emerging economies find themselves, and the ways in which these challenges might be met.

Cameo One: September 11 2001

Where were you on September 11?
It has been argued that the world changed forever the moment the four hijacked aircraft crashed on September 11. These attacks will probably, in the years to come, be seen as an historical turning point – a moment of discontinuity – which brought about a fundamental alteration in the context and content of US foreign policy and international relations. It is a moment – like the fall of the Berlin Wall or the release from prison of Nelson Mandela – in which there is a "before" and an "after".

For observers of international relations, the attacks on September 11 and their aftermath have introduced a new lexicon and new terms,

---

2 UN Integrated Regional Information Network (IRIN), 21 February 2002.
3 Cited in *Harvard University Gazette News*, 29 November 2001.

and have created both a new awareness and linkage between the United States government's interests and actions, the security of its citizens,
its foreign policy and the future of international relations. For the first
time since Pearl Harbour, America's social and economic confidence
was closely linked to the success (or not) of America's foreign policy
actions and its military prowess. Whereas before September 2001 the
focus of international engagement had predominantly revolved around
trade and investment co-operation and economic integration, after
September 11 the debate has shifted to wider concerns about terrorism and governance. The advent of the new millennium, as Tony Blair
put it, "marked only a moment in time": in contrast, the September
11 attacks "marked a turning point in history, where we confront the
dangers of the future and assess the choices facing humankind".
Although overstated in the British prime minister's own evangelical
style, this is a public declaration of intent to address the causes of
the event within a global framework.

I was in Cape Town on September 11, delivering a talk on South African regional and foreign policy to a conference organised by *The Economist* newspaper on "Closing the Perception Gap: Commercial Realities in the New South Africa" at the very moment the hijacked aircraft
slammed into their targets. At this conference, the South African finance and trade and industry ministers, among others, were pointing
out the strides made by the South African government in meeting
developmental and policy challenges, including addressing racial in-
equities since the demise of apartheid seven years before.

The September 11 attacks illustrated vividly contrasting facets of
globalisation. On the one hand, there was the grimly voyeuristic, real-
time, televised nature of the attacks; on the other, the level of social,
economic and politico-religious alienation that apparently encourages
young men to throw away their lives, along with those of many others,
in a horrific manner.

Similarly, three other contemporary events have highlighted the
cost of the emergence of such a growing gulf of prosperity and want
within and between states, despite – and, some would argue, because
of – globalisation.

The protests that accompanied the Seattle World Trade Organisation
(WTO) and Genoa G8 summits in December 1999 and July 2001 respectively showed that the debate concerning the benefits and manage-

ment of globalisation is alive, and sometimes characterised by violent division rather than consensus. While the proponents of globalisation have argued for the added value of fast- and free-moving capital, goods and services between countries, its opponents see its downsides in terms of a lack of common ethics and good exemplified by increased wealth divides and marginality from the global economy – what even Pope John Paul II has described as a "tragic fault line" between those "who can benefit from these opportunities [of globalisation] and those who seem cut off from them".[4]

Second, in contrast, the positive conclusion of the Doha World Trade Organisation round of talks in November 2001 and the commitment made to establish a new trade round exemplified the possibility of achieving consensus in devising a rules-based multilateral environment more responsive to the needs of developing states. The extension of WTO membership at this event to the People's Republic of China (PRC) and Taiwan (as Chinese Taipei) both consolidated the global trade regime and stressed the importance of economic functionality over politics, in this case that which has bedevilled the relationship across the Taiwan Strait.

Third, the fear of widespread global economic downturn at the start of 2002 and, in particular, the economic and political travails of Argentina and the negative impact on emerging markets worldwide, were evidence of the interconnected nature of the global economy, the importance of investor perception in that environment, and also the impact external shocks can have on the health of such markets.

These events raise the question: What can be done to provide a more effective framework for global governance to prevent their reoccurrence?

Cameo Two: Swaziland's Kingdom

The bus delivering us to the aeroplane taking us to Swaziland was 30 minutes late. As we waited with the engine idling, none the wiser as to the delay, an American visitor behind me asked: "What's the problem? Why are we waiting? When will we be leaving?" A grizzled South

---

4 William Pesek, "Pope appeals for a gentler and more inclusive capitalism", *The Sunday Independent*, 5 May 2002.

African sitting next to her retorted: "Don't you know TAB? You know, 'That's Africa Baby'. Don't fret, don't stress, just be patient." A bigoted comment? Probably. Yet true to the way many experience Africa, my experience of Swaziland offered a glimpse of many of the problems, challenges and difficulties facing the continent, and also its promise.

Swaziland's Matsapa International Airport is, in a word, tiny. Comprising three prefabricated huts for arrivals, departures and the VIP lounge, and enjoying half a dozen regional flights daily, the airport was in a state of comparative hyperactivity on the day I flew in. The King, His Royal Highness King Mswati III, *Ngwenyama* (Lion) of Swaziland, was expected back from a regional Southern African Development Community (SADC) summit held in Zambia. A phalanx of ten motorcycle outriders, at least five four-wheel drives, and a virtual regiment of policemen and guards adorned in scarlet tunics made up the convoy. The policemen and women were something of a colonial hangover too, their London Metropolitan police-style chequered hatbands making them look somewhat out of place in the heat and dust of Africa.

Mswati III had been in Lusaka trying to assist in bringing about a negotiated solution to the three-year war in the Democratic Republic of Congo (DRC). But President Laurent Kabila had been proving as irascible and recalcitrant as ever. The war had drawn in six nations – Angola, Namibia, Rwanda, Uganda, Zimbabwe and the DRC itself – and involved twice the number of rebel militias.

I was in Swaziland in August 2000 to address the country's diplomatic corps on the problems and prospects for modern diplomacy in the context of globalisation. My session also discussed the many challenges facing developing nations in general and Swaziland in particular. The kingdom's foreign and domestic challenges are formidable.

Swaziland's 930,000 people earn, on average, US$1,520 annually, well above the African average of US$510. The country ranked, in 2001, in 112th position on the UN's *Human Development Index*, which measures 174 countries on the basis of literacy, life expectancy, schooling, population growth, and per capita GDP. Its placing reflects in part the kingdom's HIV/Aids crisis. At around 30%, it has one of the highest HIV infection rates in the world. As a result, as can be gauged from the table below, it is expected that between 30,000 and 40,000 people will die annually from the disease, with life expectancy halving for those suffering from Aids.

Life with HIV/Aids[5]

	CHILD MORTALITY PER 1,000 LIVE BIRTHS (UNDER AGE 5) WITH AIDS	CHILD MORTALITY PER 1,000 LIVE BIRTHS (UNDER AGE 5) WITHOUT AIDS	LIFE EXPECTANCY WITH AIDS	LIFE EXPECTANCY WITHOUT AIDS
Benin	125.4	102.4	50.0	58.9
Botswana	162.5	22.7	29.6	74.4
Burkina Faso	137.0	103.2	46.9	61.4
Burundi	112.3	75.5	46.8	61.6
Cameroon	96.8	68.7	54.2	68.0
CAR	136.2	90.4	44.3	64.1
DRC	112.0	93.6	52.5	60.3
Rep of Congo	120.2	91.8	50.0	63.1
Côte d'Ivoire	116.6	71.6	44.9	63.9
Ethiopia	129.0	82.8	43.6	62.0
Gabon	118.8	84.8	47.3	61.3
Ghana	77.5	57.45	57.1	65.8
Kenya	98.7	43.0	45.5	69.9
Lesotho	132.7	52.5	38.8	68.8
Malawi	185.0	119.8	37.1	59.3
Mozambique	208.9	124.2	32.6	56.2
Namibia	15.9	37.4	33.5	70.1
Nigeria	116.3	83.6	48.6	62.8
Rwanda	157.5	106.8	37.8	59.0
South Africa	133.8	37.4	37.1	70.0
Swaziland	190.6	78.7	30.7	63.4
Tanzania	96.6	60.8	51.9	69.1
Togo	98.3	68.5	52.4	67.7
Uganda	115.6	87.8	48.3	60.1
Zambia	133.5	68.5	40.2	64.6
Zimbabwe	146.1	24.0	33.2	74.0

5 National Intelligence Council (NIC), *Global Trends 2015* on *http://www.cia.gov.*

Swaziland is not unique in facing such challenges. By 2001, seven of the 14 member-states of SADC had infection rates above 20% – South Africa, Botswana, Zimbabwe, Zambia, Namibia, Lesotho and Swaziland. About five million South Africans are, for example, living with HIV. At the current rate of infection, half of the Republic's teenagers under the age of 15 could, by 2002, expect to contract the disease.[6] Twenty-four of the 25 states with the highest infection rates worldwide are in sub-Saharan Africa. Some 25 million Africans had already died of the disease by 2000. While 2.2 million Africans died of the disease in 2001, another 3.5 million became infected with it.

Mswati III attempted, in September 2001, to stop the spread of the disease by reintroducing an ancient chastity law, whereby virgins were barred from so much as shaking hands with males for five years. They were also expected to wear traditional blue and yellow tassels to warn Swazi men against touching them. Yet the 33-year-old king himself had seven wives and two fiancées at the time. This legislation prompted something of an outcry from enraged maidens, who were concerned that the chastity provision would, *inter alia*, make them unattractive for marriage.

While Swaziland is in these respects highly traditionalist if quirky and both small and poor, there have been positive developments. The kingdom's post-independence record has been one of prudent macroeconomic policy and management, leading to average GDP growth rates of over 6% annually between 1968 and 1993. In 1998, for example, real GDP growth was 2.3%, rising to 3.7% the following year, falling to 1.2% in 2001. Inflation has remained under control at 8.1% in 1998, 5.9% in 1999 and 7.3% in 2001.

The country's growth is related to an increase in the size of the manufacturing sector, whose contribution to GDP rose from 30% to 38% over the 1990s. And there has been a shift within this sector from commercial agro-processing (sugar, wood-pulp, citrus, pineapples, cotton and meat) to higher-tech industries. Growth areas include the soft-drink sector, food products, textiles and paper products.

Swaziland's conservative macroeconomic policies are linked to the nature of its political structure. This is both a brake on radical free-market reforms (such as privatisation) and, at the other extreme, more populist pressures. As a result, this royalist system of power and decision-making has come under both domestic and international pres-

---

6 See "Fighting back", *The Economist*, 11 May 2002, pp.25-27.

sure to reform. In June 2001, the king issued a royal decree designed to curb political activity and limit independence, reaffirming his power to appoint judges, the attorney-general and the director for public prosecutions, and tightening restrictions on the media. A heavy fine or prison sentence could be imposed on those found guilty of "impersonating, insulting, ridiculing or countermanding an instruction of their majesties". The king's action, one commentator noted at the time, "carries some broader and none-too-positive messages for Africa in general".[7]

The political pressure to reform has sparked a debate within Swaziland which has resonance elsewhere in Africa. The debate is about the applicability of Western democratic norms in Africa, and the means used to pursue these. Democracy, some Swazis argue, does not necessarily mean the Western concept of multipartyism – though where Swazis stand in this argument tends to depend on their station in life. The king takes decisions in wide consultation with counsellors, who include the queen mother and a circle of princes and traditional advisers. A traditional electoral system known as *tikhundla* appoints members to the House of Assembly via a show of hands in 55 local areas, followed by two rounds of secret ballots to decide the winners. The king also appoints 10 of 65 members of the House, and 20 of 30 senators.

The reluctance of Swaziland's ruling class to reform this system has had to be balanced against its relationship with the global community. The kingdom depends on the outside world for its survival. Unsurprisingly, given the tiny size of the domestic economy, the foreign trade/GDP ratio is around 170%, and the exports/GDP ratio is nearly 80%. The country enjoys special trade status with its three main partners: the first two are the European Union and the US, with preferential market access through the Lomé Convention and the African Growth and Opportunity Act respectively. These provide duty-free and quota-free access. Its principal trading partner, South Africa, offers similar advantages through the Southern African Customs Union (SACU). South Africa takes around three quarters of Swaziland's exports and provides around 80% of its imports. Income from the SACU common tariff pool supplies more than 50% of total government revenue.[8]

---

7 See "Swaziland and the MAP", *Business Day*, 26 June 2001.
8 For a summary of Swaziland's economy, see "Swaziland", *Economist Intelligence Unit*. London: EIU.

The kingdom's small self-defence force of 4,500 personnel also illustrates Swaziland's reliance on diplomacy and alliance-building rather than confrontation. Discussions with mission heads leave little doubt of their abilities and pragmatism, and their grasp of regional problems. But Swaziland has only a small diplomatic cadre, and has scant means to project a limited influence. With a foreign service presence in just 10 centres in 2000 (Brussels, Copenhagen, Kuala Lumpur, London, Maputo, Nairobi, New York, Pretoria, Taipei, Washington DC), its missions are overstretched and understaffed.

The conference with the Swazi diplomats occurred at Nhlangano in the south of the country, named the "meeting place of kings" after King George VI travelled to the then High Commission territory in 1947 to welcome Swazi troops back from action in the Second World War and met King Sobhuza there. Nhlangano is also the site where the Swazis found their own promised land after breaking away from the Zulu kingdom in the 18th century. It remains to be seen, however, whether this promise will ever bear fruit.

Cameo Three: Quo Vadis Globalisation?

Thomas Friedman, New York Times columnist and the author of the international bestseller on globalisation, The Lexus and the Olive Tree, has argued with regard to the benefits of global integration that: "Africans themselves will tell you that their problem with globalisation is not that they are getting too much of it, but too little." As he puts it:[9]

> That's not surprising, because if you actually look around Africa you see that the countries that are the most democratic, where the people have the most freedom to choose – South Africa, Nigeria, Ghana – are the most pro-trade, the most integrated in the world economy and the most globalised. The countries that are led by dictators, are the least open and where the people have the least freedom to choose – Sudan, Zimbabwe, Liberia, Libya, etc. – are those most hostile to globalisation, openness and trade in goods and services.

This is perhaps a little crude, given that Zimbabwe is open to trade in goods and services, even if its government's politics undermine this.

---

9 "Protesting for Whom?", The New York Times, 24 April 2001.

In contrast, given its role in diamond and weapons' smuggling, Liberia is arguably too open. But two personal experiences may give the reader cause to reflect on Friedman's characterisation and also illustrate the different ways in which South Africans have responded to globalisation. The first relates to a conference held in June 2001 in Johannesburg on the topic "The Impact of Globalisation on Southern Africa", at which the participants debated the responses to globalisation of South Africans. The differences between the academics and those from the business community were stark. Whereas the academics' views could generally be termed "anti-globalisation" (because they wanted the international system to be "transformed" rather than "reformed", without apparently really knowing what this entailed), the business people were generally more accepting of the challenges and advantages that faster and deeper market access offered. The latter were aware that the cost of inputs into productive processes and services had to be viewed within a global rather than a national context, because South Africa's opportunities lie in international markets, even though these are far more competitive than local ones.

The second event was a visit that same month to Birkin Cars in Pinetown in KwaZulu-Natal. This is a business founded 20 years ago, which today manufactures sports cars for export. Only a fraction of the Birkin market is in South Africa; the remainder principally in Japan and Europe. As the founder, John Watson, put it: "There is no reason why South Africans cannot be successful in the same way as companies overseas."

Watson's comments can be related, in turn, to the experience of the Japanese motor industry during the late 1990s, again a reflection of globalisation's advantages, challenges and opportunities. For Nissan, in particular, the decade was difficult. The struggling Japanese motor manufacturer was eventually bailed out in 1999 when the French giant Renault took a 36.8% stake. Renault sent in Carlos Ghosn to turn Nissan around. By March 2001, Nissan, which had been in the red for seven years, posted its best ever profit. Ghosn had trimmed 14,200 jobs worldwide, with an additional 6,800 cuts then planned, and had become widely admired for his ability to communicate goals to workers and to commit to targets, becoming something of a celebrity in Japan, where executives tend to be faceless rather than famous.

It is perhaps no coincidence that Ghosn is a Brazilian. Key sectors in Brazil, including aviation and the motor industry, have been able to transform themselves in order to compete globally. Ironically, in doing so, they have placed a heavy emphasis on Japanese workplace ethics and techniques – among them, *feng shui*, the ancient practice of living harmoniously with the energy of the surrounding environment, which leads to the art of placement, not only of buildings, but of everything within them. In simplified form, this principle can be applied to designing a workspace in such a way as to energise and motivate those working in it.

Embraer, the Brazilian aircraft manufacturer, has turned itself around over the past 10 years from a loss-making state enterprise to a private, profitable market leader. The comparative success of Embraer's privatisation programme is linked to the popularity of the Embraer ERJ-135 and 145 series of aircraft, which is the result of a US$500 million investment made after the privatisation process initiated in 1994. At the same time, Embraer embarked on an outsourcing programme, so that not all facets of production are provided by the company directly. The ERJ-135 and 145 are cost-effective both to run and to purchase, the result of a 98% commonality of systems between the systems, components and structures of the two aircraft. Critical to the sales of the ERJ-135/145 which, by October 2000, amounted to 16 aircraft per month, is penetration of the US market, in which more than 300 have been sold. By the end of 2000, Embraer was Brazil's largest export earner.

Ghosn has disputed the attribution of any particular style of management, whether Western or Eastern, as the reason for his success. "Are they [the changes at Nissan] Japanese or Western? I don't know", he says. "I know they are global."[10] But his approach, and its successes, are revealing at a time when the Japanese economy was mired in a recession and apparently unable to respond to global pressures.

In March 2001, Prime Minister Yoshiro Mori was forced to step down and give way to the (more) populist Junichiro Koizumi. Japan's ruling Liberal Democratic Party (LDP) had struggled to deal with a decade-old debilitating slump in the world's second largest economy. As one analyst pointed out at the time, "The only way to be optimistic about Japan is to look at the charts upside down."[11] The recession had increased the political pressure on the central bank and its governor to ease credit, so as to curb deflationary, price-cutting trends.

---

10 See "Japan hails Ghosn as god of management", *Business Day*, 27 June 2001.
11 *Time*, 5 February 2001.

But there were other views as to how the crisis could be ended. First, the government believed that monetary-easing steps would encourage a virtuous circle of spending and demand-fuelled growth. However, second, analysts warned that only accelerated corporate and economic reforms could offer long-term prosperity, considering the mountain of government debt (by 2001 more than 130% of GDP), non-performing loans between US$1.25 trillion and US$2 trillion, and a 6% annual fiscal deficit, the highest in the developed world. As the LDP MP (and son of the foreign minister) Kono Taro put it in an interview in Tokyo in February 2001, "politics is preventing . . . modernisation and deregulation. Government restructuring", he said, "is long overdue". Or as Larry Summers, President Clinton's last treasury secretary, argued, "Unless Japan provides a macroeconomic vision, talk of a Japanese recovery is rather like a discussion of Hamlet without the prince."[12] And the need for vision was tied in with a third factor, the recovery of lost confidence. This, Friedman contends, is the reason why Japan had not come out of the slump:[13]

> Japan got stuck ten years ago in a psychological trap similar to what the economist John Maynard Keynes described in his 1936 "General Theory of Employment, Interest and Money". People become so worried that they won't invest in productive assets, no matter how low interest rates may fall.

A question for Japan, and indeed much of the rest of Asia, is whether the old model of development can still work, either in an economic or a political sense. The challenges faced by the state in Asia are numerous. On the political side, new pressures for democracy and human rights observance are being felt, partly as a result of influence from the West, raising new problems of legitimacy. In the economic sphere, the Asian crisis has cast doubt on the effectiveness of the Asian development model. In both cases, there is a call for a new approach to governance.[14]

The varying experiences of Japanese and Brazilian corporations,

---

12 *Asiaweek*, 9 February 2001.

13 See "Needed, New Faces to Revive Japan's Confidence", *International Herald Tribune*, 13 February 2001.

14 See, for example, Greg Sheridan, *Asian Values, Western Dreams: Understanding the New Asia*. Australia: Allen and Unwin, 1999; Bai Gao, *Japan's Economic Dilemma: The Institutional Origins of Prosperity and Stagnation*. Cambridge: CUP, 2000.

like those of their counterparts in Africa, reflect both their approaches to globalisation and the policy and governance implications of globalisation. But there are all sorts of shades of opinion in-between the anti-globalists and Friedmans, and there is no simple, consensual answer to the challenges posed by globalisation. Some analysts argue that developing countries need "to get their act together" and work in partnership to gain improved trade access, debt relief and larger aid flows. Others lobby for better global institutions to mitigate the worst effects of globalisation, while another group warns of the excesses of globalisation, especially as it affects indigenous cultures.

These differences are epitomised by the preferences of those who attend the Davos World Economic Forum (WEF) and its ideological counterpart, Porto Alegre's World Social Forum. Both parties are searching for a more inclusive global order, particularly compared to the one that we knew on September 10 2001, replete with the sort of ethics and structures to avoid a new form of economic colonisation feared by some, and to spread the benefits – put differently, to integrate – the global economy. In term of global governance, can, in a metaphorical sense, Porto Alegre meet Davos?

These concerns relate not only to the relationship between developed and developing states, however. By the end of the 20th century, doubts were already being expressed as to the sustainability of the growth brought about by globalisation, and the negative effects of the phenomenon. These concerns were heightened by the slowdown in global growth at the start of the 21st century, by ongoing trade tensions between the United States and the European Union, in which the two were increasingly seen as competitors rather than allies, and by continued volatility in international capital markets.[15]

Cameo Four: Malawi's Development Path

Malawi faces immense developmental challenges. It is landlocked, beset by malaria and HIV/Aids, and has little in the way of natural resources. The annual per capita income is just US$200. The impact of Aids has driven life expectancy down to around 36 years. Economic growth is slow, and the country is heavily dependent on foreign

15 See, for example, "The age of financial instability" and "Five reasons for gloom about global growth", on *http://news.ft.com*. Also, see "Globalisation's critics miss the point of markets", *Taipei Times*, 10 June 2001, on *http://www.taipeitimes.com/news/2001/06/10/story/0000089433*.

largesse, though it remains an isolated diplomatic outpost with, by the start of 2002, just 10 residential foreign missions in the capital Lilongwe. President Bakili Muluzi, in power since 1994, has struggled to broaden these international ties and break out of the isolation imposed by the 31 repressive years of rule of his predecessor, Hastings Kamuzu Banda.

As in Swaziland, a snapshot of the airport in Blantyre at the turn of the century is indicative of the scale of the challenge facing Malawi and the effects of its colonial heritage – a smart sergeant in British Army type garb of the 1960s complete with swagger stick barking "Morning Sah!", a filthy ceiling fan, and a poster fixed crookedly to the wall of the run-down departure lounge decorated in thick enamel boarding-school cream paint. Outside, a fire engine with the fading letters "Isle of Man Fire Service" scuttled around. Airport bureaucratic procedures were stifling. At the other major airport at the capital in Lilongwe, there were no fewer than five checks before passengers could get on the transfer bus: one to check the boarding pass and passport, another the departure tax receipt (a US$20 rip-off) and passport (again), passport control (yet again), a special one-on-one moment in a booth where a uniformed official frisked you, and then the departure gate. This is all rather old-world and somehow endearing, but while providing employment, it hardly speaks of the technologically-minded, low-cost government that is necessary to advance economies today, nor of a country trying to utilise effectively the one commodity it has in relative abundance, its tourism potential.

I was involved, in 2001, in a *pro bono* initiative to try to encourage private investment in the Malawi economy. Our mission was unashamedly ambitious: could one create conditions that could turn around a small, isolated economy like Malawi? This would advertise the benefit of sound policies even in a country beset by structural weakness. It could even create a positive regional "knock-on" effect.

Having met a variety of government ministers, aid agencies and other specialists, we wrote up a report, later presented to government, identifying the obstacles to development in Malawi. Its findings were cause for optimism. Reasons included Malawi's democratic transformation; the creation of macroeconomic stability through reducing interest rates, inflation and government spending, and stabilisation of the currency; evidence of infrastructure improvements; the advances made in social and education sectors; and the continuing commitment of donors. The challenges faced included low rates of economic growth, which were compounded by high rates of HIV/Aids infection; low volumes of FDI; high aid dependency; political instability; questions about whether President Muluzi would initiate constitutional amendments to enable him to stand for a third presidential term; slow civil service reform; allegations of corruption; food shortages; and low capacity. Overall these could be summed up by the three "C"s: Corruption, capacity and a lack of opportunities due to (economic) contraction.

The report highlighted ways in which private investment interest could be kindled. These involved faster privatisation in key sectors, notably the national airline, hotels and electricity; and the implementation of a series of investor guarantees and incentive strategies. These were particularly important in the light of the increasingly disturbing events occurring in neighbouring Zimbabwe.

The report was presented to Vice-President Justin Malewezi, and senior government officials in October 2001 at the Capital Hotel in Lilongwe. However, the vice-president responded in a lukewarm manner, even though our delegation was supported by the biggest of South African big business. He launched into an explanation of the African renaissance as a programme that demanded that Africans do things "their way", and implied that this was preferable to "other" ways, given that previous attempts at liberalisation had, from his vantage point, brought little reward.

I had to ask myself why the Malawi government did not want to carry out small but meaningful reforms that could attract investor interest. I came to the conclusion that the answer lay in a number of factors. First, this was a government highly sensitive, given its colonial past, to being told what to do – or at least being seen to obey instructions from outsiders. Second, and more important, the government was extremely insecure. In an environment where political power created access to wealth and patronage which in turn could perpetuate that position, the government was extremely reluctant either to lose control of state sectors or to create alternative centres of wealth. Third, given insecurity of tenure and the absence of other centres of wealth creation, the political elites apparently saw their job principally as a means of gaining prosperity for themselves and those close to them, and not as a mandate to rule and reform.

Concerns as to what drove the Malawian government towards its lukewarm reaction were heightened by the freezing of aid from Denmark at the start of 2002 on account of the ongoing corruption, po-

litical intolerance and judicial interference in the country. Diplomatic relations between the two countries soured in late 2001, when
the Danish ambassador left the country having been accused of insulting Muluzi, after the ambassador had reportedly questioned the
misuse of funds meant for an interparty peace initiative by some top-
tier ruling party members.[16] Its foreign ministry said that Denmark
had decided to end aid to Zimbabwe, Malawi and Eritrea and to reduce assistance to Uganda, because it "does not want to maintain dic-
tators in power".[17]

This decision led immediately to an increase in Malawi's envisaged
budget deficit (given that the Danish government reportedly used to
provide a large chunk of balance of payments support), and consequent delays in preparing the 2002-03 budget. In November 2001,
UK Minister for International Development Clare Short wrote to
Muluzi warning him that aid support from Britain was likely to be
affected by concerns over issues of overexpenditure and governance.
Shortly thereafter the UK government decided to cut development
aid. The UK was reportedly also troubled about the mismanagement
of national food reserves which had caused shortages. In addition,
the EU and the US reportedly withheld aid grants, citing corruption
as one reason for their decision, though both were reportedly un-
happy with the suspension of the privatisation programme.[18] In February 2002, the IMF warned President Muluzi's government that it
should immediately cut spending, improve governance and arrest corruption in order to reduce poverty, raise the standard of welfare of
Malawi's citizens, and "improve the depressing investment climate".[19]

With a small, declining private sector, Malawi remains highly dependent on aid, which amounted to just under US$450 million in
1999, or US$41 per capita, and 25% of GDP. This situation in turn
raises questions about the long-term efficacy of aid in Africa and elsewhere, and about the current relationship between Africa and the international community. It also provides posers about the role of aid

---

16 *Daily News* (Blantyre), 7 February 2002.

17 *New Vision* (Kampala), 1 February 2002.

18 *Daily News* (Blantyre), 15 February 2002. See also "EU, USA, UK suspend aid",
    Daily News (Blantyre), 19 November 2001. According to this last report, the EU
    decided to withhold Kwacha700 million (15 million Euros) and asked government
    to refund K400 million alleged to have been misused by government in the tender-
    ing of the rehabilitation of Blantyre-to-Chileka road project. An EU-instituted au-
    dit also reportedly revealed serious anomalies at the Ministry of Health.

19 *Daily News* (Blantyre), 8 February 2002.

conditionalities (or even sanctions) as a means of promoting democracy and good governance at one end of the scale, and the relationship between civil society and donors as a means of creating a context for political transition at the other.

Cameo Five: The Politics of Aid

The tree-lined avenues of Brussels are perhaps an odd place in which to reflect on Africa's future. But the challenges for Africa and the paradox of the role that the international community has played in Africa are arguably best exemplified by Belgium's colonial history.

It is, after all, no secret that its former African colonies (Congo, Rwanda and Burundi) have been among the most depressingly unstable since independence. It is also an illustration of the extraordinary manner in which Africa was carved up between the European powers that a country such as Belgium and its king could end up controlling, essentially for personal enrichment and aggrandisement, a country the size of Congo, 80 times larger than Belgium.

The present appears vastly different. During a visit to Brussels in October 2000, a senior government official (and Africa conflict resolution expert) commented that Belgium had "no interest any more in Africa as a result of the end of the East-West struggle". Today, he added, debate on Africa was "largely shaped and dominated by Belgium's internal politics and by multilateral contacts". This comment was more than slightly disingenuous given Belgium's ongoing role in trying to influence events in the Congo (such as during the Inter-Congolese Dialogue held in South Africa in 2002), but did reflect both the increasing importance of multilateral political interaction in Africa at international, continental and regional levels, and the role of Brussels as a location for international organisations.

More than 1,100 international agencies, including the North Atlantic Treaty Organisation (NATO), are today based or represented in Brussels. By 2000, it played host to 159 embassies, 2,500 diplomats, 600 press agencies, and the European headquarters of 1,700 foreign businesses. Additional to these international organisations, the city is home to the headquarters of the European Union (EU), the 15-state conglomeration of 373 million people, combining economies with a total value of US\$8.35 trillion.[20] The EU's relationship with the 71

---

20 By comparison, the US population is 270 million and GDP is US\$8.9 trillion.

developing countries of the African, Caribbean and Pacific (ACP) grouping through the Lomé and Cotonou Conventions raises questions, however, about the contemporary relationship Africa enjoys with the international system, with its inherent constraints and opportunities, and the difficulties Africa faces in operating in this environment.

Belgium, with Antwerp at its commercial heart, has also been a key actor in the international diamond trade. Yet diamonds, essential to development in Africa, have earned a bad reputation in fuelling Africa's wars, and enriching its leaders at the expense of their people. In Sierra Leone, diamonds have been singled out as both the cause of civil war and the resource that has sustained it for so long. Sierra Leone is a key location for the international NGO set, where the post-mobilisation programmes employ former combatants, and where the need for reconciliation has given rise to a range of related civil society movements. Acronyms abound: the National Commission for Disarmament, Demobilisation and Reintegration (NCDDR), the Sierra Leone Ex-Combatant Reintegration and Development Organisation (SLEDRO), the National Forum for Reconciliation (NFR), the Association for Sustainable Community Development (ASCOD), the Grassroots Empowerment Movement (GEM), the Global Outreach Movement (GOM) and the Commission for the Consolidation of Peace (CCP). The war-scarred streets are congested with aid agency and UN four-wheel drive-vehicles.[21] But the point to be made here is more complex.

It is not contested resources such as diamonds that are at the heart of African conflict, but the lack of conditions in which good governance and democracy are possible. And the absence of these essential features may in fact be encouraged – and not removed – where the international community is all too ready to backstop corrupt and inefficient African governments, and sometimes even to collaborate with Africa's worst elements over the distribution of Western largesse.

For example, if they had known that the world would not help them, Eritrea and Ethiopia would probably never have embarked on, or at least sustained, their two-year bitter struggle at the end of the 1990s in the midst of a famine. It is uncomfortable for the international community to sit idly by with scenes of desperation flooding television screens. It is especially difficult when African governments cry racism and global hypocrisy if little or no assistance is forthcoming.

21 See, for example, "More NGOs than sense in Sierra Leone", *The Sunday Independent*, 24 June 2001.

Simply put, the involvement of the world aid agencies and the battery of NGOs who too often adopt the same causes in the same uncritical way in dealing with humanitarian disasters can absolve governments of responsibility towards their own people. That is why African scholar-diplomats such as Abdoul Aziz M'Baye have called for the continent to work towards the cessation of aid flows within 20 years in the spirit of the much-debated and somewhat maligned African renaissance vision.[22] This is a debate that raises questions about the role of humanitarian assistance, and the link between development, governance and externally imposed conditionalities.

Cameo Six: Getting on the Industrial Chain in Lesotho and Swaziland

A watered-down version of the US African Growth and Opportunity Act finally made it through Congress in May 2000. Under the terms of the AGOA, which came into effect from 1 October 2000, eligible African states would receive zero-tariff access into the US for eight years for apparel made with African cloth. American officials predict that the Act could improve US imports of African clothing from US$250 million in 2000 to US$4.2 billion by 2008. This amounts to an increase in Africa's share of the US clothing market from its 2000 level of 0.8% to 3.5% by 2007. If achieved, this should enable Africans to establish a market presence before the expiry of the worldwide Multi-fibre Agreement in 2005.

The Act contains provisions to extend duty-free access to all products from sub-Saharan African economies. However, there are two important provisos: First, the US president has to designate those countries that will receive these benefits conditional on their commitment to "appropriate" domestic policies which support good governance, a free-market philosophy and democracy. Second, the Act's product coverage beyond apparel will have to be extended through a process of review.

There has been considerable scepticism over the benefits of this Act, over worker conditions in the apparel factories in the 35 eligible countries, and some (political) dissatisfaction expressed over the unilateral manner in which beneficiary states are designated. But it offers considerable opportunities to a number of Southern African states,

---

22 See his chapter on "Nations, States or Nation-States: Human Rights and Democratisation in Africa", in Pandelani Mathoma, Greg Mills and John Stremlau (eds.), *Putting People First.* Johannesburg: SAIIA, 1999, p.70.

among them Swaziland, Lesotho and Malawi, which have small but important clothing industries. Along with strategic investments made in these sectors, the AGOA was soon providing hitherto unexpected employment opportunities, hastening the pace of industrialisation in these impoverished nations. By mid-2002, US officials estimated that the AGOA had created an additional 60,000 jobs in Africa, increasing African exports to the US by more than 1,000% and generating nearly US$1 billion investment.[23]

By 2001, there were 25 clothing factories in Lesotho, producing three times the volume of South Africa's garment industry, and making Lesotho the largest producer of jeans in the southern hemisphere. The jeans manufactured were all for export, around 90% of them to the US market and stores, including K-Mart, Gap and Sears. In 1999, the kingdom's garment exports to the US earned in excess of US$74 million, doubling to US140.3 million in 2000, and leaping again to US$215.3 million in 2001. By 2002, 20,000 extra jobs in the textile industry had been created as a result of the AGOA. As a result, for the first time in Lesotho's history, the number of people employed in private manufacturing exceeded those in government.[24]

Much of the investment in the garment sector in these countries has been made by Taiwanese concerns. South African-based Taiwanese companies were quick to welcome the AGOA, anticipating an upsurge in export volumes. Taiwan's own economic transition might help to explain the reasons for Taiwanese investments in the clothing sector in Southern Africa, and provide some pointers for future growth strategies. Also, investors in the garment and textile sectors are not only major employers in the impoverished areas of South and Southern Africa, but they could place South Africa's poorer neighbours on industrial development paths not dissimilar to that experienced by Taiwan, once known as the "Kingdom for Clothes, Bicycles, Umbrellas and Plastics". Today the island has moved up the technological chain, producing, for example, 60% of the world's laptop computers.

As is noted above, investments in the clothing sector are having, and will continue to have, a marked effect on the micro-economies of Lesotho and Swaziland. In the former, it is anticipated that the revenue from the jeans industry could overtake the value of remittances from

---

23 Discussion, Pretoria, May 2002. See also President George W Bush's statement to the United Nations Financing for Development Conference held in Monterrey, Mexico, 22 March 2002.

24 IRIN, 22 May 2002.

migrant miners – traditionally the major foreign earner for the Basotho – by early in the 21st century. The AGOA could provide further incentives for additional industrialisation in this sector. Whether Taiwanese and other investors react to these opportunities in droves or dribbles depends largely, as one prospective investor noted, "on how the governments in the region react", particularly over the issuing of work permits to skilled foreign staff and the offering of investor incentives. This raises, in turn, questions about the necessary and sufficient conditions to attract foreign direct investment, and the nature of external and internal policy reforms and initiatives necessary for investment.

Cameo Seven: Governance in Morocco

In June 2001, in the ancient city of Fès in Morocco, which boasts a university older than Oxford and Cambridge, a music festival aimed at "putting the soul back into globalisation" – *Une âme pour la mondialisation* – was held. Clearly globalisation has touched even the more remote areas of Africa, but in more ways than can be initially imagined.

Morocco is hardly regarded as a bastion of good governance and transparency. It is arguably known more for its constitutional monarchy, appalling human rights record in the 1980s and its disputed annexation in 1976 of the territory of the Western Sahara than for its track record in economic and social reforms. It also faces considerable economic challenges, including 20% unemployment and 50% illiteracy among its 30 million people, and a US$20 billion national debt. It does not have the abundant oil reserves of its neighbours. It appears, on the surface, to offer little hope to its people and not much of an example to Africa. Yet the kingdom illustrates the advantages of economic liberalisation. It has successfully diversified its economy towards export-oriented light manufacturing, most notably in textiles, car parts and electronics, facilitated by the conclusion of free trade arrangements (FTAs) with the EU, Jordan, Egypt and Tunisia. Already two thirds of its trade is with the EU, and this is expected to increase as the FTA comes fully into force in 2008.

Since 1983, Morocco has pursued a liberal structural adjustment programme aimed at fiscal and monetary stability and convertibility. This has included the privatisation of more than half of 112 companies (comprising 75 companies and 37 hotels) earmarked, realising over US$4 billion by the start of 2001, and by a rapid reduction in external tariffs from an average of over 100% to around 10% today.

Overall improvements are reflected in increased FDI flows and in various strategies promoted by the government. These include the revision of the legal system, the development of industrial parks and of the communications network, a focus on training and management, and the introduction of a range of fiscal and financial incentives, including tax holidays. During the 1980s, the annual average FDI inflows were US$80 million; during the 1990s, US$500 million; and over the last five years, US$1.3 billion. The year 2001 was a record year, with US$3.2 billion in inflows, of which 70% was related to privatisation. Principal investors in the industrial sector are: France (37%), Switzerland (16%) and Spain (11%). In 2001, investments were sourced from France (85%), Portugal (4%), the US (3%) and Spain (3%), with 81% in the telecommunications sector. Morocco has also focused on tourism, particularly as a means to reduce income inequalities between urban and rural areas. As the second-largest foreign currency earner after the remittances of Morocco's two million expatriates, this sector employs 600,000 people and contributes 4% of GDP. The kingdom aims to double annual tourist numbers to four million visitors by 2003.

Strong efforts have also been made to instil sound corporate governance, of a type that will encourage FDI inflows. This improvement in business practice is linked to the emergence of a new generation of business leaders. Assisting the trend are the increasing influence of NGOs within Morocco such as *Transparency Maroc*, the more critical role played by the media, and the conditions imposed by external partners. Put simply, the fight against corruption has emerged as a prominent public policy issue related to the political and socioeconomic mutations under way in the kingdom. Morocco ranks 48th of the more than 150 states on the global *Index of Economic Freedom*, and is characterised as "mostly free".[25]

Much, however, remains to be done. As Hassan Alami, President of the General Confederation of Moroccan Enterprises, observed in an interview in June 2001, "Although everyone now speaks about corruption openly, previously a taboo subject, in Morocco small corruption is still considered to be normal behaviour. We also have an administration suited to the 1960s; yet possess a 21st century economy."[26]

---

25 Where a position of 1st is deemed freest. See
    http://database.towhall.com/heritage/index/country. cfm?ID=100.0
26 These comments were gathered during the course of research trips to Morocco
    in June 2001 and July 2002.

And while efforts at streamlining bureaucratic, particularly customs, procedures have helped, it is generally recognised that further attention is needed, particularly with regard to "applying and not just writing up" laws and codes of conduct.

Whatever the problems, Morocco's economic changes are fundamentally connected to political reforms undertaken by King Hassan II in the 1990s and pursued, following his death in 1999, by his son, King Mohamed VI. Before this time, Morocco had a very poor human rights record. Now, though it remains a constitutional monarchy, the country's political terrain has opened up. As Minister of Health Thami Khyari put it in an interview, also in June 2001: "Let me assure you, Morocco has changed completely. I was in prison before, but now we have a socialist government." Or as one foreign diplomat noted in Rabat the same month, "While Morocco's human rights record and political environment is not perfect, in regional terms it's an angel."

Improvements in regional relations could see the realisation of the Union of the Arab Maghreb (UMA) with Algeria, Libya, Mauritania and Tunisia, signed in February 1989, and aimed at the free movement of goods, services and workers. This has essentially been put on hold because of the Western Sahara issue. With the borders with Algeria closed, there is an awareness that, as one official observed, "The solution of the Saharan problem can contribute to the development of the Maghreb vision." Nonetheless, progress on this issue should not overshadow the strides made over the past decade in integrating Morocco with the global economy. Also, through open trade regimes and the establishment of more transparent and accountable systems of governance, Morocco provides an example of the sort of effort on which Africa's future prosperity depends.

Cameo Eight: New Roles for the Ghanaian (and Other) Militaries?

Three apparently disconnected events highlight the organisational and strategic challenges facing African and other militaries and their political masters in establishing peace and curbing crime and other destabilising elements.

In December 2000 I conducted research for a project on the nature of contemporary civil-military relations in Ghana. Eighteen months later, in May 2002, I was in Berlin to attend a conference. Adjoining

Berlin, in Potsdam, the devastating affects of the Second World and Cold Wars and 45 years of Russian occupation and Communist East German rule had left their impact, in spite of the enormous financial commitment made by the federal German government following re-unification. While I was in the German capital, for so long emblematic of Cold War divisions and the scene of military tensions, on 14 May 2002, in Reykjavik, more than 50 years after its founding and a decade after the end of the Cold War, NATO approved an agreement accepting its former enemy Russia into a new partnership on terrorism, arms control and international crisis management.

Accra's Burma Camp is a snapshot of all that is right and wrong with African militaries. Its whitewashed stone-lined roads and smartly turned-out soldiers give a good impression at first glance, one confirmed by the solid international reputation built up by the large number of Ghanaians serving on UN peacekeeping missions. Since the start of 2001, at any one time 2,000 of 7,000 Ghana Armed Forces personnel are with the UN – the fifth largest contributors to UN operations, with troops deployed from Liberia, through Sierra Leone and the Western Sahara, to Lebanon. This snapshot, however, does not tell the full story.

The Ghanaian armed forces are dependent on peacekeeping as a major source of governmental and household revenue. Each soldier retains half of the daily UN allowance (US$32,00 in 2000), no small matter to a private who earns barely US$100 monthly. This money is saved and used to buy a car, taxi or corn-mill at the end of the peacekeeping "tour"; an investment which keeps the soldier going until the next UN secondment. Knowledge that this source of income could instantly dry up if the military attempted another coup has been a critical (probably *the* critical) factor deterring the army's further involvement in politics. Also, the smart exterior of Burma Camp belies the more fundamental problems experienced by the military. The shortage of funding can be seen in the interiors of the buildings, the best of which are run down. Before the change of government from Rawlings to John Kufuor in December 2000, this situation was exacerbated by the rivalry with a relatively prosperous and well-equipped presidential guard, 64 Battalion, set up by Jerry Rawlings to provide personal armed protection. And the relatively healthy state of the military obscured the need to focus on more wide-ranging internal security problems. For example, the police force was comparatively worse off, both in terms of budget and manpower.

Ghana's armed forces stand out in the West African region not only because they compare favourably with their Western counterparts in terms of abilities and professional standards, but because they maintain them in a region which has been characterised by state collapse and military insurrection. But Ghana has not always enjoyed such stability. The first African country to receive its independence (from Britain in 1957), Ghana has a troubled post-colonial history of economic decay. The military, far from being a stabilising force, constantly meddled in politics. There have been no fewer than five successful military coups in Ghana between that in 1965, which deposed Kwame Nkrumah, and the last which brought Flight Lieutenant Jerry Rawlings to power for a second time in 1981. Since the last event, however, Ghana has reintroduced democracy and economic reforms. Rawlings voluntarily stepped down from power at the end of 2000.

The nature of Ghana's military today, and its wider role in peacekeeping in its region, raise questions about the role of police and military forces in developing countries, and the manner in which "security" is both presented and dealt with. In the case of South Africa, for example, during the Cold War debate around strategic issues traditionally involved assessments of the value of the Cape sea route to Western shipping interests, of the importance of the South African resources sector, particularly mining, to the West, and of the perceived "anti-communist" leanings of the government and the role that the then South African Defence Force might be able to play. Today, however, in spite of the positive value of the political developments in South Africa, when viewed from outside, the environment is inverted: South Africa is seen by some analysts not in terms what contributions it could make if things go well, but rather the negative "contribution" it could make if things went wrong, such as the effect of a returning diaspora from South Africa to Western countries, the impact of refugee flows, and the link between socioeconomic decay and transnational crime.

How might African security concerns be related to the NATO agreement with Russia?

The Reykjavik agreement was hailed by UK Foreign Secretary Jack Straw "as the funeral of the Cold War". The agreement was made possible not only by the reduction of Cold War tensions and the obvious rapport between Presidents George W Bush and Vladimir Putin, but by the events of September 11. Quantitatively and qualitatively, technological gaps between NATO's and Russia's military capabilities were no longer a central concern, as was the case a decade before. Of greater import, however, was the widening gap between American and European military capacity, along with the transnational threats posed by the events of September 11. These threats, as NATO Secretary-General Lord George Robertson emphasised, "can no longer be measured in fleets, warships, tanks or airplanes" and emanate from an enemy that "can strike utterly without warning".[27]

The events of September 11 and the US-led action in Afghanistan that resulted suggest three possible responses to terrorism. First, greater international collaboration is needed to meet such insidious transnational developments. Second, a focus on intelligence gathering and co-operation is required to identify terrorist and related criminal networks dealing in drug smuggling and money laundering. Third, there is a need to restore state control and its corollary, capacity, in countries or regions where this is lacking.

Here the US military and, at the opposite end of the capacity scale, the Ghanaian and other African armed forces have shared interests in developing strategies to ensure peace, whether this is achieved through a diplomatic focus on conflict prevention and resolution, or military-centred peace enforcement, peacekeeping and post-conflict peace-building. In drawing attention to the conditions and ideological differences that motivated the hijackers, the attacks of September 11 have emphasised the linkage between state capacity and dysfunction, local governance and external intervention. Yet how can an interventionist strategy be operationalised to bring about what Western policymakers refer to as "structural stability" within states?

Cameo Nine: The Folly of Geography and the Failure of Leadership

Chatting to a senior government official in steamy Kinshasa in January 2002 was akin to Alice's view through the looking glass. While he spoke of government plans and programmes for his country, he admitted that government forces nominally controlled just 40% of the territory. In reality, given the presence of Angolan and Zimbabwean forces and the limited infrastructure, such control could probably

---

27 Cited in "NATO approves pact giving Russia a voice in the alliance", *International Herald Tribune*, 15 May 2002.

only be extended by the government to the capital and its decaying surrounds. And the notion of "control" did not equate with the provision of basic services and security for the Congolese people.

The Democratic Republic of Congo illustrates the enormity of Africa's difficulties. Situated at the heart of Africa, Congo is the continent's second most populous and second-largest state (one quarter the size of the US), home to 50 million people belonging to more than 200 tribes, and sharing borders with nine countries – Congo-Brazzaville, Central African Republic (CAR), Sudan, Uganda, Rwanda, Burundi, Tanzania, Zambia and Angola. It is also one of the richest African countries, yet its people remain among the poorest. Its leaders for the most part have been more concerned with ensuring their own wealth and survival than providing for the wellbeing of Congo's diverse population. It is, in the words of the DRC's World Bank representative, "one of the five poorest countries in the world, but probably one of the ten richest resource countries worldwide".[28] It has a hydro-electric potential estimated at 100,000 MW, sufficient for the needs of at least all of Southern Africa; oil reserves of 180 million barrels; and enormous untapped wealth in other natural and mineral resources, which includes 65% of the world's cobalt reserves. Congo is emblematic, in this way, of all that is good and bad in Africa. Its huge economic potential and opportunities contrast with the challenges of dealing with corruption and venality, providing governance and ensuring state capacity to deal with the competing forces of territorial fragmentation and state consolidation, and institutionalising democracy.

War, instability and misrule have been a characteristic of the Congo since colonial times. The brutal history of colonial exploitation was followed by decades of poor governance under Mobutu Sese Seko.[29] The ending of the Cold War, followed by Mobutu's overthrow, apparently heralded brighter prospects for the continent's second-largest state. Mobutu's regime ended in 1997, after a successful invasion from the country's west by the Alliance of Democratic Forces for the Liberation of Congo-Zaire brought about the installation of Laurent-Desiré Kabila in his place. Hope that Kabila's rule would lead to a more prosperous and stable period in Congo's history quickly turned

---

28 Interview, Kinshasa, 26 January 2002.

29 See, for example, Adam Hochschild, *King Leopold's Ghost: A Story of Greed, Terror, and Heroism in Colonial Africa*. New York: Mariner, 1999; and Michela Wrong, *In the Footsteps of Mr Kurtz*. London: Fourth Estate, 2000.

sour, as his own regime was characterised by large-scale corruption, human rights abuses and a renewed round of warfare as Kabila's former allies, Uganda and Rwanda, turned against him. He sought new external partnerships with countries including Zimbabwe, Namibia and Angola. Their support prevented the overthrow of Kabila's regime, though in January 2001 he fell victim to an as-yet-unexplained assassination – most probably at the instigation of his new-found allies.

The DRC's vast geographic spread is also reflected in its relationship with its neighbours. They have both greater capacity and more direct interests than Kinshasa in various regions – whether this is Rwanda and Uganda in the eastern DRC, Zambia in the south, and Angola to the west. This resulted in peace – perhaps more accurately put, stability – in pieces rather than throughout the entire Congo under Kinshasa.

In 2002, the DRC peace process took a new, more positive turn. The Inter-Congolese Dialogue restarted in February at Sun City in South Africa, the first round in Addis Ababa at the end of 2001 having been troubled by a lack of funding and the lukewarm response of some of its participants, notably the government of Joseph Kabila. The role of South Africa in the dialogue was more than simply symbolic. As the continent's most powerful state, South Africa was expected by many to take the lead in this facilitatory role, not least because of President Thabo Mbeki's push for peace as a precursor to the successful roll-out of the New Partnership for Africa's Development (NEPAD).

The history of Africa is, of course, neither homogeneous nor consistent across and even within states. Attempts at dealing with the enormity of Africa's challenges have given rise to some extraordinary leadership, both good and bad, both complex and contradictory in its policies. The value of leadership cannot be overemphasised, however, and is key to engagement by Africa's peoples and the external community in addressing the continent's challenges.

But for 40 years Africa has been blighted by a succession of weak and failed leaders and poor, often self-serving policies. The blame for this should not, of course, lie solely at the door of Africans themselves, but was tolerated and occasionally implicitly encouraged by external powers and agencies. Too often have African leaders relied on what Patrick Chabal has termed "the political instrumentalisation of disorder" as a means of perpetuating and consolidating their

rule. One of Mobutu's "solutions" to the legacy of colonialism was
to built a cult around himself, described as *authenticité* or *Zairianisa-
tion*. In practice this amounted to little more than a selfish attempt
to deflect criticism and excuse corruption and poor governance. Opposition was not tolerated (or even legally permitted) in Zaire and
many other African states, under the pretext of "nation-building".
In Ghana, to take another example, populist and inefficient economic policies were paraded in the immediate post-independence period
as an example of "African socialism". The country's first prime minister, Kwame Nkrumah, was more concerned about seeking what he
termed the "political kingdom" than ensuring his own people's prosperity, an error of judgement which led to the first of Ghana's five military coups. Yet Nkrumah is regarded today as something of a visionary, mainly on the grounds of his postulation of the need for economic
development through political unity. Certainly he could have earned
no praise for his contribution to the welfare of the average Ghanaian.

Similar questions could be asked about other leaders who started
well but apparently ended badly. In Southern Africa, Frederick Chiluba's Movement for Democratic Change took over from the benign
dictatorship of Kenneth Kaunda in Zambia in November 1991, intent
on political and economic reform. This involved the privatisation of
some 280 parastatals, 80% of which were sold within the decade. But
Chiluba blinked when it mattered most – over the sale of the state
copper company Zambian Consolidated Copper Mines (ZCCM) –
amidst increasing concerns both about the criminal elements within
his government, and that the president might attempt to seek an unconstitutional third term of office. At the time of Chiluba's stepping
down as president in 2002, Zambia's economy was verging on collapse.

In neighbouring Zimbabwe, Robert Mugabe was widely admired
as following a pragmatic policy combination of political reconciliation and a mixed economy. In the mid-1990s, with the emergence of
post-apartheid South Africa and the deterioration of economic conditions, he resorted to using the racially discriminatory allocation of
agricultural land (inherited from Rhodesia's colonial past) as a tool
to maintain his grip on power, whatever the cost to the economy and
his people.

Such practices are in part a manifestation of Africa's inheritance,
but the performance of such leadership will condemn the continent's
future. Their type appears with a disconcerting and pernicious regu-

larity. Today Mugabe, Daniel arap Moi, Liberia's Charles Taylor, Angola's José Eduardo dos Santos, and Namibia's Sam Nujoma, to name a few, rule in the mould of Mobutu. "These men", Shyaka Kanuma observes,[30]

> . . . are not troubled by niceties such as respect for human rights, concern for their population's material welfare or consensual decision-making. Most preside over decaying military or police states. They benefit from a hybrid of African patronage and farcical parliamentary, judicial and other institutional procedures that contrive invariably to act in the big man's interests.

If the differences between the qualities and performance of African leaders have been acute, there is one common, arguably cultural thread: the cult of the African "big man", the modern day "chief". Yet the rule of such a man has more often than not been defined by impoverishment, not prosperity; corruption rather than construction; and repression rather than democratic practice. As Chabal and Jean-Pascal Daloz have argued:[31]

> Our research on contemporary Africa indicates that present political transitions have not hitherto changed either the role of the elites or the nature of leadership . . . African politicians undoubtedly have both regional and national ambitions; they aim to "represent" the largest and most diverse constituency possible. However, the strategy that they follow is essentially patrimonial: they need to accumulate clients, building up their networks from the local to the national level . . . There is no reliable evidence that this type of particularistic leadership, based as it is on communal links and clientelistic transactions, is waning on the continent – although it might be markedly weakened by the dearth of resources which the elites currently suffer.

Some of these men, as Alec Russell notes, have been responsible for the worst betrayal of their people, possibly worse even than that of the European powers, who "abandoned their colonies in unseemly

---

30 *Mail and Guardian*, July 2002.
31 Patrick Chabal and Jean-Pascal Daloz, *Africa Works: Disorder as a Political Instrument*. London: James Currey, 1999, pp.43-44.

haste", and that of the superpowers, who "used Africa as a battle-field in the fight for global domination".[32]

The contemporary debate about creating the conditions for eco-nomic growth on the continent has nonetheless centred on the need to create "African solutions to African problems". This has, ironically, been spurred on by the West, which has tired of attempting to engineer and sponsor solutions in a barren, unwelcoming environment where its efforts are inevitably dismissed as interfering, patronising and self-serving – which they often are. The Africanist tendency has (perhaps unwittingly) reinforced this trend, preferring home-grown solutions to foreign-inspired diplomatic efforts and economic recovery plans – yet simultaneously entertaining the expectation of a special global recovery plan for Africa.

But can the African renaissance in the form of the New Partner-ship for Africa's Development hope to achieve where others have failed to before? How can African leaders who are clearly part of the prob-lem, be part of the solution? Can it be made to work and, if so, how? Or will NEPAD turn out to be yet another charade that ends up ex-cusing poor governance and corruption and refusing to take respon-sibility for failure? Moreover, are African solutions necessarily the most appropriate, in a globalised world of increasing uniformity? Can so-lutions be engineered for the fundamental problems faced by states which do not possess even the capacity to fulfil basic functions, on a continent where the nature of colonial boundaries appears to defeat the logic of statehood? What does it require to make a successful state? What is the relationship between governance, development and glob-alisation? When can governance be considered as "good"? Is it pos-sible for weak, sometimes dysfunctional, and ill-formed states com-prising many different national groups to adjust to global norms and, if so, how?

Cameo Ten: Answers in NEPAD?

I was present when President Thabo Mbeki launched NEPAD in South Africa's parliament on 31 October 2001. He has pinned much on the success of this initiative. In his speech to parliament in Cape Town, the President spoke of the need for "African ownership": where African leaders had to accept "openly and unequivocally that

---

32 Alec Russell, *Big Men, Little People: Encounters in Africa*. London: Pan, 1999, p.2.

they will play their part in ending poverty and bringing about sustainable development". "We must", he said, "strengthen democracy on the continent; entrench a human rights culture . . . end existing conflicts and prevent new conflicts. We have to deal with corruption and be accountable to one another for all our actions."

A conference on NEPAD, co-hosted by the South African and Finnish Institutes of International Affairs and *Business in Africa* magazine, was staged in Cape Town the day following the parliamentary debate. At the event, South African Foreign Affairs Director-General Sipho Pityana aligned NEPAD to the Durban World Conference on Racism recently concluded, and to the need to restructure relations with developed countries to address "the abnormal relationships of exploitation and dependency" so that we can "determine our own destiny and refuse to be conditioned by circumstance".

What is NEPAD? Is it an attempt (as South African opposition leader Tony Leon argued in parliament) to replace "the old African stereotype, of the outstretched hand and the begging bowl, with a new image of Africa's place in the world"? Or is it an attempt by Africa to seek additional aid in compensation for centuries of injustice? It seems to be both of these – a cocktail of African political and economic empowerment and consciousness mixed with the promotion of African business and the hope of prosperity. In presenting this alternative within the same overarching development framework, Mbeki has sought to simultaneously address apathy, issues of political and economic governance, and the need for regional co-operation.

The NEPAD concept has been founded on two principles, the first being that Africa's chronic underdevelopment demands radical action involving resource transfers from the North to the South. As Rubens Ricupero has argued in this context:[33]

> If African countries are to overcome their aid dependency, the perverse trend of dwindling amounts to official assistance being fed into debt payments must be dramatically reversed. It may sound paradoxical, but the only way to end aid dependency is in the first instance by using more aid, and in a more effective way, to generate a positive momentum that in due course will make aid superfluous.

33 "Sustainable Development of Africa and the Role of the United Nations System". Statement by Rubens Ricupero, Secretary-General of UNCTAD to the ECOSOC, Geneva, 16 July 2001.

The second principle is that, while the assistance of the global community is critical in helping to meet these challenges, at the same time African states cannot afford to disengage from the forces (and benefits) of globalisation – that globalisation is not the polar opposite of development as some critics claim. To achieve this and to engage in collective and co-operative action with other countries, however, a strong and capable state is required, a feature largely absent from the African landscape at present.

With this in mind, NEPAD has proposed a number of interrelated objectives, including the need to address poverty, improve human resource capacity, and create a platform for private capital investment and thus economic growth. These will be achieved through the promotion of intra-African trade and infrastructure links; the establishment of conditions of good economic and political governance; the combating of regional threats (including conflict and disease); and the promotion of resource inflows. In essence, NEPAD is thus, in the words of one of its drafters, "an attempt, first, to accelerate poverty reduction and, second, to provide a platform for investors".[34]

For Africa to reach its goal of halving the incidence of poverty by 2015, its economies will have to expand by between 7% and 8% in real terms annually, well above their average growth rate of 2.2% between 1991 and 1997. Africa's economies have to grow by 5% annually just to prevent the number of poor people from increasing. Hence, in seeking to create a new, positive developmental paradigm for Africa, NEPAD is trying to change the context in which African states find (and view) themselves. The initiative is thus an attempt to redefine the power relationship between Africa and the rest of world. As is argued in the NEPAD document:[35]

> The initiative calls for the reversal of this abnormal situation by changing the relationship that underpins it. Africans are appealing neither for the further entrenchment of dependency through aid, nor for marginal concessions. . . . What is required . . . is bold and imaginative leadership . . . as well as a new global partnership based on shared responsibility and mutual interest.

Such ambitious plans are nothing new. According to one calculation, there have been 18 African developmental initiatives over the past

---

34 Discussion, Stephen Gelb, Johannesburg, June 2001.
35 See *http://www.nepad.org*.

20 years.[36] Previous attempts at partnership between Africa and the developed world have ended in failure or, at best, disappointment, as is reflected in the declining patterns of aid to the continent, and the shift in focus of the purpose of aid.

Three distinct periods of post-colonial engagement can be identified in this respect. First is the period immediately preceding the oil and related balance-of-payments crises of the mid-1970s, when aid was used mostly for poverty-related needs, mainly in the rural areas, though transfers were highly politicised according to the Cold War strategic logic of the time. A large proportion of aid found its way into white elephant infrastructure projects. Second, after the crises, aid became increasingly conditional on economic stabilisation and adjustment. Aid was used both as a source of finance and an incentive to reduce fiscal deficits, adjust exchange rates, reform monetary policy, liberalise trade, and lessen the state's role in the economy. In spite of this action, however, during the mid-1980s, exposure to the World Bank and IMF exploded rapidly, with increasing debt/GDP ratios.

Sub-Saharan African Debt

YEAR	US$ BILLION (GDP PERCENTAGE)
1960	3
1980	84 (30.6%)
1987	198 (66.3%)

Third, these conditions were further expanded in the 1990s, being focused on creating the "right" state structures and sociopolitical environment for growth – described by the term "good governance" – including support for civil society movements. At the same time, renewed emphasis was also placed on poverty reduction through debt relief initiatives.[37] The trend is now towards more focused, condition-bound aid in smaller quantities, contrary to the needs and wishes of NEPAD.

What arguably makes NEPAD different from earlier initiatives is its recognition of past failures, current state failings, the need for ownership by Africans themselves and, critically, its timing. But there is a

36 "African initiative struggles in hope for a fresh start", *Financial Times*, 13 February 2002.

37 See The World Bank, *Can Africa Claim the 21st Century?* Washington DC: World Bank, 2000, p.239. See also Carol Lancaster, "Africa in World Affairs", in John Harbeson and Donald Rothchild, *African in World Politics.* Colorado: Westview, 2000 pp.208-234.

more fundamental question arising out of NEPAD. Is NEPAD – and its focus on special developmental conditions for African states – not an admission of the "dysfunctionality" of these states, that they require huge aid transfers and special external preferences to be able to survive let alone prosper? This poses additional questions about the ability of these states to survive without external assistance, the relationship between external assistance and the creation of internal governance capacity, and, more fundamentally, about the nature and viability of state structures and the power relationships within them. Are there alternatives: both to the current aid environment and, within the context of African state failure, to these state units?

Summing up the Development Challenge

Sitting with me and discussing Ghana's development problems and prospects over beers in Accra's Sunrise Hotel just across from the World Bank offices, a hardened expatriate journalist argued that there was little the international community could do which would assist in the development of a more effective African state in the longer term, given the fundamentally artificial nature of their creation. To attempt assistance was a wasteful folly, designed more to soothe Western consciences than offer real hope. "What the international community should do", he argued, "is let the continent go – to allow it to find its natural place and state structures." The British columnist Simon Jenkins has argued for a similar response: where states should essentially fight it out to find their natural place. Multilateral military interventions lead only to what he terms "frozen societies", under the protection and tutelage of the UN and NATO.[38] Another version of the same argument is that "Africa works" if left to its own devices.

"In West Africa", my journalist friend said in Accra, "this future is likely to be one where the coast would be populated by traders and oilmen, and the interior by missionaries and mining engineers." The effect would be, he argued, mass population movements to the coastal zones and illegal immigration into Europe and North America. Africans would increasingly be involved in organised crime and other illegal transnational activities. This is a scenario termed "Continental Collapse – Islands of Resource Development" by management gurus in the 1980s. But my friend's argument was motivated less by a cyni-

---

38 See Simon Jenkins, *SAIIA Annual British Council Lecture*, Jan Smuts House, Johannesburg, 21 February 2000.

cism about Africa than a wish to shame the West into a more proactive role. This would go beyond simply maintaining a holding pattern of development and helping to preserve a modicum of African state stability. This is a point that the columnist Ken Owen has emphasised when urging greater international commitment to Africa's development challenges:[39]

> Well, we have time. We can wait while the refugees paddle across the Straits of Gibraltar, or beach ancient hulks on the shores of France or Italy, or smuggle themselves through the tunnel into Britain. It is Europe which, wallowing in limitless wealth, is most threatened by the human misery outside its gates.

The African – and, indeed, Asian and Latin American – challenge is thus to find a development path that can offset the worst effects of poverty, deal with collapsed state structures (where the distribution of nations does not always equate with state and national boundaries and state functions do not match its obligations), and accommodate the aspirations of ordinary people, aspirations that have inevitably been heightened by the advent of globalisation and satellite communications.

But is this model possible in a global environment in which, compared to the era of the Cold War where strategic and ideological logic drove engagement, industrialised countries are less inclined today to dig deeply into their pockets to ensure African state survival let alone prosperity? What mix of aid and conditionalities might assist in following this developmental path? Or is aid the best that the international community can offer Africa? Who does aid benefit? How might aid be better targeted? Should Africa not reject aid and the dependency and devolution of African state responsibilities that go with it? What should be done about collapsing state institutions, or with states that do not exhibit the elements and attributes of statehood? What are the necessary and sufficient conditions for economic reform, recovery and prosperity? Can Africa learn from the experiences of others and its own successes and failures to institute a cycle of stability and growth? Is it possible to transplant lessons of governance – or its failure – from Asia, Latin America and Africa?

---

39 "West most threatened by poverty", *Business Day*, 20 May 2002.

The Focus and Purpose of this Book

As the poorest continent and with the lowest aggregate levels of state capacity worldwide, Africa[40] thus faces a compendium of complex challenges.

One set of these relates to the international context. Globalisation brings with it increasing technological demands on states, which can create or exacerbate tensions between them. Related to this is the weakness of the relationship between the governments of developing nations, especially those in Africa, and multilateral inter-governmental institutions. This results in a failure to address economic crises and conflict.

A second, related concern is the difficulty of devising, implementing and supporting reforms to suit the particular context and circumstances of African nations. Another is linked to the regional environment and the need to deepen and widen the regional integration of markets and of people, and interlink security concerns. A fourth area of concern relates to the often dysfunctional nature of many African states. Many of these are incapable of arresting economic and social degradation because of structural inadequacies in the state itself.

With the above in mind, *two fundamental approaches* exist currently with regard to how African states might attempt to deal with the inter-related challenges of poverty, global marginalisation, instability and economic decay.

One of these approaches suggests that given the general weakness (and in some cases smallness) of African states, they have insufficient power to address in a fundamental and sustained manner the challenges they face. Any effective response has to take into account the fractured nature of global society and the inability of weak states to globalise effectively. Thus there is a need to alter the "global rules of the game" including the role and nature of the Bretton Woods institutions and the UN, and the nature of flow of global capital, trade openness and aid. These could broadly be termed *structuralist*, interventionist initiatives. IMD Little has described these thus:[41]

> The structuralist sees the world as inflexible. Change is inhibited
> by obstacles, bottlenecks and constraints. People find it hard to

---

40 Although reference is made to the experience of North African states elsewhere in this volume, this study focuses on sub-Saharan Africa, given its distinct pre-colonial, colonial and post-colonial history.

41 Cited in HW Arndt, "The Origins of Structuralism", *World Development*, 13, 2, 1985.

move or adapt, and resources tend to be stuck. In economic terms, the supply of most things is inelastic. Such general inflexibility was thought to apply particularly to LDCs [least developed countries].

As Little suggests, there would appear to be clear limits on what developing countries can do to change factors that inhibit development. Some issues cannot be changed: geography, weather patterns and other apparently exogenous factors beyond the control of states and their citizens. And for those issues which can be altered through domestic actions, it is clear too – or it should be – that we face a world in which the majority of its citizens (the 3.6 billion of the low-income developing world and the 1.48 billion of the middle-income community) see issues quite differently to the manner in which the minority (the 886 million of the high-income developed world) do. But it is more often the latter who set the agenda, both through their political and economic influence in multilateral fora and through their military power.

The second of these approaches focuses instead on the efficacy of *qualitative* or *voluntarist* "neo-classical" or "neo-liberal" policy changes for developing states. Examples are policy issues related to governance such as macroeconomic and microeconomic reforms, fiscal prudence, allocation of public resources, as well as leadership styles and practices. According to this argument, the success of global strategies is not premised entirely on the actions of the developed North, and recovery will have to involve a partnership in which the developing South plays a proactive part. These strategies include the establishment and policing of strict governance criteria essential to successfully combating poverty and ensuring prosperity, involving observation of the rule of law, freedom of the markets, and upholding of individual rights. In this vein, while it is important for the North to play its part through poverty alleviation and debt relief strategies along with improved access to its markets, developing countries will also have to clean up their own acts – removing impediments to trade, and improving the trust of investors, *inter alia* through the creation of sound domestic financial and other sectors.

This book examines the synergy of these two responses between the international and national environments. In doing so, the study seeks to provide policy-relevant options for decision-makers both inside and outside the African continent which also have resonance for developing states elsewhere. At the heart of this study is a wish to understand not what Africa *ought* to look like, but rather a desire to build on local realities about what Africa *does* look like, and *how* the situation might best be positively influenced by learning from the experience of others.

This study recognises the degrees of variance between different parts of the continent – from genuine success stories to complete disasters – and abandons, from the outset, the assumption that one formula must fit all. In doing so, it seeks to lay out alternative choices for the steps that decision-makers both inside and outside the continent can take – working with the grain of African realities, rather than against it – to help manage the forces that are rapidly and dramatically changing this important but imperilled part of the planet. The study is thus deliberately descriptive, analytical and modestly prescriptive, drawing a number of conclusions about suitable external and African policy responses.

Key questions examined include:
- What are the developmental challenges facing Africa, and how can we categorise the different levels of development in (and differentiate between) African countries?
- What is the nature of the external environment in which these challenges have to be met?
- What conditions denote a "stateless" or "dysfunctional" state, and what, if anything, can be done to remedy this condition?
- How have other developing states managed similar challenges? What policy interventions have met with success? Would those governments do things differently today – for example, in Asia following the 1997 economic crisis, and in contemporary Latin America?
- What is the relationship between external intervention and development: in, for example, the efficacy of aid?
- How might conflict resolution and post-conflict intervention efforts best be directed, especially in Africa, and what lessons can be learned from recent experiences in African countries?
- What role is there for the international community (for states and for civil society, along with business) in assisting economic reform and creating conditions of good governance?
- Finally, how can Africa fulfil its promise and create a logic of recovery and prosperity? Can this be brought about through the vision of an African renaissance, or as encapsulated in NEPAD?

The book is intended, principally, to have policy ramifications, and to be accessible to the general reader rather than the specialist academic. But it is also aimed at complementing recent major academic studies on African state behaviour and international relations.[42] It draws on studies of Latin America and Asia in an attempt to provide a comparative basis of examination, and relies heavily on fieldwork conducted on the three continents.[43]

---

42 Including: John Harbeson and Donald Rothchild (eds.), *op cit*; Jeffrey Herbst, *States and Power in Africa*. Princeton: PUP, 2000; Christopher Clapham, *Africa in the International System*. Cambridge: CUP, 1997; and, Patrick Chabal and Jean-Pascal Daloz, *op cit*. On Latin America, see Victor Bulmer-Thomas, *The Economic History of Latin America since Independence*. Cambridge: CUP, 1994; Richard Salvucci (ed.), *Latin America and the World Economy: Dependency and Beyond*. Lexington: DC Heath, 1996; Jeffrey Frieden, Manuel Pastor and Michael Tomz (eds.), *Modern Political Economy and Latin America: Theory and Policy*. Boulder: Westview, 2000; Stephen Haber (ed.), *Political Institutions and Economic Growth in Latin America: Essays in Policy, History and Political Economy*. California: Hoover Institution Press, 2000; and Julia Buxton and Nicola Phillips (eds.), *Developments in Latin American Political Economy*. Manchester: Manchester University Press, 1999. On Asia, relevant material includes Ross McLeod and Ross Gaurant (eds.), *East Asia in Crisis: From Being a Miracle to Needing One*. London: Routledge, 1998; Karl D Jackson (ed.), *Asian Contagion: the Causes and Consequences of a Financial Crisis*. Boulder: Westview, 1999; Mya Than (ed.), *ASEAN Beyond the Regional Crisis*. Singapore: ISEAS, 2001; Michael Backman, *Asian Eclipse*. Singapore: John Wiley, 2001; and Philippe Riés, *The Asian Storm: Asia's Economic Crisis Examined*. Boston: Tuttle, 2000.

43 Countries visited during the course of this research include: Argentina, Australia, Botswana, Brazil, Chile, the DRC, Ghana, Indonesia, Japan, Madagascar, Malaysia, Malawi, Morocco, Mozambique, Singapore, South Korea, Sudan, Swaziland and Taiwan.

CHAPTER ONE

DEBUNKING THE THEORIES?
Governance and the Global Environment

> Globalisation often has been a very powerful force for poverty reduction, but too many countries and people have been left out. Important reasons for this exclusion are weak governance and policies in the non-integrating countries, tariffs and other barriers that poor countries and poor people face in accessing rich country markets, and declining development assistance.
>
> NICHOLAS STERN, *World Bank Chief Economist*[1]

> It is very unjust if globalisation only goes in one direction.
>
> JUAN SOLER-ESPIAUSA GALLO,
> *Fundacón Para el Análisis y Los Estudios Sociales*[2]

The World After September 11

The Archbishop of Canterbury, George Carey, neatly encapsulated the challenges facing the international community at the start of the 21st century, in reflecting on the World Economic Forum held in January 2002 in New York.

He noted that the meeting took place in the "long shadow" of the events of September 11, which, he said, illustrated the dangers of "dearth" – that "poverty and want may offer a fertile breeding ground for the growth and practice of terrorism". But the WEF summit also took place in the shadow of the collapse of the US energy giant Enron, arguably indicative of capitalism's excesses and of the failure both of corporate governance and US government oversight. Without attempting to draw an equivalence between the two events – Enron and the September 11 bombings – the Archbishop successfully emphasised the way in which these two forces, dearth and excess, could destroy the common good.[3] The same qualities might be used to describe the world of globalisation or, indeed, the conditions present in many de-

---

1 On *http://lnweb18.worldbank.org/news/pressrelease.*
2 Interview, Madrid, 21 February 2002.
3 "Enron's collapse teaches us the dangers of excess", *Daily Telegraph*, 20 February 2002.

veloping countries: of extremes of wealth and poverty dividing nations and peoples, and the means available to address these.

★ ★ ★

The events of September 11 spotlight three features of contemporary globalisation.

The first is the increased pace and volume of technical or technological aspects, including digital communication. Along with burgeoning trade and investment ties, technological advance is apparently inevitable and unstoppable, even though its global regulation is not. In the absence of such regulation, this integration process may create ongoing tensions and even social and interstate ruptures.

Second, although the world is a wealthier place because of globalisation, societies have arguably been weakened in a number of critical respects. Examples are cultural diversity and social insecurity, relating especially to employment, marriage, and delinquency. Moreover, increasingly questions are being asked about the type of protection required for smaller, especially developing countries, many of them overburdened by social inequity, poor education standards and a fragile sense of national identity. While globalisation offers improved communications, not all have access to this technology, even though many can now see how citizens of the developed world live. This creates a tension between ordinary people, who aspire to the way of life enjoyed by citizens of industrialised societies, and their governments, which face enormous difficulties in attempting to meet such expectations. As Brian Hanrahan has observed in this respect:[4]

> [G]lobalisation, the new phenomenon that was generating such economic benefit for the United States, was also doing it enormous harm. The Internet and the boom in other media carried America's influence around the world. However, it also boosted the influence of its opponents, who were reaching layers of society that hadn't previously had a voice in politics. And their attack on America's reputation was spreading faster than America could counter it.

---

4 Brian Hanrahan, "America the Unloved" in Jenny Baxter and Malcolm Downing (eds.), *The Day that Shook the World: Understanding September 11*. Sydney: British Broadcasting Corporation (BBC) and the Australian Broadcasting Corporation (ABC), 2002, p.53.

Third, as Prime Minister Tony Blair pointed out, September 11 has stressed the connection between development and security, not only within small states, as development discourse suggested decades ago, but within the international system itself. In this new security framework, the "modalities of underdevelopment have become dangerous". This is in stark contrast to security thinking during the Cold War when "the threat of massive interstate conflict prevailed". Now the "question of security has almost gone full circle: from being concerned with the biggest economies and war machines in the world to an interest in some of its smallest".[5] There appears to be a relationship between poverty, resources, non-state actors, and weak, failing or predatory institutions and states. Their connection with crime and terrorism has come under the international microscope, as have the means of resolving these problems.

The Age of Globalisation

For many, September 11 thus offers tragic proof of the unresolved tensions between the "haves" and the "have-nots" – and, conversely, of the common interests between the countries of the developing world and their counterparts in the developed "North". As the head of the United Nations Development Programme (UNDP), James Gustave Speth, argued in 1996:[6]

> Most important are the links between development and peace. Many critics of international assistance have not paused to think about the underlying causes of the conflicts in which the United Nations and others are becoming involved. Degrading poverty, diminishing natural resources, and increasing joblessness all feed ethnic and social tensions. It is from this cauldron that crises can boil over.

In line with the increasingly violent protests at the major international summits held in Seattle, Gothenberg and Genoa, concern has shifted to addressing the uneven impact of globalisation on developing countries. Here co-operation between the North and the South in re-

---

5   Mark Duffield, *Global Governance and the New Wars: The Merging of Development and Security*. London: Zed, 2001, p.16.
6   Cited in Paul Cornish, "Terrorism, insecurity and underdevelopment", *Journal for Conflict, Security and Development*, 1, 3, 2001, p.149.

structuring the global trade and investment terrain has been deemed by many as critically important. There would now appear to be, in the light of September 11, a collective self-interest to be served in building more complete social, economic and political systems and architecture through which the root causes of terrorism, including social and economic alienation, violence, and the absence of justice, can be addressed. This shift towards coalition-seeking and consensus-building complements other efforts being made to avoid such clashes and to address issues of global governance.[7]

This was the thrust of the open letter written in September 2001 by Belgian Prime Minister Guy Verhofstadt, then president of the European Union. Addressed to the anti-globalisation movement, Verhofstadt's submission called for international co-operation rather than parochialism to develop solutions to the problems of marginalisation and exclusion, the most commonly quoted downside of globalisation. Noting that it does not make "any sense to be unreservedly for or against globalisation", he wrote, "the question is rather how everybody, including the poor, can benefit from the manifest advantages of globalisation without suffering from any of its disadvantages". He called for "ethical globalisation" – a "triangle consisting of free trade, knowledge and democracy; alternatively, trade, aid and conflict prevention".

Verhofstadt's letter both highlighted and complemented other, similar initiatives. For example, following Genoa's upheavals, Klaus Schwab, the president of the World Economic Forum, proposed a global refocus from the G8 in favour of the more diverse group of G20 industrialised and emerging markets originally created in 1999. (Members included South Africa, Brazil, China, India, Mexico and Turkey.) Schwab wrote that this would be the first step towards a more participatory management of globalisation, involving not only governments but also representatives from business and civil society. But such a broad collection of nations would arguably only hope to be effective if it sought solutions that were practical and politically feasible in both their worlds – with the consequent risk of reducing global action, in essence, to the lowest acceptable denominator.

---

7 This section is based, in part, on an article jointly written with Jonathan Oppenheimer that appeared in *The Sunday Independent*, 21 October 2001.

But globalisation is not a new phenomenon.[8]
Global trading routes and people movements are as old as maps themselves. Indeed, the transition into the information age or post-modern
era has been labelled the "Third Wave", suggesting that it is as important as the two previous historical transitions – those from hunter-
gatherer to agricultural, to industrial societies.[9] The World Bank has
characterised three periods of globalisation: that between 1870 and
1914, which was spurred by better transport links and lower freight
costs; that between 1945 and 1980, which rolled back the years of protectionism and revived international trade links; and that from 1980
until today.[10] Within this broad framework, however, societies developed at very different rates. In the 21st century, there are stark differences between developed (predominantly Western) and developing
(or Third World) states. This gives rise to different problems relating
to different levels of development, and such problems demand different solutions.

What has changed today is the pressure on states to conform and
to compete on a wider international stage. Therefore the focus is on
the depth and speed of global integration. Production has become
globalised across national borders, while information technologies
have emphasised the role of knowledge in these processes. Cultural,
even national, boundaries and communities are becoming altered,
too, by the deluge of electronically transmitted information.[11]

In this environment, "governance" – especially "good governance"
and "global governance" – has become a 21st century buzzword. Good
governance is today a concept used as a literal means test for the success and potential of economic reforms. The term is taken to encom-
pass limited but effective government, the implementation of a range
of liberal macroeconomic policies, sound and forward-looking leadership, the absence of corruption, and national and regional political
and social stability. It has become a policy end in itself, with the notion of good governance emerging in the 1990s as a political conditionality in the structural adjustment programmes of the World

---

8 For a detailed examination of the nature and impact of globalisation, see Greg
   Mills, *The Wired Model: South Africa, Foreign Policy and Globalisation*. Cape Town:
   Tafelberg, 2000; also Francis Fukuyama, *The Great Disruption: Human Nature
   and the Reconstitution of Social Order*. London: Profile, 2000.
9 See Alvin Toffler, *The Third Wave*. New York: William Morrow, 1980.
10 See *http://econ.worldbank.org/files/2896_ch1.pdf*.
11 See Fukuyama, *op cit*, p.3.

Bank, in the belief that economic reforms were more likely to succeed if the right, democratic sociopolitical context were encouraged.

However, good governance is not the only requirement for success in the harshly competitive world economy. Regional strength is another critical feature. The development of regional units is synonymous with the age of globalisation and technology in which we live today, along with faster and larger international financial flows, burgeoning global trade volumes, and reducing costs for more efficient transport and communication links. Other, sometimes more pernicious, effects of globalisation are the spread of transnational influences including crime, illegal immigration and refugee flows, and environmental and health risks.

It is said that if technology makes globalisation feasible, liberalisation makes it happen.[12] This process of trade liberalisation has taken two ultimately interlinked roads: one, global tariff reduction through the General Agreement on Tariffs and Trade (GATT) and the WTO; and, second, regional integration. With regard to the global arena, the volume of international trade increased at twice the rate of growth of world output between 1985 and 1994.[13] World output has expanded fivefold over the last 50 years, while world trade has expanded 16 times.[14] The proportion of intra-regional trade to total trade has been steadily increasing: between 1980-1989 from 51% to 59% in Europe, from 33% to 37% in East Asia, and from 32% to 36% in North America.[15] Around 60% of world trade occurs within regional trade blocs.

Tying the concepts of good governance and economic liberalisation together is the notion of "global governance". In his *An Agenda for Peace*, published in the early 1990s, then UN Secretary-General Boutros Boutros-Ghali noted the willingness of states to yield sovereign prerogatives to collective regional and international political associations. This has been made more urgent by the threat posed to state cohesion by conflict, and by the relationship between underdevelopment and deepening poverty and the causes of conflict. Boutros-Ghali argued that conflict prevention had to address the reasons behind

---

12 See Martin Wolf, "Why this hatred of the market?", *Financial Times*, May 1997.

13 See Dani Rodrik, *The New Global Economy: Making Openness Work*. Washington DC: ODC, Policy Essay 24, 1999, p.9.

14 *African Development Report 2000*. Oxford: African Development Bank/Oxford University Press, 2000, p.109.

15 These figures are cited in Samuel Huntington, "The Clash of Civilisations?", *Foreign Affairs*, 72, 3, 1993.

conflict, notably "economic despair, social injustice and political oppression".[16] Their resolution presumes the operation of liberal principles of international co-operation, intervention and partnership.

With this backdrop in mind, this chapter discusses three issues:
• First, the nature of the global environment facing developing states, especially in the post-millennium context.
• Second, an understanding of the term "good governance".
• Third, the challenges obstructing deeper integration with and between developing countries, particularly in Africa.

★ ★ ★

Globalisation circa *2002:* A World in Transition?

Globalisation has resulted in improved levels of wealth and respect for human rights worldwide.

Child death rates, for example, have fallen by half since 1965, and in developing countries the proportion of children in primary school has risen from less than one half to three quarters. People now work fewer hours for more money, even in developing countries, and they live longer. A combination of improvements in sanitation and health care, along with higher agricultural yields and better technology, have also generally translated into improved prosperity and longer life expectancy for the world population: up from 71.5 years in 1970 to 77.7 in industrial nations; and from 54.5 to 64.4 in developing countries over the same period. Worldwide GDP has increased ninefold to US$30 trillion over the past 50 years, while the share of people enjoying "medium human development" rose from 55% in 1975 to 66% in 1970. During the same time span, the share in "low human development" fell from 20% to 10%. In 1980, there were an estimated 1.4 billion people in the world living in extreme poverty – that is, on less than US$1 a day. This number had been rising since 1820. Between 1980-2000, however, it fell by 200 million to 1.2 billion.

---

16 Boutros Boutros-Ghali, *An Agenda for Peace*. New York: UN, 1995, p.43.

World poverty, 1820-1998

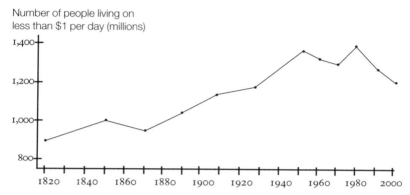

SOURCE: The World Bank, *Globalisation, Growth and Poverty: Building an Inclusive World Economy*

As the Centre for Trade Policy Studies has noted:[17]

> Because it expands economic freedom and spurs competition, globalisation raises the productivity and living standards of people in countries that open themselves to the global marketplace. For less developed countries, globalisation offers access to foreign capital, global export markets, and advanced technology, while breaking the monopoly of inefficient and protected domestic producers. Faster growth, in turn, promotes poverty reduction, democratisation, and higher labour and environmental standards. While globalisation may confront government officials with more difficult choices, the result for their citizens is greater individual freedom. In this sense, globalisation acts as a check on governmental power that makes it more difficult for governments to abuse the freedom and property of their citizens.

Personal freedoms have, indeed, improved. The late 20th century saw the rapid spread of democracy as the accepted form of government worldwide. At the start of the 20th century, only six of the 43 states recognised as nation-states could be considered democratic. In 1980, 37 of 121 countries were democracies. Today 117 of the world's 192 countries, accounting for more than 70% of the world's population, live

17 See *http://www.freetrade.org/issues/globalization.html.*

under pluralistic regimes. Even in Africa, long considered democrati-
cally backward, the number of democracies increased from just four
(Senegal, The Gambia, Botswana and Mauritius) in 1980 to over 40
today. Of course, while these figures are relevant in charting a general progress, they have to be qualified. Democracy is not simply de-
finable as the result of a "free" (or acceptably "fair") election, but entails a functioning liberal constitution and working institutions. It also,
critically, involves the presence of an effective parliamentary system
and opposition, with a balance between the influence of the executive,
government and opposition.

As the World Bank has noted,[18] the wave of globalisation starting in
1980 is distinctive for a number of reasons. First, a large group of developing nations has been able to break into global markets, increasing the percentage of manufactured goods as exports of developing
countries from 25% in 1980 to more than 80% by 1998. This occurred
as developed nations moved further up the manufacturing value-
added chain, and moved their lower-end operations to lower-cost developing countries, taking advantage of the cheaper skills available
there.

Second, those developing nations which could not (or did not) engage with the global economy became increasingly marginalised, suffering declining incomes and consequently greater poverty. Third, this
period has also been characterised by significant international increases in the movement of people and capital. In contrast, during the period of "second-wave globalisation" from 1945 to 1980, growth for developing nations was significantly slower than in richer countries. As
a result, world inequality in 1980 – measured as a sum of equity within and between both developed and developing countries – was about
the same as it had been 25 years before.

But even during the period from 1980 onwards the wealth-creation
process has not been uniform, either between or within states, as the
table below suggests.[19] For example, the gap between the world's sev-
en richest and seven poorest nations nearly doubled in the 30 years
after 1965.[20] According to the UNDP, the income gap between the

---

18 See *Globalisation, Growth and Poverty: Building an Inclusive World Economy* on
   http://econ.worldbank.org/files/2896_ch1.pdf.
19 I am grateful to Séan Cleary for the concept of this table.
20 See "Freedom's Journey: A Survey of the 20th Century", *The Economist*, 11 September 1999. The statistics in this section are drawn both from this article and
   the United Nations Development Programme (UNDP), *Human Development
   Report*, 1999. New York: Oxford University Press (OUP)/UNDP, 1999, p.25.

richest and poorest fifth worldwide was 74:1 in 1997, up from 60:1 in 1990 and 30:1 in 1960. This parallels, too, the widening income disparity between the top and bottom countries in the 19th century, from 3:1 in 1820 to 11:1 in 1913. By the turn of the last century, nearly one quarter of the world's population – 1.5 billion people – lived in absolute poverty, while the richest fifth disposed of 85% of global wealth.[21] As noted above, half of Africa's population, totalling 800 million people, exist on less than US$1 per day. This is partly a function of different starting points in the development process, but part of the reason is that many African states are dysfunctional, as are some in Asia. Dysfunctional states are unable to operate at even the most basic level, let alone fulfil the rigorous requirements of global competition.

On the effects of globalisation on the wellbeing of the world's population, Kofi Annan has observed that:[22]

> There is much to be grateful for. Most people today can expect to live longer than their parents, let alone their more remote ancestors. They are better nourished, enjoy better health, are better educated, and on the whole face more favourable economic prospects. There are also many things to deplore, and to correct. The century just ended was disfigured, time and again, by ruthless conflict. Grinding poverty and striking inequality persist within and among countries even amidst unprecedented wealth. Diseases, old and new, threaten to undo painstaking progress. Nature's life-sustaining services, on which our species depends for its survival, are being seriously disrupted and degraded by our own everyday activities.

The World Bank has identified a group of developing countries (including China, India, Malaysia, Mexico, the Philippines and Thailand) that have, over the past 25 years, managed to integrate with the world economy, and have doubled their ratio of trade to GDP in the past 20 years. Their relative growth in GDP per person has accelerated from 1% in the 1960s to 3% in the 1970s, 4% in the 1980s and 5% in the 1990s.[23]

21 See Hans-Peter Martin and Harald Schumann, *The Global Trap: Globalisation and the Assault on Democracy and Prosperity.* Pretoria: HSRC, 1997, p.23.
22 See *http://www.un.org/News/ossg/sg/.*
23 See Ross Gittins, "Globalisation's benefits starting to filter down", *Sydney Morning Herald*, 2 February 2002 on
http://www.smh.com.au/news/0202/02/biztech/comment2.html.

While income per person was growing at a rate of 5% annually in these countries, in rich countries it was growing at a rate of only 2%, narrowing the gap between rich and poor countries. But most of these globalising economies have seen only small changes in income inequality between households. In some countries, such as those in Latin America, the gap has increased, mainly due to pre-existing extreme inequality in levels of education. In China, the gap has widened because the pace of development has differed between the cities and the country. But overall rates of life expectancy and levels of schooling are rising in countries that have adapted to globalisation, to levels close to those prevailing in rich countries around 1960. Yet two thirds of developing countries, mainly including countries from sub-Saharan Africa, the Middle East and the former Soviet Union, have not gained from globalisation. This group accounts for two billion of the world's population. Such countries are predominantly exporters of primary products, and have suffered an outflow of foreign and local capital. In this group, whereas education levels are rising slowly, life expectancy is falling. As the IMF has noted:[24]

> Globalisation leads to economic growth and higher incomes. No country has benefited for any length of time from closed-door policies, and the countries that have achieved most prosperity have embraced globalisation, together with the policies that make it work. Outward-oriented policies brought dynamism and prosperity to much of East and Southeast Asia. This experience shows that globalisation offers extensive opportunities for truly worldwide development. But it is clearly not progressing evenly and countries that are integrating more slowly are seeing slower growth and more poverty.

Also:

> One very important reason that global inequality has increased – with some countries doing extremely well and others poorly – is that many countries have resisted globalisation or the policies needed to tap its benefits. In the 1970s and 1980s when many countries in Latin America and Africa pursued inward-oriented policies, their economies stagnated or declined, poverty increased and sometimes hyperinflation set in. As these regions have changed

---

24 On *http://www.imf.org/external/np/exr/ib/2000/041200b.htm#II.*

their policies, their incomes have begun to rise. . . . The trends toward openness and sound economic policies, together with strongly pro-poor policies, are essential components of effective strategies for reducing poverty in the low-income countries.

As a result, perceptions of the benefits of globalisation tend to be skewed according to where one sits ideologically or geographically. Whereas advocates cite its virtues and its inevitability, "[o]pponents proclaim its supposed vices and vincibility".[25] Jagdish Bhagwati cites a "trilogy of discontents" concerning the process of globalisation, the idea of capitalism and so-called "market populism", and the behaviour of corporations.[26] Sceptics express doubts about globalisation's ability to deliver social justice (though socialism, globalisation's apparent ideological counterpoint, aims to constrain market access), resentment at global wealth divides conveyed by media images and, ironically, reflecting the fragile nature of the anti-globalisation alliance, criticism of global monopolies (including the media). As John Pilger has argued, "There is no news from Africa. In the Media Age, the continent hardly exists."[27] Or as Edward Said has contended:[28]

The threat to independence in the late twentieth century from the new electronics could be greater than was colonialism itself. We are beginning to learn that de-colonisation was not the termination of imperial relationships but merely the extending of a geopolitical web which has been spinning since the Renaissance. The new media have the power to penetrate more deeply into a "receiving" culture than any previous manifestation of Western technology.

And as Litha Musyimi-Ogana has noted:[29]

Africa is reaping few, if any, benefits from globalisation. For the Western world, liberalisation of the global economy will translate

---

25 Jagdish Bhagwati, "Coping with Globalisation: A Trilogy of Discontents", *Foreign Affairs*, 81, 1, January/February 2002, p.2.
26 For a critique of globalisation and the so-called New Economy, see Thomas Frank, *One Market Under God*. Sydney: Vintage, 2002.
27 John Pilger, *Hidden Agendas*. South Africa: Random House, 1999, p.9.
28 Edward Said, *Culture and Imperialism*. London: Chatto and Windus, 1993, pp.352-3 cited in Pilger, *ibid*, p.9.
29 Litha Musyimi-Ogana, "For Africa, Few – If Any – Benefits from Globalisation", on *http://www.wedo.org/news/Nov99/africa.htm*.

into increased opportunities such as expanded trade, new technology, foreign investment, and media and Internet coverage.
In Africa, however, it merely means expanded domestic markets
for goods and services coming from the West. This opening up
of national boundaries for foreign trade, capital, technology and
information is outpacing governance of Third World markets at
the expense of people and their rights. . . . Africa's macroeconomic policies have been re-aligned to respond to the music of globalisation – the famous "trim" and "efficient" public sector that
can only be achieved through a painful restructuring process. This
process has rendered millions of people jobless and income-less
and condemned many others to street life. We have seen our social services collapse because governments have withdrawn subsidies from the poor and vulnerable members of society. We have
watched our environment being exploited by Westerners.

As the table below indicates, the level of GDP of 40 of 48 sub-Saharan
African countries is below the turnover of the 500th ranking company in the Fortune 500 index.

Global Wealth Index

COUNTRY/REGION/COMPANY	COUNTRY RANK	GDP BILLION (1999)[30]
OECD		24,863.1
United States	1	9,152.1
Developing Countries		5,826.7
Japan	2	4,346.9
East Asia and the Pacific		2,122.0
Germany	3	2,111.9
Latin America & Caribbean		1,989.8
UK	4	1,441.8
France	5	1,432.3
Italy	6	1,171.0
China	7	989.5
Brazil	8	751.5
Canada	9	634.9

30 These figures are calculated from the UNDP, *Human Development Report
2001*. New York: UNDP with OUP, 2001, pp.178-181.

South Asia		684.0
Spain	10	595.9
Sub-Saharan Africa		309.8
Argentina	16	283.2
Belgium	18	248.4
Exxon/Mobil	*#1 (Fortune Global 500)*[31]	210.392
Wal-Mart	2	193.295,0
General Motors	3	184.632,0
Ford	4	180.598,0
Daimler-Chrysler	5	150.069,7
Royal Dutch/Shell Group	6	149.146,0
BP Amoco	7	148.062,0
General Electric	8	129.853,0
Mitsubishi	9	126.579,4
Toyota Motor	10	121.416,2
South Africa	27	131.1
Nigeria	51	35.0
Sodexho Alliance	*#500 (Fortune Global 500)*	10.306,3
Tanzania		8.8
Angola		8.5
Botswana		6.0
Zimbabwe		5.6
DRC		5.6
Mauritius		4.2
Sierra Leone		0.7

Thus the advantages accruing to some countries and sectors through globalisation have not stopped the debate about how to cope with, and benefit from, its technologies. The debate also concerns how to develop institutional and other global norms to manage the problems of this new operating environment.[32] It should also continue to ponder how smaller, less developed states may benefit from globalisation.

---

31 These figures are for 2002. See *http://www.fortune.com*.
32 This section draws on the address given by Fred Phaswana, SAIIA National Chairman, Cape Town, 22 August 2001. See also Nicolas Guyatt, *Another American Century? The United States and the World After 2000*. Cape Town: David Philip, 2000.

In the decade immediately following the collapse of the Soviet Union, a number of different theories were advanced regarding the future of international relations. Generally, it was suggested that in the global system the state would no longer be the centre of attention, and that engagement would shift – at least in part – towards business as the centrepiece of economic activity, and to civil society. In this new environment, there would be both a "peace dividend", as armies became increasingly redundant, and a "democracy dividend", as a more stable and prosperous Western, liberal model of democratic capitalism took root. Foreign policy, it was suggested, would in part be geared to the creation of democracies as the most accepted form of government. And for many states, "commercial diplomacy", where business, government and civil society would work hand-in-hand to tap into external markets, would supplant previous patterns of foreign engagement.

Looking back on the post-Cold War decade, I can identify five issues which provide the overall policy context for this study.

Identifying the Policy Issues

Issue One: The Pursuit of Democracy, Modernity, Security and Stability

The rapid growth of the economies of the East Asian tigers from the 1960s onwards stimulated three related areas of debate over economic reform in developing societies. These revolved around, first, the relationship between authoritarian government and economic development; second, what methods could best be adopted to achieve political and social stability to provide a secure context for economic growth; and third, the role of special values in assisting this process. The difficulties that Southeast Asian economies found themselves in at the end of the 1990s raise additional questions about the need for transparency, accountability and democracy to safeguard the path of economic development, and stress the importance of outside players to this process.

This Asian experience illustrates the changes brought about by the end of the Cold War. During this period, superpower rivalries ensured that "world politics remained a zero-sum game in which the success of one side was defined by the failure of the other".[33] Since then, the

---

33 "Principles of a Modern Global Community". Speech given by UK Foreign Secretary Jack Straw at the Lord Mayor's Banquet, Mansion House, London, 10 April 2002.

dissipation of such rivalries, combined with the spread of free trade, mass tourism and global communications, has served to draw people, states and values closer together, to share both a common understanding and a sense of a global community. As noted above, the world now has more democracies, and nations have embraced the rule of law, market economics and human rights in increasing numbers.

In spite of globalisation and the apparent spread of common values, a number of problems still exist.

First, democracy as a model for all states was (and remains) a contested notion, not least in Asia and parts of Africa, where the state is sometimes weak, ill-formed or even dysfunctional. As Robert Kaplan reminds us, "States have never been formed by elections. . . . Social stability results from the establishment of a middle class."[34] Nonetheless, although the promotion of democracy might not have brought tolerance, respect for human rights and a deeper "culture" of democratic values, the link between democracy and sustainable economic development is apparently more widely accepted. Where there is democracy, there is more likely to be observance of the rule of law and of human rights, and the existence of a stable, free-market economy.

Second, the *promotion* of democracy has not necessarily brought stability. Indeed, in some cases it has not brought democracy at all. The "democratic peace" thesis, which was linked to the notion that the end of the Cold War symbolised the "end of history" and a vindication of the Western democratic-capitalist model, rested on the ability of countries successfully to promote and consolidate democracy. In practice, however, Western democracies have been reluctant to commit resources to this task, especially in countries where their own interests are minimal (as in much of Africa). In their defence, it has not always been clear how foreign interests can create the conditions necessary to help democracy take root. Nor has the West used the existence of democracy as a condition for aid and engagement in undemocratic countries where it has strategic interests, notably in China and the oil-producing countries of the Middle East and Africa.

Third, though it is generally accepted (especially after the attacks of September 11), that the international community should play a more active role in dealing with conflicts within states and with state collapse, the appropriate policies to achieve this are unclear. Military

---

34 "Was democracy just a moment?", *The Coming Anarchy: Shattering the Dreams of the Post Cold War*. New York: Vintage Books, 2000, pp.69-70.

intervention and humanitarian and development aid do not create
states.

Fourth, state dysfunctionality – or insufficient capacity – is linked
to entrenched security difficulties, which increase poverty and threaten
both the sustainability of democratic practices and economic progress.
The US National Intelligence Council's (NIC) *Global Trends* 2015
notes that in sub-Saharan Africa:[35]

> The interplay of demographics and disease – as well as poor gov-
> ernance – will be the major determinants of Africa's increasing
> international marginalisation in 2015. Most African states will
> miss out on the economic growth engendered elsewhere by glob-
> alisation and by scientific and technological advances. Only a few
> countries will do better, while a handful of states will have hardly
> any relevance to the lives of their citizens. As sub-Saharan Africa's
> multiple and interconnected problems are compounded, eth-
> nic and communal tensions will intensify, periodically escalating
> into open conflict, often spreading across borders and sometimes
> spawning secessionist states.

According to the report, "in sub-Saharan Africa, persistent conflicts
and instability, autocratic and corrupt governments, overdependence
on commodities with declining real prices, low levels of education, and
widespread infectious diseases combine to prevent most countries from
experiencing rapid economic growth". In summary, it cogently notes,
"The quality of governance, rather than resource endowments, will be
the key determinant of development and differentiation among African
states." What remains unclear, however, is: How can policy interventions be made which will improve this environment and positively influence the pestiferous cycle of disease, failing governance and divided
societies?

Fifth, modernity is increasingly seen as synonymous with state stability, being linked to the adoption of the aforementioned economic
policies, and the sort of values enshrined in the Universal Declaration of Human Rights, which should transcend cultures and religions;
and of legislation reflecting developments in international law (such
as the creation of the International Criminal Court). However, the
debate concerning special social and economic routes for development

---

35 See *http://www.cia.gov/nic/nic_publications/index.htm.*

is still simultaneously promoted and contested. While the World Bank has acknowledged that many countries take different paths to development and to good governance depending on "culture, geography, political and administrative traditions, economic conditions and many other factors", it also believes that governments "share many features". These include the "need to establish a basic policy framework, provide critical goods and services, protect and administer the rule of law, and advance social equity". "Good governance", the Bank notes in its 1998 report on *Governance in Asia: from Crisis to Opportunity*, "is good government". It argues, "The concept relates to the quality of the relationship between government and the citizens whom it exists to serve and protect."[36] Is it thus possible to pursue different economic development paths along the lines suggested by the debates over "Asian" values or, for that matter, an "African" renaissance?

Issue Two: Good Governance and the Global Environment

It has been shown that there is no alternative to good governance (that is, transparency, and accessible, responsive government) in ensuring economic prosperity and stability. This was the principal lesson to be learnt, for example, from the collapse of Asia's economies in the late 1990s. But what do we understand by the notion of "good governance" and its relationship to policy?

Former EU Development Commissioner João de Deus Pinheiro is reported to have said that "Good governance is like love: you can't define it, but you know that it's there."[37] A more exact definition was provided by Sudanese Foreign Minister Mustafa Osman Ismail, in July 2001, when asked in an interview what he understood by the term "good governance". The minister replied that he viewed it in terms of the need to instil eight elements in his government: democracy; respect for human rights; peace, stability and national unity; economic stability; intolerance of corruption; openness; good neighbourliness; and integration with international values.[38] Although these are hardly concepts synonymous with Sudan, the minister's statement is an indication of how far different countries have come together in their identification of common challenges, and in a common understanding of what governance implies.

---

36 World Bank, *Annual Report 1998*. Washington: World Bank, 1998, p.16.
37 I am grateful to Abdul Minty for this anecdote.
38 Interview, State Guest House, Pretoria, 25 July 2001.

The UNDP has pinpointed a number of "subjective" and "objective" indicators of governance. The former group includes civil liberties, political rights, press freedom, levels of violence and political stability, law and order, rule of law, government effectiveness, and perceptions of graft and corruption. The latter involves political participation, the number and role of nongovernmental organisations (NGOs), freedom of association and collective bargaining, and the ratification of international conventions on civil and political rights.[39]

More specifically, in an address given in 1998 entitled "The IMF and Good Governance",[40] then Managing Director of the Fund Michel Camdessus described what was needed to promote good governance. The IMF, he noted, believed that the value of good governance lay in its "ensuring the rule of law, improving the efficiency and accountability of the public sector, and tackling corruption". He said, "in a world in which private capital has become more mobile, there is mounting evidence that corruption undermines the confidence of the most serious investors and adversely affects private capital inflows – this is the case in all too many countries in Africa". The IMF, he said, helps to promote better governance by assisting its members to "improve the management of their public resources and establish a stable and transparent regulatory environment for public sector activity, a *sine qua non* for economic efficiency and the eradication of corruption". This included the minimisation of *ad hoc* and preferential decision-making; the simplification and strengthening of tax and customs regimes and systems, and of business legislation; and improving the transparency of budgetary procedures and the quality of government expenditure (reducing outlays on costly unproductive projects such as military expenditure, and increasing spending on primary health care, education and basic infrastructure).

The UN's Economic and Social Commission for Asia and the Pacific (ESCAP) has identified eight major features of good governance in decision-making – it must be participatory, consensus-oriented, accountable, effective and efficient, equitable and inclusive, and be compliant with the rule of law.[41]

To a great extent, however, good governance is linked with economic policy and the attitude of government towards corruption. This

---

39 UNDP, *Human Development Report 2002: Deepening Democracy in a Fragmented World*. New York: UNDP with Oxford University Press, 2002, pp.38-45.
40 See *http://www.imf.org/external/np/speeches/1998/012198.htm*.
41 See *http://unescap.org/huset/gg/governance.htm*.

in turn reflects not only the practices of individuals, but also the legal, administrative and, indeed, political environment in which they operate. Although corruption takes many forms and is often linked to economic and cultural environments, and can introduce numerous distortions and costs (not least the discouragement of higher FDI inflows), self-interest lies at its heart.[42] For this reason, corruption is not uniquely African or Asian; nor is it confined to developed or developing states. It is a global phenomenon, costing an estimated US$80 billion annually.[43]

Good governance has thus become one of the keystones for development co-operation and assistance, and "most often appears as conditionalities intended to promote accountable government and democratisation in aid-receiving countries". It is seen as entailing much more than the promotion of liberal economic policies. It refers also to "the nature and style of political systems", and is associated "with a range of political conditionalities such as democratisation, promotion of multiparty systems and commitment to free elections".[44] But good governance, it can be argued, is largely a concept advocated by the developed North, which ignores the systems of governance practised in pre-colonial societies, and in its current form obscures the linkage of policy with culture, human rights and wider developmental concerns.

Three principal questions thus arise: first, what can be done to instil practices of good governance, both domestically and further afield? Second, what is the relationship between policy and good governance? Third, can nations follow different development paths and yet practise good governance?

Issue Three: Trade, Regionalism and the End of History?
In spite of the arguments put forward by those who foresaw the "end of history" and the centrality of good governance to economic advancement, globalisation and global capitalism are still not universally accepted as a recipe for uniform global economic prosperity. One

---

42 For a comprehensive discussion on the causes and costs of corruption, see Susan Rose-Ackerman, *Corruption and Government*. Cambridge: Cambridge University Press, 1999.

43 This World Bank figure was cited on SABC Radio, 15 June 2001. See also *http://www.transparency.org/documents/cpi/2000/cpi2000.html*.

44 See Anje Kruiter, "Good Governance for Africa: Whose Governance?", on *http://www.oneworld.org/ecdpm/pubs/govahk.htm*.

reason is that the relationship between business and government –
the practical counterpart of the globalisation thesis – is at times still
characterised by tension and disputes, especially in Africa, where the
relationship is generally either too close or too contested.

Furthermore, as was noted in the Introduction, the increasingly
violent demonstrations at international summits in Seattle, Prague,
Gothenburg, Genoa and Barcelona over the past two years illustrate
the contested nature of the economic debate. Although this anti-globalisation movement originates from diverse social forces, they are seen
to have both comparable values, norms and discourses, and increasingly parallel strategies and tactics. In the former, they are opponents
to "neo-liberal capitalism". In the latter they lobby for the cancellation of Third World debt; the meeting of basic developmental needs
through local, not hard currency, loans; the subsidisation of interest
rates for development loans; the increasing use of grants, not loans,
for development purposes; the ending of neo-liberal aid conditionality; the acceptance of national control on capital movements; and
the decommissioning of the IMF and the World Bank. As Patrick Bond
has argued:[45]

> The political strategy . . . global attacks by the working class and
> allies from social and environmental movements against financial/
> commercial capital's nerve centres in Washington and Geneva,
> combined with local, national (and then regional) class struggles
> to re-establish radical development visions . . . [invokes] the need
> for critique of the neo-liberal Washington Consensus as a pure
> form of capitalist economic doctrine . . . and for the global target-
> ing of the multilateral institutions that are the most direct sites of
> the command and control functions that subordinate much of the
> world to neo-liberalism.

Less controversial is the acknowledgement that globalisation and the
end of the Cold War have made it possible once more for nations to
rediscover and strengthen regional links. In this process, it is acknowledged that the development of economies cannot occur in isolation. As
Omar Kabbaj, President of the African Development Bank, has observed:[46]

45 Patrick Bond, *Against Global Apartheid*. Cape Town: UCT Press, 2001, p.235.
46 African Development Bank, *African Development Report 2000*. Oxford: OUP,
    2000, p.i.

With about 800 million consumers, the importance of economic co-operation for Africa derives mainly from the opportunities that emanate from integrating the markets of individual countries on the continent. Large markets matter because they create new investment opportunities, enhance the production of tradable commodities, and encourage the flow of foreign direct investment. Regional integration could also help in building efficient infrastructure, strengthening regional security, improving human capital, and natural resource management.

There are, nonetheless, a number of constraints on regional free trade initiatives, particularly those involving African states (where attempts at regional integration, represented by a flood of acronyms, have mostly proved short-lived). There are two schools of thought on the value of regional economic and political units. The first is that these represent building-blocks or a stepping-stone towards fuller participation in the global economy – so-called "open" integration. The second is that these units provide a developmental bulwark against deeper global integration – the so-called "closed" integration thesis.

These two approaches are not necessarily mutually exclusive. It is important to recognise differences between the needs of developing countries, in relatively immature stages of industrialisation, and those of states higher up the industrial chain. These are issues which the WTO and regional bodies such as the European Union will have to take into account in the creation of liberal trade and developmental regimes. It cannot be just a case of seeking *freer* trade, but of securing *fairer* trade too.

There are also analytical misgivings about the untoward impact of rapidly liberalising economies, especially when attempts are made to strike a balance, as intimated above, between domestic needs and greater openness. Openness can have a significant impact on economic growth along with work conditions, gender issues, and environmental standards, *inter alia*. We should also realise that liberalisation can leave countries more vulnerable to external shocks. This is applicable particularly to those countries where the economic fundamentals are shaky and state institutions weak.

Such concerns are related also to the recognition that tariff liberalisation is but one of a series of economic and political initiatives which need to be implemented to achieve growth. Others include the establishment of a domestic investment strategy, the development of technologies and skills, the implementation of a sound macroeconomic and fiscal policy, and the existence of efficient but not overbearing domestic institutions. Thus, *openness alone cannot bring about economic competitiveness*.

But the fact remains that countries that trade more grow faster: that *openness can work*. And it works partly because it sends out a signal about what sort of economy the liberalising state wants to have: one that is open to trade, as well as to ideas, people, skills, and investment; one that wants to compete on the global stage; and one that stands for internationally acceptable political values and social practices.

Studies show that developing countries with open economies grew by 4.5% annually in the 1970s and 1980s; while those with closed economies expanded only by 0.7%. Developed, open economies grew by 2.3% annually during this period; closed ones by 0.7%.[47] Closed economies are regarded as those with the features of high import tariff and non-tariff barriers, a socialist economic system, a state monopoly on important exports, and a big gap between official and black-market exchange rates. It is, admittedly, sometimes difficult to work out whether protected economies do badly because they are cosseted, or because they have unsound macroeconomic practices. Yet this does not challenge the essential argument of the free-trade growth thesis applied to developing countries – that there is a striking correlation between export growth and overall GDP growth. When assessing the value and practice of integrative attempts, the analyst should also distinguish between the formal intergovernmental process of regional integration and the value of people-to-people contacts. In Southern Africa, for example, while the process of integration between the governments of states has been comparatively problematic and slow, the integration of people and economies through increased movement, investment and trade has been rapid. The involvement of South African companies in Africa is a positive illustration of this process.[48]

47 See Jeffrey Sachs and Andrew Warner, "Economic Reform and the Process of Global Integration", *Brookings Papers on Economic Activity,* 1995 cited in "The never-ending question", *The Economist,* 3 July 1999.
48 Since the end of apartheid, South African firms have been able to trade and invest without political handicap in Africa. In the trading domain, South Africa's overall trade with Africa increased by 130% from R10.9 billion in 1994 to R25.3 billion in 1998, totalling R22.7 billion in SA exports and R4.3 billion in imports in 1999. The increase in involvement by SA-based firms in Africa has been replicated in sectors beyond mining, notably in banking, brewing, retailing, cellular communications and insurance.

Issue Four: **The Death of the Nation-State?**

Whatever its challenges (and challengers), the nation-state is still very much at the centre of international relations. It has not been supplanted by civil society, as some predicted, in its principal problem-solving function. The state may today not be the only problem-solving unit in global politics, and may in some areas of the world be the problem to *be* solved, especially in areas of Africa, Asia and Latin America, where the state can be ill-formed, weak and even dysfunctional. But a strong state is necessary for social and economic effectiveness. As a result, the debate has shifted towards questions on how civil society can work with the state in invigorating and strengthening, rather than supplanting, its capacity.

Arguably more relevant than the future of the nation-state in the context of developing countries are two related questions. First, the population of some states comprises members of many nations. The socioeconomic conditions and political strategies employed by their governments do not treat all citizens equally, as in Europe, but capitalise on (and thus exacerbate) ethnic divisions. How can such states function effectively?

The second question relates to the previous one. In some states, the machinery of government does not reach all of the populace. In others, for example Argentina, the state is neither respected nor capable. What can be done to create a sense of national identity in such cases? Or, put differently: must the sovereignty of a state be matched by internal effectiveness?

These questions have special pertinence to African countries. Many African states are small and comparatively underpopulated. The continent covers 18% of the world's surface area, but is home to just 11% of its population. African countries are frequently afflicted by low state capacity: where many cannot extend state control over the entire territory nominally under their control, and possess only low, even rudimentary, levels of technological sophistication. Their boundaries, as Jeffrey Herbst reminds us, have not necessarily been determined by how far these states can extend power. Instead they are a reflection of imposed colonial structures, which have been retained as key to state consolidation by African political elites.[49] He argues:

---

49 See Jeffrey Herbst, *States and Power in Africa.* Princeton: PUP, 2000, especially pp.252-3.

The African successors to the colonialists adopted the European position on colonial boundaries; indeed, they created a new state system, based on the Addis rules, that was dedicated to reinforcing the salience and viability of the received boundaries. The relatively well-defined and consequential boundaries created are no longer a good mirror of state power, which tends to continue to be fractured, weak and contested . . .

He notes:

The fundamental problem with the boundaries of Africa is not that they are too weak but that they are too strong. It is not that they are artificial in light of current political systems but that they are too integral to the broadcasting of power in Africa. It is not that they are alien to current states but that African leaders have been extraordinarily successful in manipulating the boundaries for their own purposes of staying in power rather than extending the power of their states. To say that the boundaries have been a barrier to state consolidation in Africa is largely a non sequitur. The states, to a certain extent, are their boundaries.

At one level, this raises questions about whether African countries can make the transition necessary from *nations*-states to *nation*-states; at another it invites debate on the distribution of power within these societies, which focuses on who (if anyone) benefits from continued instability and state weakness, and on whether anything can be done to reverse this decline.

Issue Five: **Cultural Value Convergence or Divergence?**
September 11 and the questions it raises about a resultant possible "clash of civilisations" have rekindled a discussion of the role and management of values in international relations, and the relationship between economic reform, regional integration and value congruence.

The values debate is certainly not new. The role of so-called "Asian values" received prominence during the phenomenal growth phase of both the Asian tigers (Singapore, Hong Kong, Taiwan and South Korea) and that which followed in Southeast Asia in the 1970s. The more pernicious effects of these values came under the microscope as a result of the Asian financial crisis in 1997, shifting the focus of debate from their benefits to their compatibility with global standards of good governance, human rights and democracy.

The relationship between processes of integration and the establishment of common regional identities has also highlighted the importance of achieving congruence in policies and trajectories, so as to encourage regional economic and political co-operation, co-ordination and ultimately integration. Conversely, the role of leadership in moulding and organising a common regional identity in the face of diversity and countervailing forces (including conflict and the role of external actors), is also critical in achieving such congruence. Put differently, regional co-operation can shape a common identity; and the shaping of that identity can promote a regional regulatory framework, institutions and architecture.[50]

As a result of the difficulties experienced by some Asian economies in the last five years, arguments have emerged about the efficacy of applying global models of economic reform and development to particular cultural contexts – not least in Africa and Asia.[51] This raises further questions about the relationship between internal economic strategy and institutions of governance on the one hand, and global economic development and precepts on the other. Put differently, are "Asian" values, much vaunted during the 1970s and 1980s, now inimical to sustained economic growth in the 21st century? As noted in the previous chapter, in the case of Japan, is it possible to adapt the economic structure that put the country on its feet after the Second World War – the so-called "1940 system" – but which had, by the start of 2002, brought the economy to the brink of breakdown? This is a system that centres less on consumer power and choice, and domestic demand than on government preferences and interference.[52] After all, no business consultant would dare suggest that a single strategy would work for a global corporation for a period of 50 or even 20 years.

Finally, the relationship between values and political and social life in contemporary times has also received prominence as a result of the terrorist attacks of September 11. In particular, it has emphasised the need to forestall social alienation and state collapse, breeding grounds of terrorism, and so avoid a repetition of such events.

---

50 For example, for a discussion of these issues within an Asian context, see Amitav Acharya, *The Quest for Identity: International Relations of Southeast Asia.* Singapore: Oxford University Press (OUP), 2000.

51 See, for example, Bai Gao, *Japan's Economic Dilemma: The Institutional Origins of Prosperity and Stagnation.* Cambridge: CUP, 2001.

52 See William Overholt, "Japan's economy at war with itself", *Foreign Affairs,* 81, 1, January/February 2002, pp.134-147.

Conclusion: *Societies and Global Practices in Transition?*

Globalisation has thrown up a new set of challenges for the world community. In summary, the first of these, as the table on page 69 suggests, is to achieve congruence between societies. This entails equality of access to technologies, and the bridging of the development divide, as well as the adoption of similar policies. While global integration offers huge opportunities for development, the volatility and uncertainty of capital flows and the differences in the developmental starting points of states suggest a new role for international financial institutions. There is a need for the opening of markets along with the universalisation of key political and cultural values. If September 11 made the world aware of the extent of global diversity and societal fragmentation, then the response has to involve the development of a new global polity involving, *inter alia*, the transformation of the existing global architecture of the WTO, the UN, the IMF and the World Bank as the axes of trade, conflict management, finance and development respectively.

For many in the developed world, the positive changes wrought by the new technological age have also brought changes for the worse, most notably in altered social norms and pathologies. These manifest themselves in less job security, higher divorce rates, large numbers of children born out of wedlock, higher rates of crime, fewer marriages, depopulation, and an overall decline in society's trust of institutions amidst growing individualism.

For the states in the developing world, the challenges include most of the above, with the exception of depopulation, but including the need for radical political and economic as well as societal transitions. The challenge is thus not so much to adapt existing social norms but to create them altogether.

Both developed and developing nations are thus "societies in transition". In squaring up to this environment, four different sets of transitions emerge:

• Global political and economic institutions with developed nations largely at the helm must change to accommodate the ambitions, fears and insecurities of countries in the post-post Cold War era.

• Business practices and social norms within OECD states should alter to reflect the demands of the new technological economies and hyper-competitive global capital and trade patterns.

- Developing (or semi-developing, ex-Soviet bloc) states must convert to developed economies and Western, liberal political systems.
- Mostly developed states must make the transition from the industrial to the information age. A number of developing states are attempting to "leapfrog" development in this way, notably, for example, Brazil, South Africa, India, China, Malaysia and Argentina.

In the contemporary era, in the shift from industrial to information societies where services increasingly displace manufacturing, the role of knowledge and intelligence and information is critical, as is the education of people and the development of technology. This environment produces freedoms and equality, partly by reducing bureaucratic controls. Just as in businesses, states also have to become leaner and more effective in harnessing technology and individual expertise. As Nicholas Stern, the World Bank's chief economist, has argued:[53]

> Some anxieties about globalisation are well founded, but reversing globalisation would come at an intolerably high price, destroying the prospects of prosperity for many millions of poor people. We do not agree with those who would retreat into a world of nationalism and protectionism. That way leads to deeper poverty and it is fundamentally hostile to the wellbeing of people in the developing countries. Instead, we must make globalisation work for the poor people of the world.

But it is unclear how developing states can make the sorts of economic advancement necessary for political and social stability in this environment. Put differently, it is critical to reconcile good governance and global best practice (including the application of so-called neo-liberal macroeconomic fundamentals) with the provision of welfare to citizens and the reduction of poverty, especially within fledgling democracies.

Increased capital flows and improved technology appear to offer Africa the opportunity to leapfrog ahead in its development. The scale of the continent's challenges demands policies based on engagement and not on isolation. For the continent to reach its goal of reducing poverty by half by 2015, the UN Conference on Trade and Development (UNCTAD) estimates that Africa's economies will, as noted

---

53 *http://lnweb18.worldbank.org/news/pressrelease.*

in the Introduction, have to grow by between 7% and 8% a year in real terms, well above their average performance of a little over 2% from 1991 to 1997. This increase is likely to require, among other things, raising the level of investment from 16% of GDP to between 22% and 25% over the next decade, and increasing aid by US$10 billion annually.[54]

But FDI to Africa dropped by 13% in 2001. Financing for development projects is unlikely also to come from African countries themselves, given their low savings rates. And the requisite capital is unlikely to come from donors, because total global aid flows have been declining: in real terms, they are less than half of what they were two decades ago. International donors or institutions would be reluctant to invest more where previous contributions brought about so little improvement. Another point to consider is that in states where governance is minimal or absent, aid is likely to distort the delivery of government and exacerbate the situation rather than assist development. Nicolas van der Walle reminds us that, while calls for an "African Marshall Plan" might be fashionable, the total aid flows of the Marshall Plan between 1948 and 1952 did not exceed 2.5% of Western Europe's GDP. By comparison, by 1996, excluding Nigeria and South Africa, African countries received on average 12.3% of GDP in aid.[55]

In summary, globalisation is not a linear phenomenon, and does not necessarily mean global growth equally for all. It has enabled and simultaneously disabled key constituents within states. There is a need to manage the disparity that some states can take advantage of globalisation in a high-tech sense, some in other ways, and some scarcely at all. Its impact has been exaggerated (in both positive and negative aspects) by the high-tech, digital explosion. It is characterised at times by a systemic dysfunctionality of state and interstate systems alike. In an environment of faster, deeper and more volatile globalisation and where some sectors of society (and some states) have apparently benefited more than others from globalisation, a number of critical issues arise in the debate around the development of a new global order (and a corresponding concern with the problems of Africa and emerging markets on other continents).

---

54 See the address on the "UN's Role in Africa" given by Rubens Ricupero, Secretary-General: UNCTAD, Geneva, 16 July 2001.
55 "Africa and the World Economy", in Harbeson and Rothchild, *op cit*, p.271.

The first focuses on the link between domestic reforms and external action. The historical evidence from Europe and elsewhere is that countries must build up their national structures if they are to benefit from regional integration, and not be misled by the belief that continental, regional or international initiatives will somehow compensate for a lack of domestic capacity.

Second, and related to the above, is a need to identify the means or avenues through which governance, stability and modernisation, as prerequisites for peace and stability, can be achieved.

Third, there is a need to explore ways of developing the conditions in which business can prosper, at the core of which is an improved understanding between business and government. This relationship – the practical counterpart of globalisation – is unfortunately at times still characterised by tension and disputes, especially in Africa.

Fourth is the need for means to resolve tensions within regional groups, necessary if such bodies are to successfully represent their member-states' interests. Value and policy congruence, visionary leadership and the construction of norms and institutions are arguably both a reflection of and necessary for a common regional project.

The scale of the challenge facing Africa, and the response of Asian and Latin American states to the globalising environment are the subjects of the following three chapters.

CHAPTER TWO

THE AFRICAN CONDITION

The continent is a tragedy; it is also a challenge. Africa's variety inhibits concerted action; the scope of its crises nevertheless demands significant response.

HENRY KISSINGER[1]

Issues of international development are no longer foreign issues but domestic issues.

JAMES WOLFENSOHN, *February* 2002[2]

[W]e place great importance on addressing the underlying causes of conflict [in Africa]: poverty, inequality, intolerance, weak civil society, bad governance. We will redouble our efforts within the international community to curb trade which fuels violence, such as trafficking in conflict diamonds and weapons. We must all do more to heal war-torn societies so that violence does not recur.

US SECRETARY OF STATE COLIN POWELL, *May* 2001[3]

Introduction

Sub-Saharan Africa is officially the poorest region in the world. Consider the following statistics:[4]

- The total combined annual GNP of its 48 economies is just US$300 million (roughly the same as that of Belgium, with just ten million inhabitants), of which more than 40% is contributed by South Africa and 11% by Nigeria. The remaining 46 countries – or 450 million people – survive on US$140 billion.
- This combined GDP is less than the US$350 billion agricultural subsidies allocated annually to the Organisation for Economic Co-operation and Development (OECD) countries.
- It accounts for less than 2% of world trade, down from 3% in the

---

1 Henry Kissinger, *Does America Need a Foreign Policy?* New York: Simon and Schuster, 2001, p.210.
2 Appearing on *CNN Q&A*, 22 February 2002.
3 Address to SAIIA/Wits University, 25 May 2001.
4 These statistics are drawn from a variety of sources including the World Bank, *Can Africa Claim the 21st Century?* Washington DC: World Bank, 2000.

1950s. Without South Africa, sub-Saharan Africa's share of world trade is just 1%.

- Aid transfers amount, on average, to 9% of GDP.
- 250 million (40%) of people lack access to safe water.
- 200 million (33%) have no access to health services.
- More than 40% of its 600 million people live below the internationally recognised absolute poverty line of US$1 per day.
- Its share of the world's absolute poor grew from 25% to 30% in the 1990s.
- Two million children will die before their first birthdays.
- At the start of the 20th century, there were 223 deaths from malaria per 100,000 people annually: today this figure is 165/100,000.
- Seventy percent of the world's Aids cases are to be found on the continent.

In addressing this environment of dearth and disease, the continent faces three sets of broadly inter-related challenges: per capita economic contraction; at best limited, weak governance and, at worst, collapsing, ill-formed states; and the existence of widespread conflict and politico-socioeconomic vulnerability and instability. Yet, as the World Bank has noted, "Explaining Africa's slow growth remains a major challenge."[5]

This chapter examines each of these challenges in turn.

★ ★ ★

Economic Contraction and Collapse

The African challenge is complex, rooted in history and defined by ill-formed, sometimes dysfunctional geographic and state units. Its problems have domestic, regional and international dimensions, relating to both its colonial history and the nature of the region's transition to independence. Africa's economic decline reflects both political and institutional failure, along with the growth of corruption, nepotism, populist redistribution and patronage politics. This has manifested itself in a number of ways:

- *Political instability and conflict.* Africa has more armed conflicts than any other continent. During the second half of 2001 the number of internally displaced persons in Africa reached 13.5 million, an in-

---

5 *Ibid*, p.23.

crease of more than five million since 1998, and more than three
times Africa's estimated refugee population. While many of the conflicts are internal in nature, they are sustained by external, cross-
border linkages.

- *Skills and Capital Flight.* It is estimated that 60,000 doctors, engineers and university staff left Africa between 1985 and 1990, and that
  since 1990 this figure has been 20,000 per year. The gap created by
  this loss has had to be filled by expatriates. Also, Africa has lost an
  estimated US$150 billion in capital flight, with around 40% of pri-
  vate wealth held outside the continent, a higher percentage than in
  any other region.[6]
- *Low investment returns and high transaction costs.* Poor infrastructure,
  distant geographical location, low productivity and a high-risk environment in combination led to lower returns (around one third of
  the global average) on capital investments in the three decades from
  1960. This trend was aggravated by state expenditure that was principally focused on reinforcing patronage rather than promoting
  economic growth. Although returns on African investment rose considerably in the 1990s, high transaction costs, coupled with a high-
  risk premium, have deterred many investors outside of the mining,
  oil and tourism sectors. Indeed, the outcome is that only projects
  that offer exceptional returns are undertaken because of the real or
  perceived risks attached to them. Transport costs are on average
  three times more than global levels. Freight rates by rail are on average around double those in Asia, and air transport is four times more
  costly.[7] There are just 55 kms of rural roads per thousand square
  kilometres of surface area in Africa, compared to over 800 in India;
  and in Africa there is only one tenth of the number of telephones
  per capita in Asia. Freight and insurance charges amount to 15% of
  export earnings, whereas the average for developing countries is
  just 6%. Africa's transportation costs have also been rising – the comparable figures for 1970 were 11% and 8% – whereas those of the
  rest of the world have been falling.[8]
- *Commodity price decline.* Oil prices rose dramatically in 1973. Paradoxically, African oil producers did not take advantage of this opportunity, owing mainly to ongoing civil strife in producing states.

---

6 See Alan Gelb and Rob Floyd, "The Challenge of Globalisation for Africa",
South African Journal of International Affairs, 6, 2, Winter 1999, p. 13.
7 See the World Bank on *http://lnweb18.worldbank.org/news/pressrelease*.
8 See *http://econ.worldbank.org/files/2896_ch1.pdf*.

The share of commodities (excluding fuels) as a share of world exports decreased from 33% in 1970 to 15.5% in 1991; while for developing countries this went down from 50% to 18% over the corresponding period. In the case of South and East Asia, 80% of their exports in 1991 were made up of manufactures (with commodities at 13%), although their share of world commodity exports nearly doubled over this period (from 7.5% to 12.6%). Latin America's share of world commodity exports decreased from 13% in 1970 to 3.1% in 1991, when commodities made up 40% of Latin American exports. Africa's share of world commodity exports shrank, however, from 8.4% to 3.1% over this period, even though commodities and fuels accounted for 24% and 60% of African exports respectively in 1991.[9]

- *Weak agricultural and manufacturing sectors.* While 80% of South and East Asia's exports were comprised of manufactures in 1991, and this sector accounted for two thirds of Latin America's exports, the picture is very different in Africa. In 1965, manufacturing accounted for 9% of African economic activity: yet by the late 1980s this had risen to just 11%. Poor policies, ineffective agricultural and farming methods, as well as lack of proper marketing systems, have also prevented the continent from meeting the achievement of continental food self-sufficiency. Africa's grain deficit doubled between 2000 and 2001, reaching 44 million tonnes, leaving the continent locked in an acute food crisis.
- *Embryonic regional units.* Although the route to global integration and competitiveness runs through regional consolidation and the harnessing of regional economies of scale, intra-regional trade, which accounted for 6% of African exports in 1990, grew to just 10% by the end of the decade.

These issues are highlighted further below.

Global Marginalisation

Evolving the correct strategies for African economic renewal is dependent on the correct identification of the core problems. In particular, the extent (and importance) of Africa's participation in the

---

9 See Lodewijk Berlage and Guy Vandille, *Commodity exports of the developing countries: A survey of post-war experience.* Brussels: Flemish Inter-university Council, August 1995, p.5.

global economy has been declining. This marginalisation has occurred for a number of inter-related reasons, including Africa's low growth in merchandise exports (partly due to policies that discouraged such growth); reliance on, and deterioration in, the terms of trade of narrowly-based traditional commodity sectors; a failure to industrialise; economic stagnation; and political-security upheaval. Ironically, given that African countries were locked into the global trading system through their colonial history and were dependent on trade for a high proportion of their GDP, the diversification (and expansion) of trade was limited, too, by these colonial networks, being usually directed towards the former colonial power.[10]

A core problem is thus: African countries remain on the margins of the global economy, and increasingly so. Attempts to restructure and diversify their economies have met with only limited success, owing to a range of factors that undermine the consistency and content of policy reforms and deter investment. These factors include a low quality of governance, instability, overvalued exchange rates, high levels of taxation, and excessive regulation.

The issue is that African problems are large and structural as well as voluntarist. This means that they may persist beyond isolated reforms, which include debt relief and policy changes. Also important is that the uncertainty created by the macroeconomic environment, poor governance (especially as exemplified in administrative incapacity, corruption and physical insecurity) and inadequate monetary policies points to another failure – that of external actors to devise and implement acceptable policy regimes.

Investment Confidence and Stability

Africa today accounts for less than 1% of annual global capital flows, declining from 4.5% a decade earlier. Put differently, Africa has failed to capitalise on the advantages of globalisation. These factors help to explain why, by 1999, according to UNCTAD, Africa's total accumulated FDI stock was just US$93 billion, compared with US$485 billion for Latin America and the Caribbean, US$769 billion for Southeast and East Asia, and US$3.2 trillion for the developed world as a whole.

What are the reasons for such low investment levels?

---

10 See "Africa in the World Economy", in Harbeson and Rothchild, *op cit*, p.266.

What Multinational Companies Say Dissuades Them from Investing in Africa[11]

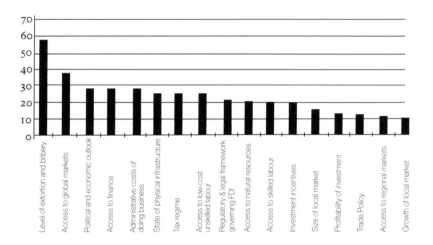

The relevance of this table can be gauged, for example, by the relative success of China versus Africa in obtaining foreign investment. The former has attracted more than US$350 billion in FDI over the past decade, as a result both of the size of the increasingly wealthy market represented by its more than 1.2 billion people and the global competitiveness of its cost of production. While not democratic, China is politically stable. Sub-Saharan Africa's population of 600 million is, by comparison, increasingly poor, attracting less than 10% of China's FDI figure, and, while democracy has spread, the subcontinent is characterised by widespread conflict and instability. Whereas China's GDP per capita growth rate was 9.5% between 1990 and 1999, sub-Saharan Africa's was -0.4%.

Other studies point to similar perceptions in foreign investors. South Africa, for example, has been largely unable to translate its positive attributes – a first-class infrastructure, declining fiscal deficits, low inflation and high investment ratings – into high rates of both inward FDI and growth. According to one World Bank study in 2000,[12] top-

---

11   This table is taken from the UNCTAD *World Investment Report 2000*. New York: UN, July 2000.

12   See "SA can still improve its economy, says World Bank", *Business Report*, 8 August 2000.

ping the list of constraints on growth in South Africa are: crime (with firms spending an average of 1.6% of sales revenue on crime prevention), the cost of capital and credit, the depreciation of the rand, inflexible labour regulations, government corruption and poor local bureaucracy, and a shortage of skilled labour. It is, however, important to point out the positive indicators for FDI in Africa. According to the same UNCTAD study (as in the table above), these include the growth of the local market (cited by 60% of respondents); the profitability of local investment (over 60%); the size of the local market (60%); access to regional markets (60%); trade policy (just under 60%); the political and economic outlook (over 50%); and the tax regime (50%).

Differentiation and Conflict

Africa's situation is, however, not homogeneous, contrary to the generally held stereotypes which reduce all African states and all state capacity to the lowest continental denominator. At one end of the scale is the modern, industrialised economy of South Africa, a global exporter of automobiles, services, technology and, increasingly, skills. At the other, the collapsed, dysfunctional entities of Somalia, Congo, Liberia and Sierra Leone are characterised by outward rather than internal displays of state capacity, and by seemingly endless internal conflict. As the Polish author Rysard Kapuščiñski has observed:[13]

> The continent is too large to describe. It is a veritable ocean, a separate planet, a varied, immensely rich cosmos. Only with the greatest simplification, for the sake of convenience, can we say "Africa". In reality, except as a geographical appellation, Africa does not exist.

A number of Africa's so-called "big states" – including Nigeria, the DRC, Ethiopia and Sudan – have performed particularly badly since independence. All have experienced economic collapse, social and political unrest, state decay and open civil war in varying intensities. The 12 smallest African countries[14] by population have had a very

---

13 Rysard Kapuščiñski, *The Shadow of the Sun: My African Life*. London: Penguin, 2001.
14 Seychelles, São Tomé and Principe, Cape Verde, Equatorial Guinea, Comoros, Swaziland, Mauritius, Guinea-Bissau, Gabon, The Gambia, Botswana and Namibia.

different development profile than the 12 largest,[15] averaging more than US$2,000 annual per capita income by the end of the 1990s compared to the little over US$500 for the larger states. The three largest states (DRC, Ethiopia and Nigeria) average around US$200. Importantly, the total population of the 12 smallest countries amounts to just 1.7% of the continent's total. In contrast, over 70% live in the 12 largest states, and 36% in the three largest.[16] This has impeded the progress towards regional integration, with the need instead to isolate against the potentially destabilising impact of these powers. This was true even for the continent's economic superpower, South Africa, under apartheid.

In spite of the differentiation, the impact of conflict has costs for all. It raises the costs of doing business. It worsens perceptions of the whole continent, raising premiums for entering the African market. It creates opportunities for regional actors to extend their influence, not always in a positive manner. It permits the criminalisation of economic activity, with or without state involvement. It degrades or, in its worst form, destroys already weak state capacity. As the World Bank described the rise of a new "arc" of conflict from Sudan in the east to Congo-Brazzaville in the east in the late 1990s, these conflicts pose "the biggest threat to sub-Saharan Africa's near-term prospects, derailing still fragile recovery and threatening the stability of the entire central African region".[17]

The need to end conflict and create conditions of stability necessary for a virtuous circle of economic growth, social and political inclusion and prosperity is thus an African priority. An estimated 18 sub-Saharan African countries were, in 2001, directly or indirectly involved in wars, and as many as 12 others were in unstable situations which threatened to erupt into violent civil conflict. For example, at the start of the 21st century, the war in the DRC alone involved six countries in the fighting, nine armies and 23 movements.

What are the possible responses in this environment? It cannot be desirable to create and maintain new colonies through external intervention, as has been attempted through large-scale British aid and military assistance in Sierra Leone. Artificially created or sustained societies, though infinitely preferable to conflict-riven ones, do not address the core problems of state incapacity that created the condi-

15 Côte d'Ivoire, Madagascar, Mozambique, Ghana, Uganda, Sudan, Kenya, Tanzania, South Africa, DRC, Ethiopia and Nigeria.
16 I am grateful to Jeff Herbst for this observation.
17 Cited in Thomas Callaghy, "Africa and the World Political Economy: More Caught between a Rock and a Hard Place" in Harbeson and Rothchild, *op cit*, p.62.

tions of conflict in the first place. Such new "colonies" would also re-main vulnerable to the political whims of the foreign (mainly Western) powers which have the means to prop them up. Devising strategies for intervention and recovery depends, however, on identifying the rea-sons for persistent conflict and underdevelopment in African states.

The Logic of African Decline, Collapse and Conflict

Although violence is endemic and persistent in Africa, it exhibits a constantly changing and challenging dynamic. There are, for example, shifting patterns of international and regional engagement, while new threats, such as the role of warlords and militias and the effects of re-gional contagion, continuously emerge.

Africa's wars have their origins in a complex compendium of social, leadership, resource, personality, class, ideological, colonial, post-colonial, ethnic, territorial, religious and Cold War divisions – at times one, some or even most of these factors. The end result of this is that in many cases, the inheritance of an already weak state has been fur-ther undermined or has collapsed as a result of a vicious cycle origi-nating in a shortage of skills, poor management, the abuse of leader-ship, and even through war itself.

In the post-Cold War world, the existence of large numbers of weapons, the continued involvement of the former colonial powers (notably France), the creation of a new trend of resource wars (most-ly over diamonds and oil), the emergence of patterns of unequal dis-tribution of wealth between urban and rural areas, and the impact of new factors such as Aids and disputed access to water can lead to instability both within and between states. Wars that were earlier sus-tained by external actors during the Cold War continued, partly be-cause they could not simply be turned off, especially where the exter-nal powers had little at stake and where no serious attempt at conflict resolution was made. As a result, belligerents were not reconciled, and continued to fight because resources were available to sustain the conflicts and weapons could be easily obtained. This was because Cold War surpluses meant arms were cheap; the supply of arms had been privatised; and governments were unable to control existing stocks. Mercenary contacts – guns for hire, often in exchange for diamond and oil leases – also contributed to the background of continued war.

However, in both the Cold War and post-Cold War environments, the inability of governments to manage these issues without conflict reflects a core problem with the African state itself: that the state and its leadership is weak and insecure, and its response to challenges is through patronage, divide-and-rule tactics, and external aggression towards its neighbours.

The political context of Africa's economies is a critical determinant of its deterioration and, conversely, its prospects for recovery. In many of Africa's states, politics could be described as "clientelistic". This condition is related to economic scarcity and the specific African environment of social (in)stability and stratification. As Chabal has argued,[18] the problems behind African conflicts are complex with at their heart the nature of the patrimonial system on which African politics function and leadership depends. He has argued that such a system is inimical to long-term economic growth and development, given its diversion of resources into non-productive sectors. Combined with the collapse of African economies from the 1970s, the relationship between the state and ruling elites on the one hand and populations on the other, has increasingly involved repression and violence, in spite of the emergence of democratic systems. This has been exacerbated by the state's failure to discharge even its nominal responsibilities to its citizens.

The Logic of Conflict and State Decay: A Vicious Cycle

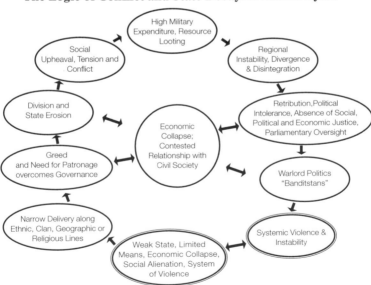

18 These comments were made at a conference on Africa organised by the Japan Institute of International Affairs (JIIA), Tokyo, February 2001.

In this environment, as Chris Patten illustrates in *East and West*, the policy choices facing African leaders are both complex and difficult. The spiral of decay is easier to identify than it was to avoid. Patten is well worth quoting at length:[19]

> Take any old Joe Tyrant in Africa – or Asia or Latin America for that matter – the political and economic journey was similar everywhere from the 1960s onwards. Joe wanted to keep the urban masses quiet, so he subsidised their food and their electricity. That meant less money for their education and their health care, and less money for agriculture research stations and the proper maintenance of power plants, which therefore soon broke down. He raised taxes to meet the bill for subsidies and guns. Fewer people could afford to pay them, so he confiscated the assets of those who could. Subsidising food was getting more expensive, so he held down the prices paid to his farmers. They produced less, so he had to import more and was then obliged to try to get his farmers to grow more expensive crops for export to pay for the basic crops he was importing. Joe had already taken over the main industries and helped himself to what was in the till, when the need arose, so he would not invest in new capital equipment. As he became more unpopular he had to spend more on his armed forces, so that they consumed an increasing share of his budget – far more than was allocated to development. He could not afford to stop paying the soldiers, so the teachers and the nurses had to go without. Joe printed more money, so that its value plummeted and inflation soared. The economy and the political structure spiralled down through subsidy, regulation, imprisonment without trial, deficits, welching on debts, locking up opponents, closing down newspapers, persecution of ethnically different but successful traders, overproduction, underproduction, inflation, famine – all into the Noah's flood or the slash-and-burn forest fires or the dust bowl of ecological catastrophe.

He continues:

> Once you began to open up and reform these economies, to regenerate enterprise, to scrap regulations, to privatise industries, to curb inflation, to cut army bills, to fight corruption, to use

---

19 Chris Patten, *East and West: The Last Governor of Hong Kong on Power, Freedom and the Future*. London: Pan, 1998, pp.186-7.

prices to encourage farmers and food production, to welcome foreign investment, to invest in basic infrastructure and social development, it became rapidly apparent that a political agenda was appearing as well. A more open economy lets in more ideas as well as more goods. Devolving economic decisions leaves less power at the centre. Fewer regulations and subsidies means less jobbery and graft. Dismantle economic controls and in most places political repression founders too.

Of course no single cause (or outcome) can be applied universally. Different reasons for conflict exist in different areas, sometimes in the same region or state. But the common thread is that state decay, dysfunction, weakness or even failure exists in varying forms and degrees in most African countries.

State Failure, Instability and Conflict

The post-independence history of Africa is of governance apparently more concerned with the trappings than the function of statehood.

The colonial template seemingly assumed that function followed form: that motorcades were more important than governance; that the smartness of uniforms spoke louder than the creation of prosperity; and that the existence of national airlines was more than just a symbol of independent statehood (even though they were most often run at a loss, on borrowed money and using expatriate crews). These were "pretend" states, though the venality of their leadership was anything but pretence, as rulers secured fortunes at the expense of their populations, and kept power through an intricate process of vertical linkages buttressed by ethnicity, religion and familial ties.[20] Why did this happen?

The post-colonial world accorded statehood to entities that possessed neither the underlying foundations of coherent, indigenous units nor the skills to allow them to function effectively. As Crawford Young has argued,[21] "Colonial heritage is a necessary point of departure for analysis of Africa's international relations", where only "a few African states have any meaningful pre-colonial identity (Moroc-

---

20 For a detailed explanation of this argument, see See Patrick Chabal and Jean-Pascal Daloz, *Africa Works: Disorder as Political Instrument*. Oxford: James Currey in Association with the International African Institute, 1999.

21 "The Heritage of Colonialism" in Harbeson and Rothchild, *op cit*, p.23.

co, Tunisia, Egypt, Ethiopia, Burundi, Rwanda, Madagascar, Swaziland, Lesotho and Botswana)", and rather "most are products of the
competitive subordination of Africa . . . by seven European powers".
In explaining the roots of the problems facing African states and
their (lack of) powers, Henry Kissinger has argued that:[22]

> In Africa, borders not only follow the demarcations *between* the
> spheres of influence of the European powers, as in Asia; they
> also reflect the administrative subdivisions *within* each colonial
> area. . . . Most importantly, the administrative borders in each
> colony were drawn without regard to ethnic or tribal identities;
> indeed, the colonial powers found it useful to divide up ethnic or
> tribal groups in order to complicate the emergence of a unified
> opposition to imperial rule.

Whereas, he notes, "[I]n most countries of the world, a society or nation preceded the state; in most African countries, the state precedes
the nation and must wrest a national consciousness from a plethora
of tribes, ethnic groups, and, in many cases, different religions". In
his fictional account of war in West Africa, James Cobb provides a
vivid narrative of this impact. A French naval captain explains the continent's problems thus:[23]

> Let me tell you of Africa, my friends, and what we have done to
> her. . . . We came with the other Europeans, back when the con-
> tinent was an honest wilderness and each black tribe and king-
> dom held what land it could by tradition and by the strength of
> its spears. It was a system that worked well for them and they
> were content. We Europeans, however, had a different idea. We
> divided Africa up like a pie, each colonial power taking its own
> juicy slice. We drew lines on maps, governing those lines with
> colonial administrators and enforcing them with garrison bay-
> onets. We did not care that our lines had arbitrarily been drawn
> across tribal territories or cultural and language groupings. Our
> system worked well for us and we were content. But the day of
> the colonies passed, and the Europeans all went home, taking our
> administrators and garrisons with us. But we left behind those
> lines on the map. We left Africa divided into all these damn little

---

22 "Does America Need a Foreign Policy", *op cit*, pp.202-3.
23 James Cobb, *Seafighter*. London: Headline, 1999.

boxes; each box inhabited by broken and separated peoples and by nervous and fragile little governments.

It took a while for the impact of the colonial inheritance to become apparent, however, as "the tremendous euphoria surrounding independence and the success that African leaders had in delegitimating claims of self-determination initially masked the incompleteness of state consolidation".[24] Deriving notions of statehood from the European Westphalian experience, colonialism (or, more accurately, post-colonialism) transferred rights and responsibilities to the new governments, but scant means to pursue or fulfil these. Today the seemingly interminable nature of the continent's conflicts and crises has produced a burgeoning literature on the subject of dysfunctional – or "failed" – states in Africa. This term describes those entities which no longer exhibit even the most fundamental attributes of statehood, such as the provision of individual security and basic services such as tax collection and primary health care. Indeed, in many cases, the contemporary African state would seem to exist only to perpetuate the inefficient rule of elites and to sustain the patronage links on which this rule is founded and maintained.

The image of these failed states was brought home vividly by Robert Kaplan's article on "The Coming Anarchy", which described them in terms of his experience in West Africa:

> West Africa is becoming the symbol of worldwide demographic, environmental, and societal stress, in which criminal anarchy emerges as the real "strategic" danger. Disease, overpopulation, unprovoked crime, scarcity of resources, refugee migrations, the increasing erosion of nation-states and international borders, and the empowerment of private armies, security firms, and international drug cartels are now most tellingly demonstrated through a West African prism. West Africa provides an appropriate introduction to the issues, often extremely unpleasant to discuss, that will soon confront our civilisation. . . . There is no other place on the planet where political maps are so deceptive – where, in fact, they tell such lies – as in West Africa.

24 Herbst, "States and Power in Africa", *op cit.*

And there are other anecdotal, but no less revealing, means of measurement. Take the plight, for example, of the African rhino. In 1960, the African black rhino population numbered more than 100,000. By 1999, a combination of mismanagement and poaching had brought numbers down to just 2,600, of which 40% were in South Africa.[25] This "rhino index" tells a vivid tale of the extent of transnational influences and the abilities of African states to protect sovereign assets.

Until now, much of the debate around failed African states has made a number of presumptions. Put crudely, these take it as given that there was a state to begin with, and that it exhibited formal, juridical sovereignty and possessed institutions of state behaviour and control. It is also necessary to distinguish between different types of state transition and collapse – between, for example, a predatory/kleptocratic state (Mobutu's Zaire), one which is weak because of the impact of transnational events (Colombia and crime), where there is organised and orderly state devolution (Canada), and finally, one where there has been a (sometimes failed) political and economic transition (Russia, former Yugoslavia).

If a failed state is one in which there is no identifiable government with bureaucratic capacity, then Liberia would not fall into this category. After all, Monrovia still issues passports – with some degree of consternation for the international community. Neither would the DRC qualify. If defining the conditions for a successful state is ruling with respect for civil niceties, then undemocratic regimes could be said to have failed, even though the authority at the centre still holds. Some degree of subjective assessment would thus seem to be necessary to establish a criterion by which states can be said to fail.

Clearly, however, we are mainly not concerned with all these different versions and permutations, but rather, as William Zartman has argued, with those states in which "the structure, authority (legitimate power), law and political order have fallen apart and must be reconstituted in some form, old or new".[26] Put differently, it is when states fail to exhibit those functions associated with statehood – a functioning national social, political, security and economic order. To a great extent, such states can be identified through empirical means (the declines in economic output, *Human Development Index* ranking – including levels of life expectancy, adult literacy and infant mor-

25 See W Taylor *et al.*, *Africa's Big Five*. Rivonia: Southern, 1999.
26 William Zartman (ed.), *Collapsed States: The Disintegration and Restoration of Legitimate Authority*. Colorado: Lynne Reiner, 1995, p.1.

tality – as well as the increases in the extent/number of conflicts). But failure is at least as much about degrees of collapse as it is about pinpointing the event itself.

It is also necessary to distinguish between those states which are weak, and in which violence may result as a consequence of this weakness, and those that have been weakened because of violence. Put differently, it is necessary to distinguish between wars that emerge in the context of state collapse (Liberia and Sierra Leone) and those which are the result of a struggle for the control of assets or for control of the state itself.[27]

Do states have characteristics which predispose them to collapse or conflict? And to what extent are these characteristics of a sort that states can do something about (as in policies or personalities)? Or are these issues beyond their control (as in structural deficiencies)? This debate is central in assessing the conditions necessary for African economic recovery.

A brief typology of a failed state identifies the presence of the following conditions: low (or no) capacity, low (or no) legitimacy, and poor, short-sighted, often narrowly focused policies. These conditions are expounded below.

Explaining the Reasons for and Relevance of State Dysfunction

By the time of the fall of Mobutu Sese Seko in 1997, the state of Zaire had ceased to exist. More than 80% of the roads had been destroyed through neglect, as had most of the railway. As one South African diplomat based there in the mid-1990s noted in private conversation, "How can they call a place where the two main cities [Kinshasa and Lubumbashi] are not connected by road, railway or waterway, a single country?"

How could this happen in a territory that is adjudged to be one of the ten most rich in natural resources in the world? Arguably the collapse of Zaire's infrastructure was by Mobutu's tactical design, as a more effective means to prevent a coup than the payment of the army. Such an argument would probably be as specious as it would be flattering to Mobutu, though many Congolese interpreted the disintegration of the transport network as a deliberate ploy by Mobutu to

---

27 See Jeffrey Herbst, "State Failure in Theory and Practice". Paper presented to the Failed States Project, World Peace Foundation, Harvard, 2-3 June 2000.

reduce Zaire to "a handful of isolated city enclaves, cut off from the outside world and each other".[28] The collapse of the central African state was partly attributable to Zaire's colonial inheritance, given the size and impassability of the territory (eighty times larger than Belgium), and also the style of exploitative, brutal, repressive rule inherited from the Belgian colonial authorities. As Alec Russell has argued in *Big Men, Little People*, "Indeed it could even be argued that King Leopold II of Belgium, the founder of the Congo and the driving force behind the 'Scramble', was a role model for Mobutu."[29]

Zaire's failure was also partly a result of the Cold War, in which the superpowers (in this case the United States) blithely turned a blind eye to Mobutu's excesses in order to maintain a grip on Africa's largest territory. Even during the relatively benign presidency of Jimmy Carter, Zaire consumed half of the US aid budget for Africa – and this after Zaire's own resources had been milked dry by Mobutu and his inner circle. The Cold War was costly for Africa: elsewhere on the continent, it led to disastrous leftist policies and bloated bureaucracies, a distracting arms build-up (Angola alone is estimated to have accepted US$800 million annually in Russian military assistance in the 1980s, while the opposition UNITA received US$60 million annually in aid from the US), and costly, dead-end ideological follies such as collectivised agriculture. To Zaire's ruling elite, it simply presented another means of income and source of patronage. Two thirds of the aid budget never reached its intended destination.

A number of different viewpoints can be identified regarding this question: What is the cause of state incapacity and, at its extreme, failure?

Clearly a distinction has to be made between factors internal to states, and those external. Regarding internal factors, Van der Walle has argued persuasively[30] that fiscal extractive capacity is important in determining "the activities that states can sustain and the quality of the public infrastructure available to the state to undertake its functions". State capacity is, put simply, a reflection of its tax-generating capabilities. This is dependent, in turn, on the economic foundation

28 Cited in *The Annual Register*, 1995. London: Cartermill, 1995, p.265.
29 *Op cit*, p.16.
30 "The Economic Correlates of Failed States". Draft paper presented at a meeting of the Failed States Project, World Peace Foundation, 2-3 June 2000, Harvard.
31 Organisation for Economic Co-operation and Development.
32 *Ibid*, p.7.

of these societies; and on governmental, institutional (personnel) capacity. With regard to the former, agrarian societies characterised by low levels of urbanisation and population density and low value-added economic activity are likely to be less successful at fiscal extraction. State capacity is also influenced by the historical process of state formation, in particular the role of mineral (extractive) industries which generally – at least in Southern Africa – served to assist in a process of public investment and provide a higher share of tax revenue. Typically, however, African countries have a low share of tax income relative to GDP (21.1% of GDP from 1990 to 1996) compared to the OECD[31] states (32.8% over the same period), though they experience a higher share of taxes on international trade (6.2% versus 0.8%).[32]

The reasons behind state dysfunction can thus be broadly grouped into two inter-related areas: historical/political and economic. In each a complex set of compounding factors has worked to erode statehood.

State Failure: The Reasons

Historical/ Political Factors	• The effect of colonialism on state formation and leadership.
	• Arbitrary borders.
	• External intervention and relationships, including clientelism.
	• Strategic interests of other nations.
	• Ethnic, religious and class divisions.
	• Use of repressive and exclusionary policies, including terror.
	• Poor leadership and role of central authority.
	• State capacity.
	• Nature of external intervention.
	• Regional environment.
Economic Factors	• Type of economy – agrarian/industrial, and the impact on fiscal management and global integration/competitiveness.
	• Levels of external dependency.
	• Extent of natural resources.
	• The impact of globalisation.
	• Impact of external policy prescriptions and interests.
	• Impact of, and reliance on, foreign aid.
	• Levels of integration with the global economy.
	• Strategic/geographic location – particularly in terms of access to the sea and ports.
	• Disease and demographics.

But is state failure relevant?
The story of the rise and fall of the Roman empire suggests that history, even at its documented start, is a continuum. Statehood and its attributes are not fixed, nor should they be taken for granted. Modern Europe rose out of the collapse of states and empires as recently as the last century. This is why there were just 43 states worldwide at the start of the 20th century, and 192 by its end. It is also generally accepted that the state is, in an age of globalisation, a locus of diminishing rather than increasing power. Thus, it is unclear whether any one contemporary state requires (or, for that matter, can possess) all aspects of Westphalian statehood. Indeed, one could question whether this is desirable. And states are not necessary for international relationships – nongovernmental organisations, businesses and other organs of civil society can forge links without (and often better without) the state in evidence. Should we thus worry about state decline and collapse?

There are a number of factors why a study on state failure is today pertinent and relevant in Africa.

- First, over the last 50 years the state has become the basic building-block of the post-1945 world order.
- Second, there is a changing relationship between territory and wealth. There is a certain attractiveness in being seen as "small", partly because military and territorial vulnerability are no longer such threats to state existence in the same way that they were 50 years ago. As the adage has it, size is not everything with regard to state power: compare the extent of the territory of the DRC to that of the economic powerhouses of Taiwan, Singapore or Hong Kong, for example.
- Third, there is a widespread awareness that modernity and democracy are two sides of the same coin; that advancement is largely dependent on high levels of industrialisation, innovation and education; and that peace and social harmony are products of better governance.
- Fourth, there is a realisation that the supreme power of the state has given way to greater sovereignty by the people with the concomitant spread of systems of accountability and justice both within and between states. Unlike the case of medieval Europe and its experience of fluid state formation, the world today has considerably more power at its disposal to influence events in Africa, a function not only of relative state power but also of the spread of information technology.

- Fifth, African state failure matters, to put it bluntly, to those caught
  up in their disintegration. Living conditions have scarcely improved,
  and in many cases have declined, in an environment of economic
  collapse in Africa. The bottom 20 of 174 countries ranked in the
  UN's *Human Development Index* are all African. In strife-torn Sierra
  Leone, at the foot of the list, life expectancy at birth is today the
  lowest in the world, at just 37 years.
- Sixth, state failure matters because states are required to do certain
  things. These include providing a framework for economic growth,
  national and border security, and domestic law and order. State capacity is vital for implementing economic reform and setting conditions conducive to performance and development.

NEPAD, as noted in the Introduction, appears to assume that the
African states are dysfunctional in advocating a special set of developmental circumstances without which these states will be condemned
to a poverty-stricken future. The question remains, however, how state
capacity can be created where there is little or none, especially since
the evidence from aid regimes and African regional integration experiences points to the unlikelihood of success in attempting to supplant
(a lack of) internal capacity from outside.

Conclusion: *An African Picture?*

While recognising the importance of acknowledging (and developing
policy according to) differences between African states, in considering the policy options for the continent, it is necessary to paint a picture of the "average" African state. Most countries in Africa are likely
to display the following characteristics:
- They are primary exporters of a narrow range of products.
- They have a lower output per capita than they had in the 1960s. The
  continent experienced a deceleration in growth from 5% per annum
  after 1973 to 1%, concurrent with a decline in investment productivity from 25% to 5%, just half the rate (12%) of that of South and
  East Asia (23%) during this time span.
- They are capital exporters. The savings rate of Africa is the lowest
  worldwide, totalling 16.3% of GDP in 1997 compared with 37.5%
  for East Asia and 24% for Latin America.
- They are aid dependent and heavily indebted.
- They are mired in poverty, with 40% of sub-Saharan Africa's pop-

ulation under the international poverty datum line of US$1 per
day.

- They are seriously affected by HIV/Aids and other diseases, especially malaria and illnesses caused by waterborne bacteria.
- Their agriculture and industry have been decapitalised, with degrad-
  ed infrastructure.
- They are in or near conflict, with one in three African states and one
  in five African lives affected.

Any attempt at reforming African countries has to address these realities. Such an attempt should centre on the three core, inter-related
objectives on which this book is focused. First, there is a need to end
conflict; second, there is an imperative to reduce poverty through
economic growth; and third, it is vital to improve the conditions in
which business – and economies – can prosper. Such reforms have to
take place within the context of a radically changing international
order, where concerns about democracy and governance – encapsulated by the term "good governance" – have become a key concern
of international policy and a prime objective of aid transfers.

CHAPTER THREE

NO MIRACLES
Lessons from Asia

Asia's experience shows that Africa's challenges in accelerating development can be overcome.

The World Bank[1]

The success of economic plans in Taiwan is that they are never carried out. The success of Taiwan is down mainly to the effort of people; not the policy of the government.

DR PO CHIH CHEN,
Taiwan Council for Economic Planing and Development[2]

The real Asian "miracle" is that the region-wide economic crisis of 1997-98 didn't happen earlier. The problem for Asia is just how many of the bad old ways remain.

MICHAEL BACKMAN[3]

Introduction

The forest fires that shrouded much of Southeast Asia in dense smog four years ago could also be taken as a metaphor for the economic and political downfall of a number of the region's high-flyers. In September 2001, the toll roads leading from Jakarta's Soekarno-Hatta international airport displayed a "wanted" poster. This was no ordinary criminal, but Tommy Soeharto, younger son of the Indonesian president who led his country for 32 years before resigning amidst scandal and political upheaval in May 1998.

The warrant for Tommy's arrest on charges of corruption and murder was an indication both of the problems at the heart of Indonesia's financial and political crisis, and the steps government would have to take to get things right again.

These events pose questions about the reasons behind the Asian economic "miracles", not least in Indonesia, and the directions that recovery from the subsequent economic crisis could take.

---

1 *Can Africa Claim the 21st Century?, op cit*, p.19.
2 Interview, Taipei, 4 May 2001.
3 See Michael Backman, *Asian Eclipse: Exposing the Dark Side of Doing Business in Asia*. Singapore: John Wiley, 2001, p.3.

Since 1997, Indonesia, the world's most populous Islamic nation, spanning one eighth of the globe, has experienced unparalleled political and economic convulsions. But before its 1997 economic crash and consequent political crisis, Indonesia was seen as an Asian tiger in the making. In the wake of the crisis, however, the Indonesian rupiah declined in value by more than 600% in 12 months. The economy, which had been expanding by over 6% annually during the decade, fell by 20% in 18 months.

Indonesia's economic collapse raises fundamental questions about what sort of government is appropriate – and possible – in developing societies, many of which share similar problems of state consolidation. The advent of democratic politics has not brought stability. Nor, indeed, has it yet altered the web of cronyist military-business-familial linkages, which have for so long determined and dominated Indonesia's political economy. It remains to be seen whether it can change the perceptions of unreliability resulting from the 1997 crisis and compete in a comparatively unfavourable global economic environment.

Kuala Lumpur's international airport leaves one in no doubt about how Prime Minister Mahathir Mohamad envisioned his country's future: of a high-tech society in the image of his "Malaysia 2020" vision. The modern three-lane highway from the airport to the city was originally designed as part of a "Multimedia Superhighway" technology corridor. At the one end is the spectacular Petronas Towers, at the time of completion the world's tallest building; at the other end, the airport and the Formula One Grand Prix circuit, the latter annually hosts, among others, to the Petronas-sponsored Sauber team.

Malaysia's economic recovery and policy of social upliftment are results of the government's recognition of two priorities, economic growth alongside improving social and racial equity. An extensive national affirmative action scheme for indigenous Malays, the *Bumiputra* ("sons of the soil"), was developed, which involved preferential access to state finance, contracts, government positions and educational opportunities. The aim was to create a Malay capitalist elite and redistribute wealth between the races. The government introduced its New Economic Policy (NEP) in 1970 shortly after the "race riots" in the capital, Kuala Lumpur, which claimed the lives of 196 Malaysian Chinese in May 1969. The NEP was designed to achieve national unity by eradicating poverty among all racial groups, and by restructuring society to achieve inter-ethnic economic parity. This vision and Mahathir's drive saw the Malaysian economy average over 8% GDP growth during the 1990s, while the percentage of those adjudged as living below the poverty line declined from 49.3% in 1990 to 6.8% in 1997.

Despite the advantages accruing to Malaysia's economy due to increased levels of foreign direct investment and trade flows, Mahathir's relationship with global capital and its institutions has been both complex and ambiguous. Mahathir responded to the 1997 financial crisis by placing a (temporary) moratorium on capital flows out of Malaysia, and banned trade in the fast-devaluing ringgit outside the country. Although observers saw this at the time as a radical move contrary to Malaysia's longer-term economic interests, with the benefit of hindsight many can now see structural economic advantages in what Mahathir did (see Chapter Five).

But Malaysia's economic growth is arguably an illustration of what can be achieved through greater integration with the global economy and through well-thought-out, even visionary, social and economic reforms. But, as will be seen, while recognising the need for social equity, the Malaysian experience raises questions about the relationship between political and economic elites. For example, although Malaysia is often held up as a model of social harmony, political support for the ruling United National Malay Organisation (UNMO) is dependent on the system of patronage set up under the *Bumiputra* system. Why else, for example, would Malaysia have 800,000 civil servants, when Australia, with the same size of population, only has 130,000? As with other examples in Asia (such as Indonesia), this raises questions about the nature of governance in such countries. Why has there been at times an indistinct separation of powers and interests between politics and business, or between politics and the judiciary? What is the relationship between state capacity, cultural make-up, the particular colonial history and inheritance, and governance? And, contrary to the generally-held assumption that radical economic reforms are only possible in authoritarian regimes: Is sustainable economic growth possible in the absence of democracy?

Malaysia's (temporary) imposition of exchange controls after 1997 raises a more technical poser about the sequencing of economic reforms. The relationship between FDI and economic growth and the potential dangers that financial inflows pose for macroeconomic balance and exchange rate stability in the absence of domestic regulatory and prudential controls are, among others, also worth examining. Finally, questions which go beyond simple (and simplistic) measure-

ments of corruption need to be asked, involving the broader association between politicians and the private sector and their mutual reliance for support, money and contracts. What sort of institutions and
practices can most positively influence this relationship?

★ ★ ★

East Asian nations are thus held up as examples *both* of what to do
and what not to do in reforming the national political economy and
adapting to the wider, external market forces characterised by globalisation. Indeed, the Asian financial crisis which started in 1997 has
brought to light marked differences between states in what had previously been seen as a regional success story – with the result that today there are probably as many doubters as there are believers in the
path followed by Asia's economic "tigers" and "cubs".

Asia has come under a spotlight which has revealed striking examples of poor governance and corruption, especially following the 1997
crash. This crisis was brought on by financial shock, but the market
collapse served to expose poorly regulated, opaque, nepotistic and
corruption-ridden systems of governance, particularly but not exclusively in the banking sector. All of these exacerbated the negative
economic impact. In 1997, East Asian economies (excluding China
and Japan) contracted by some 6%.

Nonetheless, whatever its more recent difficulties, East Asia's performance has been remarkable, the more so when it is measured
against Africa's rate of decline. In 1965, for example, Nigeria had a
higher per capita GDP than Indonesia: by 1997, just before the financial crash, Indonesia's per capita GDP had risen to more than
three times the level of Nigeria's. Ghana, the first British African colonial state to acquire independence in 1957, then had a higher GNP
per capita than South Korea: today the average income of Koreans is
around 20 times that of Ghanaians. When Malaysia gained independence in 1957, it had a per capita income less than that of Haiti. Whereas Haiti was, at the end of the 20th century, the poorest country in the
Americas, Malaysia has a standard of living higher than that of any
major economy in the Americas save for the US and Canada.[4] And despite the 1997 crisis, regional economic growth has quickly recovered

---

4 This point was made by Prime Minister Mahathir. See Dato' Seri Dr Mahathir bin Mohamad, *The Asian Values Debate*. Kuala Lumpur: ISIS Perdana
Papers, 1997.
5 World Bank, *World Development Indicators*. CD Rom Version, 1999.

in East Asia, with most countries – with the notable exception of Indonesia – proving more resilient and adaptable than many expected. With 1999 GDP growth rates in the 5% margin for Malaysia and Thailand, and touching 10% for South Korea, the East Asian success story is not a mirage but a reality, if an imperfect one.

The contrast between Africa and Asia and the lessons to be learnt by the former from the latter are all the more appropriate given Africa's search for a continental developmental framework that will help it to meet its challenges. With this in mind, this chapter examines three issues.

- First, it provides the historical backdrop to the reforms of three different East Asian economies – Taiwan, Malaysia and Indonesia – with different social, historical backgrounds and in different time series. In doing so, it identifies the conditions that gave rise to the 1997 economic crisis and its political consequences. To what extent did the crisis occur because of "bad governance"? Or to what extent was the crisis out of the control of Asian leaders?
- Second, it extracts lessons to be learnt from the Asian experience, and uses them to create a template for development pertinent to African and other developing nations.
- Third, it provides pointers to areas of concern for the future of the Asia-Pacific region, and examines ways in which these challenges are being addressed within the context of globalisation.

★ ★ ★

Asian Growth: The Historical Context

At the time of the 1997 crisis, East Asian economies accounted for nearly one quarter of global GDP and trade.

Economic Growth by Region[5]

	1965-97 (real GNP)	1991-97 (real GNP)
Latin America and Caribbean	1.3	3.4
East Asia and Pacific	5.4	10.7 (excluding Rep. of Korea)
Sub-Saharan Africa	-0.2	2.2
Europe and Central Asia	. . .	-4.4
Middle East and North Africa	0.1	2.9
South Asia	2.3	5.7
WORLD	1.4	2.3

This growth was linked to an upsurge in private capital flows to the region, which grew steadily to around US$30 billion in 1993 and touched US$80 billion in 1996. The table below illustrates the symbiosis between improved volumes of foreign capital and rates of economic growth.

Foreign Direct Investment by Region (US$ billions)[6]

	1990	1997	1999[7]
Latin America and Caribbean	8.2	61.6	90
East Asia and Pacific	10.3	61.4	93.25
Sub-Saharan Africa	0.8	5.2	10 (incl. North Africa)
Europe and Central Asia	1.1	22.3	25.8
Middle East and North Africa	2.8	5.4	—
South Asia	0.5	4.7	3.2
WORLD	192.7	395	800 (208 for developing courntries)

What made Asian economies so successful, yet apparently, in the light of the events of the late 1990s, so vulnerable? Taiwan, Malaysia and Indonesia offer instructive, if different, answers.

The Taiwan Model

In 1952, Taiwan had a per capita GDP of US$196.[8] Twenty years later this had risen to US$522, by 1982 to US$2,653, by 1992 to US$10,506, and by the end of the millennium to US$13,248.[9] Importantly, the island has been able to weather economic storms successfully. In 1998, Taiwan notched up over 4% growth, the fifth highest worldwide. Growth increased to 5.7% in 1999 and 6% in 2000. Between 1955 and 1999, Taiwan's average growth was 8.1%, South Korea's 7.7%, Japan's 5.8% and the Philippines' 3.9%.[10] Critically, this has been achieved alongside price stability.

6 *Ibid.*
7 This year is calculated from the UNCTAD *World Investment Report 2000* on *http://www.unctad.org/en/docs/wir00ove.en.pdf* .
8 At 1996 prices.
9 See *Taiwan Statistical Data Book 2000.* Taipei: Council for Economic Planning and Development, 2000.
10 The data for these figures and the two tables which follow are derived from *Taiwan's Economic Development and Outlook.* Taiwan: Council for Economic Planning and Development, March 2001.

NO MIRACLES 113

Taiwan Growth and Price Stability

	Economic Growth %	CPI Increase %
1955-99	8.2	5.1
1960s	8.5	3.0
1970s	9.0	8.5
1980s	7.4	2.6
1990s	5.8	2.5

There has also been a consistent spread of economic benefits between the wealthy and the poor. The ratio of income of the top to the bottom income quintile was 5.3 in 1964, 4.2 in 1976 and 5.5 in 1999.

Comparative Wealth Distribution: Top versus Bottom Quintile

Japan	4.7 (1994)
South Korea	5.3 (1993)
Taiwan	5.5 (1999)
Singapore	8.5 (1992-93)
USA	9.5 (1997)
Brazil	25.7 (1995)

Taiwan's long-term economic success has been due to both internal and external factors. A number of clearly identifiable developmental stages can be seen.[11]

First, during the 1950s the government embarked on a land reform process (the "land-to-the-tiller" programme), transferring 37% of land from landlords to tenants. This in turn encouraged harder work by the new owners, and resulted in improved domestic purchasing power. Industrialisation was promoted by compensating the landlords by giving them shares in government-owned companies; import substitution; and, later, concessions offered by the government to stimulate exports. At the same time, the government, realising that no macroeconomic policy could work without education and training, spent

11 See *The Taiwan Experience: Implications for South Africa.* Johannesburg: Consulate-General of the Republic of China, December 1995; Yu Tzong-shian, *The Story of Taiwan.* Republic of China: Government Information Office, undated; and Joseph S Lee (ed.), *The Emergence of the South China Growth Triangle.* Taipei: Chung-Hua Institution for Economic Research, 1996.

heavily on education. Positive economic influences included close ties with the Japanese economy, and a strategic relationship with the US granting Taiwan trade access to this important market. Trade links between Taiwan and the US intensified during the Korean War. And while establishing extensive trading links, Taiwan built up its own internal industrial production system.

Second, export development followed a path progressing from agricultural goods, processed food, light machinery and textiles, heavy industry (steel, ships) to today's shift away from labour-intensive industry towards high-tech goods.[12] Four-yearly developmental plans that were conceived and implemented by central government took the shape, in the 1960s, of a focus on light industry and exports such as textiles. The annual rate of increase in exports and imports during the 1960s was 20.4% and 15.1% respectively, increasing to 33.3% and 30.8% during the 1970s, but falling again to 15.7% and 14.9% during the 1980s and 6.5% and 8.1% in the 1990s. Taiwan recorded its first trade surplus in 1971.[13]

Third, during the 1970s oil crisis, growth was sustained by means of government investment in infrastructure. This included the construction of harbours, the establishment of a petrochemical industry to mitigate the effects of the oil price rise (Taiwan is dependent on imports for 96% of its energy needs), the building of a new international airport and freeways, and the electrification of the railways. The establishment of the petrochemical industry provided an impetus for the manufacture and export of plastic products. By the 1980s, when manufactures accounted for 38% of GDP, the economy had reached something of a manufacturing peak. Since that time, as labour costs have risen and competition increased, particularly from other countries in the region, and coupled with the floating (and appreciation in relative NT$-US$ value) of the New Taiwan Dollar, the focus has shifted to higher-tech, higher-value products in the Information Technology (IT) sector. This growth took advantage and underpinned the emergence of high-tech globalisation in the 1990s. Taiwan may even be said to have provided a massive boost to global technology. Today, Taiwan's manufacturing (secondary industry) accounts for 33% of GDP, and services (tertiary industry) 65%.

---

12 See, for example, "In praise of paranoia", *The Economist: A Survey of Taiwan*, 7 November 1998; Koo Chen-Fu, "The 'Economic Miracle': A Commentary", *Free China Review*, 48, 12, December 1998, pp.37-39.
13 *Taiwan's Economic Development and Outlook, op cit.*

Taiwan's relatively low ratio of non-performing loans (officially 5%, but probably closer to 12% by 2001) and low debt-to-equity ratio (30%) helped to spur competition and to demonstrate greater prudence and transparency in banking operations and fiscal rectitude than was shown by some of its Southeast Asian counterparts. This openness is backed up by Taiwan's rigorously free press – an anomaly in much of Asia even today – which has helped to forestall nasty surprises for investors (and their consequently often panic-stricken responses). As Chu summarises:[14]

> The Nationalist government has invariably maintained a positive real interest rate, minimum public-sector foreign debt, small fiscal deficit, a fixed exchange rate pegged to the US dollar, restrictions on the convertibility of the NT dollar, a rigorous regulatory regime over financial institutions, and a conservative ethos that permeated the entire financial sector.

What motivates this fiscal conservatism?
The Taiwanese prefer not to talk about their economic transition in terms of a "miracle". Most put their economic success down to a combination of simple factors like hard work, investment in education, improvement of skills, their habit of saving rather than spending, and the more efficient application of limited resources through small- and medium-sized private (often family-run) industries. There are some 1.2 million of these enterprises: 98.5% of all companies on the island belong to the small- and medium-sized sector.[15] This is one of the reasons, the Taiwanese maintain, that their economy was comparatively unaffected by the Asian financial crisis, which exposed the frailty of those economies that had been built on political and economic patronage often reliant on large industrial conglomerates.

There is no doubt that Taiwan's relationship with the mainland

---

14 Yun-han Chu, "Surviving the East Asian Financial Crisis: The Political Foundations of Taiwan's Economic Resistance", in TJ Pempel, *The Politics of the Asian Economic Crisis*. Ithaca: Cornell University Press, 1999, p.190.

15 See Garth Shelton, "Taiwan's Economic Success and the Role of Education and Small and Medium Sized Enterprises in Development", *East Asia Project Working Paper Series* 28. Johannesburg: Wits University, April 2001; and "Small and Medium Sized Enterprise Administration", *White Paper on Small and Medium Sized Enterprises in Taiwan*, 2000. Taipei: Ministry of Economic Affairs, 2000. Also, Monika Glinzler *et al.*, "The Asian SME Experience: Lessons for South Africa?", *SAIIA Report*. Johannesburg: SAIIA, 2002.

PRC also helped to concentrate efforts aimed at national survival –
what could be described as "performance through paranoia".

The fear of isolation has also helped to drive this success. Diplo-
matically isolated, Taipei knows that if it gets into financial trouble,
it cannot hope for an international, IMF-type bailout. This has contributed to the government's reluctance to fully liberalise its current
account. Ironically, the fear (and increasing reality) of isolation also
keeps Taiwan engaged with the rest of the region – especially the mainland. In spite of the absence of political ties and despite a ban on direct contacts, by 2002 Taiwan was the fourth largest investor in the
mainland, with an official stake of an estimated US$60 billion (though
some put it as high as US$100 billion). This is more than Taiwan has
sunk into all of Southeast Asia. The PRC was also Taiwan's second
largest export market.[16]

Taiwanese Outward Investment[17] (US$ billion)

	To China	Other Countries
1997	4.3	2.9
1998	2	3.3
1999	1.25	3.3
2000	2.6	5

Taiwan's cautious macroeconomic policies were also a product of the
stability provided by the long-lived ruling Kuomintang (KMT) party, which was defeated in the 2000 presidential election. Relating to the
hyperinflation of the late 1940s which contributed to its defeat on the
mainland, the KMT focused on central bank independence and the
(largely) state control of the banking system and its credit practices.

Put simply, enlightened government policies guiding a private
enterprise system have been at the heart of Taiwan's success.

The Malaysian Experience

Prime Minister Dato' Seri Dr Mahathir bin Mohamad attempted
to shift the blame for Malaysia's economic troubles in the late 1990s

16 Statistics supplied by the Taiwan Institute of Economic Research, May 2001.
17 These figures are for approved outward investment from Taiwan, and do not
necessarily include all investments passing through third countries and entities
such as Hong Kong. Supplied by the Taiwan Institute of Economic Research,
May 2001.

from the internal to the external domain, thereby taking a different route from what most others saw as the root causes of the crisis.[18] The dramatic 50% fall in the value of the Malaysian ringgit in 1997 was met by his attack on market speculators (most notably George Soros), and the implementation of restrictions on financial outflows. Local challenges to his rule were countered by the arrest (and subsequent imprisonment) of his deputy and heir-elect, Anwar Ibrahim, on sex and corruption charges on 2 September 1998, the day after Mahathir had imposed comprehensive controls on capital outflows. This split came after public disagreement over Anwar's imposition of IMF-style high interest rate policies to stabilise the falling exchange rate. As the prime minister noted at the time:[19]

> What we are doing is actually defending our independence, no less than that. Do remember, those who created the economic turmoil that we are facing now are just like the colonialists who once colonised us. Do not think their behaviour has changed. As the Malay adage goes, "Tigers will always have their stripes".

At the end of 1996, Mahathir had presided over the roll-out of the one-millionth Malaysian-made vehicle from the *Preusahan Otomobil Nasional Berhad* (Proton), which had recently purchased legendary British sports-car maker Lotus. He began 1997 by promoting the advantages of his plans for a Multimedia Super Corridor – an Asian Silicon Valley. Ironically, his country was among the main beneficiaries of increased worldwide capital flows. The 7.5% contraction in the economy in 1998 contrasted with an annual growth of 8.7% between 1990 and 1997.

Following the financial crash, Mahathir called for austerity and sacrifices from his people, including the encouragement of self-sufficiency. He urged farmers to grow vegetables on a large scale, so reducing spending on imports. The irony of the shift in stress from high technology to cauliflower was not lost on commentators. Calling on Malay-

---

18 For an excellent summary of the reasons behind the Asian crisis, see both Philippe Riés, *The Asian Storm: Asia's Economic Crisis Examined*. Boston: Tuttle, 2000; and Backman, *op cit*. For a description of Malaysia under Mahathir, see KS Jomo (ed.), *Malaysian Eclipse: Economic Crisis and Recovery*. London: Zed Books, 2001; and RS Milne and Diane K Mauzy, *Malaysian Politics Under Mahathir*. London: Routledge, 1999.
19 This quotation is taken from his book, *The Challenges of Turmoil*.

sians not to convert their money into foreign currencies, Mahathir said, "We must be willing to face challenges and willing to sacrifice in defending our independence and dignity. In fact, our unfinished struggle has become even more critical."[20]

Whatever his idiosyncracies, Mahathir is seen as the principal architect of both Malaysia's economic recovery and its social upliftment. Analysts point to three core features of the Malaysian economic model – leadership, discipline and central planning. The NEP had two pillars, the eradication of poverty and the restructuring of the economy so as "not to link race and occupation, and to correct social and geographic imbalances".[21] With this overarching framework in mind, and using centralised planning structures, the First (five-year) Malaysia Plan concentrated on rural development to offset the "benign neglect of the colonial authorities". This was followed by a focus on industrial growth during the 1970s, as Malaysia reached the point of maximum land utilisation, with the additional aim of creating a *Bumiputra* industrial and commercial community. This was followed in the 1980s by a focus on the development of the petro-industry, followed by a stress on the IT sector, though mainly as an assembling rather than a manufacturing facility. This was followed by changes to the structure of state-owned organisations through privatisation in the 1990s, with preference given to *Bumiputra* ownership.

There have been remarkable gains, including developments in Malaysia's infrastructure, poverty reduction, a rise in real incomes and a lessening of income disparities among ethnic communities. Yet, following the Asian crash, the Malaysian economy also revealed high levels of inefficiency, patronage and nepotism.

While the prime minister may have laid the blame for Malaysia's economic downturn at the door of capitalism's excesses, his country's difficulties also illustrate the dangers of lack of control. As long as the Malaysian economy performed well (which it did for most of the 1990s), most chose to ignore the danger signals. In the region, the decline in the currency value of Malaysia during 1998 was second only to that of Indonesia. It was countered only by pegging the ringgit. Without this intervention, the Kuala Lumpur stock market might have gone into freefall, as in Jakarta, with potentially serious consequences for the rule of the UNMO and Mahathir. However, this strat-

---

20 "Mahathir tells nation to veg out and grow your own", *The Australian*, 2 January 1998.

egy caused a perceived overvaluation of the currency, which hampered Malaysian exports, compounded by a reduced economic demand worldwide.

Non-performing loans, the most obvious of the side-effects of a lack of accountability and transparency, were, at the time of the crisis, estimated to be around 33% of the total in Malaysia, compared to 7.5% in Singapore, 12% in Taiwan, 70% in Indonesia and just under 50% in Thailand. The domestic debt/GDP ratio in Malaysia stood at 170% in 1997, making it one of the highest in the world. A number of key *Bumiputra* businesses remain protected by political largesse and national pride. Proton, for example, was in 2001 dependent on a 40% tax on imported, unassembled vehicles. The estimated price for Protons is around 20% more than that of their global competitors.[22]

Kuala Lumpur's skyline remains dotted with half-empty buildings erected during the bubble period, which have little or no productive value. The Petronas Twin Towers are the best (or worst) example. Rather than symbols of Asia's modernisation, "composed mostly of elevator shafts because of their height, the towers are symbols of excess and inefficiency".[23] Even those who benefited from the *Bumiputra* policies became critical of the cronyism and corruption which dogged the system. In particular, the financial bailout of *Bumiputra* businesses and notable Malay businessmen by the government, including Mahathir's youngest son, raised a storm of protest which threatened to destabilise the political environment. But these measures, financed largely by the state oil company Petronas, plus the regional "bounceback" from panic and the maintenance of low interest rates (partly made possible by exchange rate controls), saw an almost immediate reflation of the Malaysian economy to 4.7% growth in 1999. The discovery and production of oil (accounting for around 10% of government revenue and between 2% and 3% of GDP) has stimulated (and sustained) economic growth, and should not be overlooked.

The Malaysia model of economic development had a number of positive and negative components:

21 Interview, Tan Sri Thong Yaw Hong and Dr K Govindan, Economic Planning Unit, Prime Minister's Department, Kuala Lumpur, 30 April 2001.
22 Dwight Heald Perkins and Wing Thye Woo, "Malaysia: Adjusting to Deep Integration", in Wing Thye Woo, Jeffrey D Sachs and Klaus Schwab (eds.), *The Asian Financial Crisis: Lessons for a Resilient Asia*. Cambridge: The MIT Press, 2000, p.248.
23 Backman, *op cit*, p.3.

Malaysia's Positive and Negative Aspects

Positive Policy Lessons	• The initial importance of agricultural and land reform. • The use of infrastructure spending to stimulate economic growth. • The link between economic growth and social equity through the development of the *Bumiputra*. • The encouragement of private-public sector partnerships. • A focus on education, health and poverty alleviation. • The importance of stable relationships both within and without the region. • The need for skills building, both inside government and within the wider economy. • The key role played by the state and individuals in policy planning.
Aspects to Avoid	• The pursuit of white-elephant projects related more to national pride than economic good sense and functionality (for example, the Petronas Towers and the new government town at Petra Jaya). • The presence of widespread cronyism and corruption. • The absence of a free press. • The use of government income, notably from the oil parastatal Petronas, to pursue ambitious development projects and using it as a cash cow when these failed. • Investment in unproductive areas, notably golf courses (47 in the Klang Valley/Kuala Lumpur area alone in 2001) and hotels. • The institutionalisation of inefficiencies, notably in the loss-making national car maker Proton and Malaysian Airlines. • The cost of affirmative action – or Bumiputraism – "where things have gone wrong, those guys who were unsuccessful were not punished, but instead rewarded".[24] • The squandering of key national resources, such as Petronas, to bail out economic failures and follies.

In summary, Malaysia's economic success was constructed on an interdependent mix of political stability and sound economic policy. The former was established through a coalition government with 14 partners, and through the interventionist *Bumiputra* policy intended to redress social and economic imbalances. An absence of trade unions,

---

24 Interview, Foreign Diplomat, Kuala Lumpur, 30 April 2001.

inter alia, helped to attract foreign capital, while the payment of salaries sufficiently high to support a decent standard of living for civil servants helped to bring corruption down to "acceptable" levels. This was in stark contract to Indonesia, the Philippines and Thailand. Although Malaysia, like other Southeast Asian nations, managed to rebound more quickly than expected from the economic crisis, the nature of its socioeconomic model could prove increasingly costly, with related concerns about regional economic competitiveness and domestic political continuity and stability. The former is linked to the pegged valuation of the ringgit and the dangers of bailing out *Bumiputra* firms rendered non-competitive for reasons other than the financial panic. The latter goes to the heart of Mahathir's attempts to economically subsidise a wider *Bumiputra* political vision. As a result, "Malay leadership is caught between short-run political expedience and long-run economic competitiveness".[25]

Indonesia: *Nepotism and Collapse*

Before the 1997 crash, Indonesia was seen as an Asian tiger in the making. In the immediate wake of the crisis, however, the Indonesian rupiah declined in value by 600% within 12 months. The economy, which had expanded by 9% in 1990 and 4.7% in 1997, fell by 13.2% the next year, suffering a 36% drop in real fixed investment in 1998 and a 21% drop in 1999.[26]

Why the sudden collapse?

The simple answer is that Indonesia's growth had been built on a web of nepotism, and was not supported by the necessary political reforms. When then President Soeharto started, following the 1997 financial crisis, to dismantle the tight control that his family-run businesses had over the economy, he inevitably weakened the system of political patronage and egregious corruption that had sustained it. As *Newsweek* noted at the time:[27]

---

25 Perkins and Woo, *op cit*, p.254.
26 For background on the collapse, see Grayson Lloyd and Shannon Smith (eds.), *Indonesia Today: Challenges of History*. Singapore: Institute of Southeast Asian Studies, 2001.
27 See "Suharto Family Values", *Newsweek*, 26 January 1998, p.24. For an excellent appraisal of life under Suharto, see Adam Schwarz, *A Nation in Waiting*. Australia: Allen and Unwin, 1999 (second edition); and Geoff Forrester and RJ May (eds.), *The Fall of Soeharto*. Australia: Crawford House, 1998.

How do things really work in Indonesia? Even the most casual
visitor gets a clue. You arrive at Jakarta International, built by
Bambang Trihatmodjo, the second of President Suharto's three
sons. The jet that brought you might have been a European
Airbus leased by Sempati Air, the airline controlled by Hutomo
Mandala Putra, popularly known as "Tommy", the President's
youngest son. Your taxi may belong to eldest daughter Siti Har-
diyantti Rukmana, "Tutut", who also built the toll road that
whisks you into the city. If you're a flush expense-accounter, you
might stay at the Grand Hyatt, another of Bambang's properties.
An evening stroll could bring you to the Plaza Indonesia, a 170-
store mall that's home to Tiffany, Gucci and Bulgari – yet another of Bambang's baubles.

Indonesia's problems have thus stemmed from the nature of the relationship between its economic and political domains, where there
is little distinction made between public and private accounts. This
environment is both reflective of, and encouraged by, the weakness
of institutions (notably the central banks) and regulatory systems.
In this sense, Indonesia differs little from a number of African nations. More controversially, where this "Asian way" has been different
relates to both the manner in which business is conducted in Indonesia and the relative efficiency (and thus spread of the benefits) of the
economy. Whereas General Sani Abacha of Nigeria or, for that matter, other rulers of Western Africa's oil-rich states, was known to have
brazenly diverted public income to their own accounts, in Indonesia
(and elsewhere in Asia) this took on an outwardly apparently more
acceptable form. It was seen as a way of "doing business" rather than
outright theft. This perception arguably results from the conditions
of relative prosperity within these states as opposed to those in Africa.
It also results from the relative distribution of the proceeds of development.

Soeharto's rule was built on an absence of basic political freedoms,
though the political legitimacy of his group, Golkar, was constructed
on its revival of the economy, which had collapsed under the rule of
his predecessor, Soekarno. Hence the slogan, "Development Yes, Politics No!" Soeharto's "New Order" was underpinned by introducing
policies to attract foreign investment (mostly to take advantage of
Indonesia's vast natural resources, especially oil), and by efforts to improve agricultural production (particularly of the staple, rice).

In this respect Indonesia was not outwardly different from Singapore, Taiwan or Malaysia. But Indonesia's collapse when apparently on the brink of becoming a substantial economic and political power is due to key differences. In Taiwan, for example, while the Kuomintang, the ruling party until 2000, has substantial business interests, these "serve as investments to generate earnings to run the party rather than for the benefit of any one individual or family".[28] They are also subject to the general "rules" that pertain on the island with regard to business; where commercial expansion is reliant more on retained earnings than on external financing.[29] In Indonesia, by comparison, the private and central banking system was compromised by political connections, the state coffers were used as a familial financial feeding trough, and the practice that public positions could be used to ensure private benefits followed the example of the political leadership. Or as Backman argues, "Simply, the Soeharto empire was the biggest 'kleptocracy' that the world has ever seen", with more than 1,250 companies at least partly owned by the Soeharto family, which had amassed a fortune estimated at its peak to be as large as US$25 billion.[30]

There was a close relationship between Soeharto's political support base (especially in the army), the country's stability and geographic political consolidation, and continued economic growth. Yet Soeharto's failure to liberalise made the economy vulnerable. The economic contraction, the lack of means to engineer a domestic rescue package as in Malaysia, plus an absence of channels for political dissent led to violent unrest in Indonesia, which ultimately led to Soeharto's departure.

By 2001, the archipelago of more than 13,600 islands and 225 million people, comprising the world's fourth most populous nation, threatened to disintegrate, as it struggled to pick up the pieces after Soeharto's departure. The ageing president relinquished his 32-year reign in the midst of the dramatic fall in GDP in 1998, a 50% drop in real wages, and rioting across the country which included the torching of Jakarta's Chinatown. The government of his chosen successor, Bacharuddin Jusuf Habibie (installed in May 1998), was followed shortly afterwards by that of the elected president, Abdurrahman

---

28 Backman, *op cit*, p.181.
29 *Ibid*, p.180.
30 *Ibid*, p.237.

Wahid, the leader of the country's largest Muslim organisation. But neither president brought economic or political stability. Habibie's rule was characterised by the August 1999 East Timor debacle, while Wahid was caught up in a corruption scandal and accused of chronic incompetence. A pension fund fraud led to his censure by parliament in May 2001, and increasing pressure was put on him to resign in favour of his deputy, Megawati Soekarnoputri (whose father had, ironically, been toppled by Soeharto in 1965). Political uncertainty almost paralysed economic policy-making, and exacerbated social divisions and instability. In 1999, Stephen Redelet and Wing Thye Woo described the economic picture:[31]

> The financial system is dysfunctional: the seven state banks that dominated the financial system before the crisis are now insolvent. The corporate sector is mired in debt, and owners of bankrupt firms are reluctant to embrace formal bankruptcy or to engage in debt-equity swaps because of the possible loss of control over the firms. The hope is that the rupiah will appreciate when political stability is restored, thence the debt-servicing problem will be greatly diminished. However, without a marked improvement in the economy, and with it the generation of economic rents to co-opt political opposition, it is unlikely that political normalcy will return any time soon.

Megawati assumed the presidency needing to balance a number of different, but inter-related imperatives, including liberalising the economy; ridding the country of "KKN" – korupsi, kolusi and nepotisme – partly through the institution of prudential controls; and reforming the banking system. Another urgent priority was to reorder the relationship between the executive and the military, while simultaneously relying on military support to deal with secessionist and radical religious groupings. The development of a new social contract is critical if political stability is to be achieved, and only then can Indonesia's economic growth be restored. Strong leadership is needed to bring these improvements.

One foreign diplomat based in Jakarta observed in 2001 that most of his focus was on the internal security situation rather than the po-

---

31 Steven C Radelet and Wing Thye Woo, "Indonesia: A Troubled Beginning",
    in Woo et al., op cit, p.166.

tential for investment and trade, as it had been during the early to mid-1990s. He envisaged two kinds of problems from Indonesia: first, in increasing numbers of refugees; and second, in terms of the impact of a weakening of control by the central state, taking the forms of increasing transnational crime, including drugs and piracy and possibly Islamic terrorism. (The deputy chief of the Indonesian army acknowledged Osama bin Laden's presence in the archipelago in 2001.)

Despite these fears, Indonesia's economy grew by more than 4% in 2001. The crowds shopping for designer labels in Jakarta's huge malls, such as Plaza Senayana, underscored this upward economic trend. But economic expansion has not kept pace with population growth. Nor have reforms yet addressed the core reasons for the 1997 collapse – notably, poor governance, rampant corruption and nepotism. This meant, for example, that around 50% to 60% of the holdings of local banks were, by the start of 2002, technically insolvent. Indeed, eradicating the practices of "KKN" would also have to be accompanied by measures such as the sale of state-owned institutions through the Indonesian Bank Restructuring Agency, set up as a condition of a US$80 billion bank bailout in 1998. This will involve coming up against cronyist politics, as many of those who benefited from Soeharto's rule are still in business. For example, his eldest daughter, Siti Hadiyantti Rukmana, controls the toll road that displayed the wanted poster of her younger brother.

There is little doubt that the armed forces still have to be brought under control – to be "debrutalised", as the president put it. The military have themselves pledged to leave the political arena. This would involve the removal of non-military tasks (and assets) from its control. The role of the military in managing such enterprises as hotels, shopping centres, tourist resorts, taxis and shipping lines is referred to as *dwifungi* (dual-function). However, not only was the military likely to resist this, but with an estimated 60% to 70% of the military's income "off budget", to do so, Megawati would, put crudely, have to find the cash to bring them under civilian control. Moreover, she (or any other Indonesian leader for that matter) would have to simultaneously continue to rely on the army to provide the authority to back up her rule and reinforce her nationalistic urge to keep Indonesia intact.

It is not clear how any Indonesian leader can reconcile the converging and sometimes contending forces of nationalism (and national identity), ethnic and religious tensions, and globalisation and liberalisation with the need to ensure delivery and political support. Indonesia has relied on a paternalistic (and patronage-reliant) central authority to maintain rule in the tradition of the Javanese, Mataram dynasties. This is why many analysts, even those in the *reformasi* democracy movement, are ultimately pessimistic about the ability of the Indonesian state to simultaneously reform and remain intact; and why some Indonesians hanker for the so-called "golden age" of Soeharto's rule.

In the external domain, the fortunes of the United States economy have a major impact on all of Southeast Asia's economies, given their heavy reliance on exports, especially electronics. Exports accounted in 1999 for 35% of Indonesia's GDP, but 180% of Singapore's and 54% of Taiwan's, the two countries which suffered the most in the high-tech depression, with −3.0% and −2.0% growth in 2001 respectively.

One of the anticipated impacts of this vulnerability, coupled with the global economic downturn in 2001-2, has been an expected refocus on the advantages offered by deepening integration among the 10 members of the Association of Southeast Asian Nations (ASEAN) including Indonesia, which have committed to the creation of an Asian Free Trade Area (AFTA) by 2003. But ASEAN has also faced a number of core problems. These include the potential for instability in both Indonesia and, with Mahathir's presumed hand-over of power, Malaysia; differences in expectations and degrees of development between the established six ASEAN members (Malaysia, Indonesia, Singapore, Thailand, Brunei and the Philippines) and the newcomers (Laos, Burma, Cambodia and Vietnam); and tensions between ASEAN and the neighbouring "big brother" and potential arch-competitor China. By 2001, China received around 80% of East Asia's FDI and ASEAN members 20%, a reversal from just a few years before. To a great extent, much of Indonesia's – and indeed Southeast Asia's – economic future hinges on what happens in China. As one diplomat put it in an interview in Jakarta in September 2001, "If China does well economically, Indonesia suffers as investors will move to their north. If it does badly, then Indonesia probably will benefit, at least in the short term."

Within the regional context, too, Indonesia brings into focus an important feature common to developing areas elsewhere, as in Latin America and Africa. This is the acute difference between nations within the same regions, in terms of their developmental environment and strategies, and their respective historical contexts.[32]

In general terms, Taiwan and South Korea followed the Japanese model of development – that is, state intervention plus domestic capital, first with a focus on heavy industry, followed later by manufactures. Many of the goods produced in Taiwan and South Korea were Japanese manufactures assembled under licence, a feature that was later copied by other developing Asian economies.

Another important characteristic of the Japanese model adopted in both countries was the interlocking relationship between business and government: government exercised strong control over economic direction and policy. It not only sought opportunities for business, but also channelled capital towards business, ultimately, in the case of Japan and South Korea, causing a great waste of resources and inefficiency. The US was important, both as a backer and a market, providing more than US$500 per capita in aid to South Korea for three decades from the late 1940s. From 1949 until it stopped in 1968, US aid to Taiwan totalled US$4.1 billion, of which US$1.7 billion took the form of direct economic assistance (while the remainder was allocated to military aid). The latter enabled Taiwan to divert resources to economic development.

But there were (and remain) important differences between these three countries. For example, Taiwan relied on smaller industries to provide the engine of its economic growth. South Korea placed emphasis on the creation of Japanese-style conglomerates, or *chaebols*, though there was much greater labour unrest there than in either Taiwan or Japan.

The other two tigers, Singapore and Hong Kong, followed their own paths, both operating as entrepôts for capital and trade. Hong Kong's economic activities were facilitated by its status (until 1997) as a British colony. It had little government investment, with industrial growth being driven, as in Taiwan, by small- and medium-sized enterprises. Singapore relied on a mix between strong-minded leadership, high government credibility, and high rates of public investment to develop both its services and its manufacturing sectors.

In contrast, the development of Malaysia, Thailand, Indonesia and, more recently, Vietnam pursued a course which involved less heavy

---

32 For a clear understanding of these differences, see Danny M Leipziger (ed.), *Lessons from East Asia*. Ann Arbor: University of Michigan Press, 2000.

industry and more manufactures, and less (virtually no) domestic, but instead foreign capital. Again there was a close association between a patriarchal and patrimonial political leadership and business. In certain cases this resulted in extreme forms of institutionalised corruption (notably in Indonesia), to the detriment of long-term development. Vietnam has its own peculiar characteristics, given its one-party, communist nature. China is similarly a special case, with an enormous, ethnically and geographically diverse population, and a unique political set-up.

East Asia's nations have different starting points and success rates. In Japan and the Asian tigers, there is little in the way of natural resources, though the Southeast Asian cubs as well as China are much better endowed in this respect. And there have also been exceptions to the regional growth trend: the Philippines, Myanmar/Burma, Laos and North Korea have all, for a variety of reasons, failed to deliver growth, stability or improved social equity. Finally, although the Asian crisis was a major setback to most of these economies, by 1999 only Indonesia had not returned to pre-crisis GDP levels, though it showed signs of economic recovery.

Bearing in mind this important caveat stressing regional diversity, what are the common foundations of Asian success?

Lessons and Templates?

From the Upside: *Ten Factors for Success*

In East Asia the performing states of the 1990s had a number of factors in common: the elements of labour, capital and human resources, and the ability to combine these effectively.[33] From their experience, it is possible to create a typology of what made these states successful.

The first of these is *the role of the state in creating the right conditions to attract local and foreign investors*.[34] There is a critical link between the ability to attract direct investment and economic growth, which

---

33 "A Survey of Asia", *The Economist*, 30 October 1993. See also Gary Gereffi and Donald L Wyman (eds.), *Manufacturing Miracles: Paths of Industrialisation in Latin America and East Asia*. Princeton: PUP, 1990; and Richard Maidment, David Goldblatt and Jeremy Mitchell (eds.), *Governance in the Asia-Pacific*. London: Routledge and The Open University, 1998.

34 See, for example, Peter Drysdale (ed.), *Reform and Recovery in East Asia: The Role of the State and Economic Enterprise*. London: Routledge, 2000.

is necessary to arrest poverty and build a stable and non-belligerent society. There is another link between the commitment of local investors and consequent flow of foreign investment. Robin Renwick has listed five requirements that overseas investment institutions look for when deciding which countries to invest in: political stability, observance of the rule of law, sound macroeconomic policies, sensible monetary policies, and effective, transparent, predictable regulations.[35] These conditions are echoed in the ranking criteria used by the World Economic Forum's *Global Competitiveness Report*, which investigates the underlying conditions to achieve rapid economic growth: labour, management, institutions, the state's role in the economy, the trade and investment regime and infrastructure conditions. Some of these factors are examined further below.

The second issue is *the need for domestic and regional stability and absence of violent conflict*. These are at the head of a list of investor concerns, particularly with regard to physical investments. Stability includes freedom from political and civil conflict, as well as control of the overall criminal-security situation. So-called grey-area risks, which include crime, security, corruption, cultural differences and cronyism, are said to cost multinational companies over US$20 billion annually – or 10% of the expected returns of foreign investment.

The third is paradoxical. *National vulnerability can serve to drive economic success*. By "national vulnerability" I mean not outright warfare or conflict, but a situation of threat. In many of the successful states, populations were linked by a common cause, which might be intensified by cultural and ethnic homogeneity. This was certainly true for Taiwan, South Korea, Japan and also Singapore after the break-up of the federation.

A fourth factor is *the need for a sound policy and institutional framework*. In the case of Asia this did not, at least until 1997, include the features of what has become known as good governance (accountability, transparency, the rule of law, democracy), but it did include high saving ratios (generally taken to be more than 23% of GDP), low fiscal and current account deficits, sound monetary policies, and flexible labour markets. The flexibility of the latter is tied to the need to improve productivity and employment levels, which in turn are re-

---

35 These comments were made at the Commonwealth Business Council forum held in Johannesburg on 10 November 1999 and reported in *Business Day*, 11 November 1999.

lated to conditions of political stability.[36] This also presumes that the right people are employed in bureaucratic structures. They should not only exhibit qualities of apolitical efficiency and be free of corruption, but it is critical that they understand and see the world in the same way, in a manner that is directed at safeguarding economies rather than personal benefits. It would, however, be foolish to suggest that the introduction of liberal market economies will necessarily be rapid or trouble-free. Inevitably in a developing country wealth disparities will be a source of tension. Economic reformers are likely to have difficulties in managing both high expectations and bureaucratic structures.

A fifth factor concerns *the need for acceptable levels of government credibility.* This is related to leadership and to policy. When national leadership loses that credibility – as happened in Indonesia after 1997 – it is most difficult, if not impossible, for that country to regain investor confidence.

Sixth, *education is the bedrock on which successful nations are built,* particularly those populations skilled in the occupations needed most in the 21st century – notably engineering and information technology. Education is perhaps the key component of the Confucian view of the world. The East Asian experience illustrates the positive combined effects of education, demographic change and improving gender equality.[37]

The changing role of East Asian women in society in this equation is reflected in the elimination of the gap in education provided to boys and girls. A decline in birth rates has reduced the number of people to be educated in East Asia, which has in turn allowed for the provision of better than just basic education, with a substantial increase in

36 For evidence to support the idea that flexible labour markets promote employment, see "Working man's burden", *The Economist,* 6 February 1999. See also "Desperately seeking a perfect model", *The Economist,* 10 April 1999.

37 Between 1965 and 1980, developing regions of the world experienced a marked decline in death rates, averaging 30% to 40%. In sub-Saharan Africa this was between 2% and 10%; in South Asia, between 10% and 30%; in Latin America, between 30% and 40%; and in East Asia, between 40% and 50%. This was accompanied by a sharp decline in population growth rates in East Asia: in South Korea this went down from 2.6% per annum in the 1960s to 1.1% in the 1980s; in Hong Kong from 2.5% to 1.4%; and in Thailand from 3.1% to 1.8%. But in sub-Saharan Africa, the combination of sudden and sharp declines in death rates and only modest declines in birth rates led to a substantial acceleration in population growth. See World Bank, *The East Asian Miracle: Economic Growth and Public Policy.* Oxford: OUP, 1993, p.39.

per pupil expenditure. A sufficient quality of labour, coupled with investment in primary and secondary education, proved a cocktail for success in Asia. A surge of highly-trained young people entering the economy at the same time can provide the necessary kick-start. However, in the longer term, this can bring down the rate of population increase, particularly where girls have been educated as extensively as boys and remain in the labour market. Labour productivity in manufacturing is also a critical element in GDP growth.[38]

Seventh, as is noted above, a critical element that distinguishes successful states in Africa has been *leadership's commitment to popular welfare*. In those emerging economies which are successful, leadership has often taken on an iconoclastic character: see, for example, Lee Kuan Yew in Singapore; Chiang Kai-shek and Lee Teng-hui in Taiwan; Kim Dae Jung in South Korea; and Mahathir Mohamed in Malaysia. But the common thread among successful leaders has been realist pragmatism rather than idealism. In Africa, colonial paternalism has, in all too many cases, been replaced by autocratic government – the African "big man" – which has not only been unrepresentative, but for the most part also intolerant, repressive and corrupt. It is the Asian commitment to popular welfare that has – in the absence of democracy – offered political stability to its peoples.

Eighth, there is *a need for a suitable and versatile technology accompanied by an appropriate mindset*. Effective technological development entails quality control and an ability to respond both to market demands and those of the domestic environment. The role of technology has been critical in economic history both from the outset and in the subsequent promotion of growth through export access to the global economy. In China, where 7% of the world's surface supports 21% of its population, development and growth defy economic history, but at its core is the search for higher yields and new export markets.

---

38 For example, consider that between 1950 and 1987, Japan's GDP growth rose annually by 7.9% while labour productivity increased by 8%. In Germany the corresponding figures were 4.6% and 4.3%, in the UK 2.5% and 2.8%, and in the United States, 3.2% and 2.6%. See Michael Porter, *The Comparative Advantage of Nations*. New York: Free Press, 1990, pp.279-80.

Annualised % Growth in Goods and Services
(and trade % of PPP GDP, 1998)[39]

	1965-97
Latin America and Caribbean	1.8 (19.1)
East Asia and Pacific	9.7 (15.5)
Sub-Saharan Africa	-0.3 (16.8)
Europe and Central Asia	... (21.1)
Middle East and North Africa	... (17.4)
South Asia	5.1 (4.8)
WORLD	3.2 (28.3)

Ninth, *ethnicity and culture counts*, if not in terms of a country's work ethic, then certainly in terms of connections. This factor, which is sometimes attributed to the philosophy of Confucianism, includes the following virtues: having a strong work ethic and practising self-discipline; acknowledging hierarchy and showing obedience to authority; having respect for scholarship; noting family unity and linkages in the formation and operation of business; and demonstrating thrift, flexibility and adaptability.[40] This also manifests itself in a "propensity to defer consumption, even across generations", and a willingness to "sublimate individual interests to those of the group".[41] In one survey of societal values, those chosen as most desirable by East Asians were, in order, an orderly society, social harmony, public accountability, openness to new ideas and respect for authority. By comparison, in the same survey Americans chose freedom of expression, individual rights, personal freedom, open debate, thinking for oneself, and public accountability.[42]

Although seen in somewhat hackneyed terms, the Chinese *diaspora* has played a crucial role in pre-colonial, colonial and post-colonial developments in East Asia. Some analysts have even described East and Southeast Asia's success as an "ethnic" or "cultural" triumph. In

39 World Bank, *World Development Indicators*. CD Rom version, 1999.
40 Leung Cheun Chau, "Hong Kong: A Unique Case of Development", Leipziger, *op cit*, p.63.
41 Greg Sheridan, *Asian Values, Western Dreams: Understanding the New Asia*. Australia: Allen & Unwin, 1999, p.10. For a discussion on Asian values, see also Han Sung-Joo (ed.), *Changing Values in Asia: Their Impact on Governance and Development*. Singapore: Institute for Southeast Asian Studies, 1999.

Thailand, the Chinese – entrepreneurs and middlemen par excellence – represent more than 90% of the richest families and own a similar proportion of commercial and manufacturing assets. In Vietnam, the Chinese Cholon area of Saigon/Ho Chi Minh City is the epicentre of economic activity;[43] while in Indonesia, the ethnic Chinese, comprising under 2% of the overall population, controlled more than 70% of the country's top 300 corporations before 1997. Approximately 6% of the aggregate total population of Malaysia, the Philippines, Singapore and Thailand are ethnic Chinese, who control as much as 70% of the region's corporate wealth.[44]

Overseas Chinese Economic Power (Pre-1997)[45]

	Total Population Million	Ethnic Chinese %	Ethnic Chinese % Control of Private, Corporate Domestic Capital
Indonesia	201	3.5	70
Malaysia	20	29	60
Philippines	73	2	55
Singapore	3.5	77	8
Thailand	60	10	75

The role of the Chinese diaspora and the network of personal ethnic and familial connections outside the East Asian region is important in the infusion of capital, skills and technology. Connections – or *guanxi* – are critical for doing business both inside and outside Asia. This both reflects and undermines conditions of sound corporate governance, because the ability both to obtain and enforce contracts is dependent not on the legal system but rather on familial and ethnic ties. Another downside is that the divisions of wealth between this grouping and the local ethnic population(s) is a "recipe for calamitous social unrest", as was shown by the events in Indonesia in the late 1990s, and in the late 1960s, pre-NEP, in Malaysia.[46]

---

42 *Ibid.*
43 David Landes, *The Wealth and Poverty of Nations.* London: Abacus, 1998, p.478.
44 Backman, *op cit*, p.193.
45 *Ibid.*
46 *Ibid*, p.194.

Tenth, and last, related to the above factors, *growth has been export-led*. The external trade and capital environment is critical. For East Asia, this has been assisted not only by strategic relationships – as with the US – but also by the use of other direct economic mechanisms, including the maintenance of a deliberately undervalued exchange rate.

To the Downsides

Before the 1997 crisis broke, there was tangible evidence that the pendulum of global economic activity was swinging towards developing economies. The 1997 World Bank annual report projected that developing countries would double their share of global GDP, to account for nearly one third of global output, by 2020. The global share of the exports of the big five developing countries – China, India, Brazil, Indonesia and Russia – was expected, according to this report, to rise from 9% (in 1992) to 22% in 2020. At the time, the so-called Washington consensus on the need for liberal economic reforms – the thesis that growth and stability hinged on a rapid increase in investment and capital inflows dependent on macroeconomic policy reforms including privatisation – was apparently epitomised by the performance of the Asian tigers and cubs.

How quickly do fortunes change. But what caused the crisis?

As Jeffrey Sachs and Wing Thye Woo have noted, there is great division among analysts on the sources of Asia's crises (national *versus* international); the reasons for the rapid decline (government policies *versus* private sector weakness); the responses (IMF orthodoxy *versus* a more heterodox approach) and the means recommended to guard against a recurrence (national reforms *versus* the establishment of an appropriate global architecture).

Nonetheless, there are three main strands to the collapse of the Asian currencies and economies in 1997. First, there were the common structural problems in the economies, relating to poor supervision and regulation, and the corrupting effect of a nepotistic business-government relationship. Second, there was the contagion – or "herd"-effect of the crisis, as irrational panic spread among investors, who moved quickly from over-optimism to over-pessimism. And third, there was the inadequacy of the response of the global financial institutions, notably the IMF, leading to "overly tight macroeconomic policies and badly designed and badly handled restructuring programmes".[47] The extent of the damage, of the reforms required and

---

47 Jeffrey Sachs and Wing Thye Woo, "Understanding the Asian Financial Crisis", in Woo *et al., op cit,* p.14.

of the prospects for recovery in each of the affected countries depended on the structural and political conditions, and leadership and policy responses.

It is also important to note the relationship between political consolidation and economic growth in East Asia. In the case of Malaysia, Taiwan, and even Indonesia, political consolidation, support and even survival was dependent on continued economic expansion. At its worst extreme, this led to corruption and unregulated, preferential economic favours and access. Opposition movements, unsurprisingly, gained from the Asian crisis (notably in Thailand, Indonesia and Korea), both because of economic contraction and because a link was established in the public mind between the crisis, government policy and a lack of democratic oversight.

As has been noted above, the most crucial point is that while this crisis had implications for all of Asia, one cannot generalise and say that this was an Asia-wide problem, or, at least, that it affected all countries equally. The region is vast, both in terms of its geographic spread and of the conditions, systems and styles of governance, and economies in the countries it covers. Put simply, it is not possible to lump Japan, Korea and Australia (members of the Organisation for Economic Co-operation and Development – OECD) together with Malaysia, Singapore and Taiwan on the one hand and Thailand and Indonesia on the other. What does appear unique about the 1997 crisis, however, is that its spill-over affected the entire region (perhaps not surprisingly, given its economic interdependence) and that, unlike the Mexican peso crisis of 1994, it continued well after the intervention made by the Bretton Woods institutions. This might reflect a combination of the wrong policy medicine, a failure to identify accurately the causes of the crisis, and also problems of perception of the region.

Sachs has distinguished three variants of emerging market problems:[48]
- First, there are *fiscal crises*, such as the state sector bankruptcies which lay behind the debt problems of the 1980s in Latin America;
- Second, there are so-called *exchange rate crises*, such as the collapse of overvalued exchange rates in Mexico in 1994; and
- Third, there are *banking crises*, such as the collapse of poorly supervised institutions in Bulgaria in 1996 and Thailand in 1997.

48 See "A Guide to 1998's crises", *The World in 1998*. London: Economist Publications, p.69.

These variants, Sachs notes, can crop up in a number of combinations. In Asia, the financial fundamentals behind the plummeting currencies are relatively easy to identify. The combination of currency depreciation and fall in asset prices placed a great strain on countries which have "poorly supervised, poorly functioning, badly regulated, corrupt and government-directed financial markets". These features in turn lay partly behind the volatility caused by the removal of the fixed exchange rate regimes. In Southeast Asia, non-performing loans were successfully hidden, as governments allowed – often for political rather than sound economic reasons – the flow of borrowed money into unproductive assets. Before the crisis, there was a disproportionately high percentage of loans in Asia going into condominiums, high-rise buildings, flashy cars or golf courses instead of manufacturing plants and machinery. Without a productive value to these assets, banking systems then became hostage to fluctuations in the price of commercial buildings and, ultimately, wavering market confidence, exacerbated by dollar-denominated loans and rapidly declining local currency values.

At the time of the crisis, the World Bank estimated that non-performing loans across the region, including Japan, could total US$660 billion. This debt overhang may yet take many years to work through. In Southeast Asia alone, it has been estimated that it will cost 13.3% of the region's combined GDP to fix the problem of non-performing loans, which totalled, in 1997, an estimated US$73 billion.[49] The result is that after a decade-long borrowing binge, Southeast Asia shifted to experience something of a capital famine. Investors became markedly more risk-averse, except in the strongest economies. From a peak of US$80 billion in private capital inflows in 1996, East Asia has suffered a sustained haemorrhage of capital since that time, with outflows averaging around US$20 billion annually between 1997 and 2001.[50]

Banking and financial deregulation are some the reasons for these problems. Although banking deregulation opened up many banking institutions to outside competition, it also exposed economies to excessive risk-taking and bank insolvency. The dollarisation of these economies – where money was borrowed abroad in dollars and re-lent

---

49 See "Capital Punishment", *The Australian*, 17 December 1997.
50 Dr Ken Henry, "Restoring Growth to the East Asia Region", *The Third Monash APEC Lecture*, Melbourne, 19 March 2002.

to domestic investors – rendered these countries vulnerable to an in-creased credit risk in the event of a currency depreciation, since many of these borrowers (such as those who borrowed for property develop-ment) had difficulties in honouring loans.

An enormous volume of funds had rolled into these economies from the US at the pegged interest rates in the early 1990s, resulting in a dramatic increase in (domestic) money supply. Local currencies were unable to appreciate as market forces intervened. Much of this mon-ey went into unproductive loans, though at the time issues of crony-ism and corruption, poor governance and lack of accountability were simply glossed over by foreign investors, given Asia's position as the "darling of the world".[51]

This politics of corruption or bad governance or cronyism, which in many instances lay at the heart of the economic success of Asia (because it provided stability to the government/business nexus at the heart of the social compact) ultimately proved both overly expen-sive and counterproductive.[52] It is important, however, to distinguish two different, if overlapping, aspects of corruption. One took the form of a nepotism that was closely aligned with nation-building strate-gies, as in Malaysia and Indonesia, where preferential contracts were given to ensure racial harmony and political stability. Another was a more blatant corruption of the sort that characterised the relationship between the Chinese minority and the Indonesian ruling elite during the time of Soeharto. This was less an issue of political stability than an issue of enrichment.

Although Indonesia is probably the best (or worst) example of both types of corruption, it is not alone. And this phenomenon is not con-fined to those relatively underdeveloped environments. For example, in both South Korea and Japan, which are two of Asia's most devel-oped economies, the linkages between government and business are clear (and have been costly). The South Korean economy was, pre-1997, dominated by five conglomerates (*chaebols*) – Hyundai, Samsung, LG, Daewoo and Sunkyong – which together accounted for around half of the country's GDP. This was unhealthy in a number of respects,

---

51 Backman, *op cit*, p.294.
52 *Ibid*. Also, for a good explanation of the impact of the Asian crisis on develop-ing countries (especially the Middle East) and summary of its causes, see Alan Richards, "The Global Financial Crisis and Economic Reform in the Middle East", *Middle East Policy Journal*, VI, 3, February 1999 on *http://www.mepc.org/journal/9902_richards.html*.

particularly in terms of a lack of competition. In South Korea, the combined net profit in pre-crisis 1996 of the top 49 *chaebol* amounted to only US$65 million.[53] Also, growth and diversification (or "conglomeration") rather than profit appeared to be the major motivation of these companies, with a consequent lack of focus on core business areas and competencies. In this, too, there appeared to be a confusion between the sheer size and the apparent health and creditworthiness of these companies, a condition exacerbated by implicit government involvement in the direction taken by the *chaebols*.

South Korea has responded, post-1997, by reforming its banking institutions and practices, reducing employment in this sector by 40%, closing banks, and shutting down 14 of the top 30 *chaebols*. Japan, by comparison, has done relatively little. Although its liabilities are – unlike those of most of Asia – denominated in yen rather than dollars or Euros, and it has avoided a foreign exchange crisis, Japan's economic problems are arguably no less severe. Indeed they may be more difficult to resolve, given the "structural corruption" within the political environment, where the distinction between party and bureaucracy could hardly be said to exist, which is neither healthy, nor desirable or efficient. For example, bureaucrats control around 50% of the government's revenues, and are free from parliamentary scrutiny.[54]

The relationship between big business, politics and the bureaucracy in Japan is epitomised by the practice of big business of hiring ex-bureaucrats – known as *amakudari*, meaning "descent from heaven". This almost incestuous relationship is exacerbated by the weakness of the country's regulatory agencies, such as the Fair Trade Commission (FTC) and the Securities and Exchange Surveillance Commission. The business-government relationship has been characterised by high-level, large-sum bribery and corruption scandals, far exceeding the scale of the petty corruption rife in parts of Southeast Asia, and is often linked to public works programmes, especially in the construction sector. And where South Korea has its *chaebols*, Japan has the *keiretsu* (bank-controlled companies), and, before that time, its *zaibatsu* (family-controlled interests).

The importance of democratisation is another lesson we can learn from collapsed Asian economies. For developing nations elsewhere, there is also an illustration of the need for greater investment in so-

---

53 Backman, *op cit*, p.77.
54 Overholt, *op cit*, p.142.

called "software infrastructure", such as laws and regulations, and support for systems and institutions which commit governments to, and encourage, transparency and corporate good governance.

It is clear, however, that there are different, if narrowing, perceptions within the East Asian region about the nature and outcomes of democracy. Where South Korea's President Kim Dae Jung[55] equated the end of the Cold War with the "triumph of democracy over dictatorship", Mahathir said:[56] "The Cold War was won not by Western diplomats or generals. It was won by the workers of the West with their Chevys and Plymouths parked outside Western factories. It was won by well-stocked supermarkets and shopping malls." Such differences of interpretation have sometimes found expression in the debate concerning the role of Asian values and in the priorities identified by leaders. The debate has, however, been used to hide shortcomings of governance and a reluctance on the part of leadership to subscribe to the increasingly globalised values of transparency, accountability and openness.

In this regard, the role of a sound work ethic has been taken as an argument for the perpetuation of so-called "Asian values" and of authoritarian governments as a necessary precondition for economic growth. Asian values have too often been used as a pretext for collusion and corruption, where "know-who" has been more important than "know-how". As the Asian crash demonstrated, an environment where ideas and people can circulate freely is necessary for the establishment of transparency, accountability and good governance.

From a global perspective, the notion of different values may be viewed as an increasingly hollow mantra. Values are increasingly perceived as universal, despite the differences in ethnic origin of the world's people. Asia has witnessed the emergence of raucous, healthy democracies such as those in Taiwan and South Korea.[57] This has not been to their cost, but instead has contributed much to Asia's long-term economic benefit. Indeed, both of these countries displayed relative economic strength in the Asian crisis. As Freedom House has noted, "Democracy, prosperity and economic freedom are all part of the same bundle." The message is the same everywhere when giv-

---

55 Cited in Riés, *op cit*, p.207.

56 "The Asian Values Debate", *op cit*, p.1.

57 On Asian "values", see ET Gomez and KS Jomo, "Authoritarianism, Elections and Political Change in Malaysia", *Public Policy*, II, 3, July/September 1998, pp.113-144; also, Mahathir, (1997), *op cit*.

en by undemocratic leaders who presume to speak for their electorates. As Patten argues persuasively:[58]

> Without contesting for the moment the erroneous suggestion that people are more likely to enjoy economic rights if they are denied political ones, it is surely sufficient to suggest that perhaps they should be asked to make this choice for themselves rather than have their decision presumed by those who customarily speak out for the political illiteracy of the poor at a considerable social distance from them.

This might be dismissed as coming from a former (and the last) British governor of Hong Kong, which has never been a democracy. Less facetiously, however, especially in an age of globalisation, it is important to remember the need to avoid triumphalism in favour of a set of Western values, and consequently to see Asian values as representing forms of government and social condition inferior to those offered by democracy. While some Asian societies have, for example, maintained segregation of the sexes and the allocation of "traditional" roles to women, this should not be used to obscure the contributions made by Asians and their so-called "culture", on the one hand, and the many negative social pathologies of the West towards the East on the other. Asian values are not just about authoritarianism or corruption, and are much more than just political values. It is important to realise, too, that no one set of values applies in all of Asia.[59]

Although Asian values – once viewed as the reason for economic growth – are now seen by some as contributory causes of the recent economic failure, as Han Sung-Joo points out,[60] there are at least two reasons why they are still relevant. First, regardless of their functionality, Asian countries will "continue to be guided by such values". Secondly, though Asian values are viewed as antithetical to globalisation's precepts, a country such as Singapore (which weathered the Asian crisis better than the rest of the region, and has apparently adjusted well to the demands of the global environment), remains an ardent advocate of these values.

---

58 *Op cit.*
59 See Sheridan, *op cit*, esp. pp.293-317.
60 Han Sung-Joo, "Asian Values: An Asset or a Liability?", in Han Sung-Joo (ed.), *op cit*, p.4.

Moving Ahead

By the start of the 21st century, most of the Asian economies affected by the economic crisis were showing unexpectedly rapid signs of recovery partly as a result of rapid growth in the US economy and the comprehensive reforms undertaken throughout much of Asia. The pace of recovery also reflected the soundness of many of the economic fundamentals in spite of the crisis. Questions remained, however, as to whether the reforms undertaken had completely eliminated risk factors, and whether the economic reforms were politically or institutionally sustainable in the relative absence of technical capacity, given high degrees of governmental political vulnerability. Moreover, as the above analysis suggests, Asian countries have taken (and are taking) vastly different routes towards economic recovery and reform at the start of the 21st century. For example, in some countries such as Indonesia and the Philippines, contemporary policy is more a matter of party-political (and governmental) survival than growth. But where there is political stability, as in much of East Asia, plans are being made to move into a third generation of economic growth, leaving behind manufacturing and the IT sectors as the principal suppliers of performance.

There is thus no single Asian "model". But despite the differences between nations within regions, there is arguably one characteristic common to Asia's economies at present: the need to match openness and global competition with a clear social agenda. This is particularly true of the more vulnerable economies, and relates to the need for political certainty and stability, which is in turn dependent on strong leadership, good governance and a more equitable distribution of income. In the past, rapid economic growth offered stability and social mobility, underpinned by a Confucian ethic stressing the importance of social order and hard work. Today, the need to retain stability amidst increasing economic and political liberalisation – of a move from, at worst, coercion and corruption to, at best, democratisation and transparency – will demand of governments the development of a new social contract with a higher priority given to welfare provisions, and a relationship with business defined less by political connections than by the demands of corporate governance and open competition. The need for such a new Asian model is also made more urgent by the effects of an ageing population and continuing urbanisation, along with rising disparities in income and wealth. All this is linked to improving democratic conditions. As Stephen Haggard notes:[61]

---

61 Stephen Haggard, *The Political Economy of the Asian Financial Crisis.* Washington DC: The Institute for International Economics, 2000, pp.213-4.

The crisis made clear that the next generation of poor people could not necessarily count on unremitting growth to lift them out of poverty. . . . the problems of devising social policy are not limited to the administrative; social policy also engages broader political interests. . . . although it is not a foregone conclusion, the prospects for social protection of the poor seem more, rather than less secure under democratic rule which seeks to incorporate urban middle- and working-class interests.

Can the lessons from Asia's successes and failures be universally applied to other developing countries in general, and to Africa in particular?

Asia's Lessons – How Applicable?

It should be stressed once more that Asia is not a homogeneous region. It has varying and different situations, problems and policy solutions. No one size fits all. It is thus difficult to identify universal, region-wide remedies to Asia's problems or reasons for its success.

Five fundamental lessons stand out, however.

As is intimated above, the *first* is that there is no easy route to development – there is no silver bullet to solve regional or national problems. Hard work and good policies are the core ingredients.

In this respect, as noted in Chapter One, "good governance" has acquired a meaning beyond simply avoidance of corruption, to include a range of wider policy concerns of interest to the investor, which also provide an index of a country's economic potential. Direct investment is critical for success, and is linked, in turn, to rapid privatisation, the establishment of liberal regimes in respect of skills inflow and exchange controls, and a domestic emphasis on education and training.[62]

In the light of the Asian crisis, a table of economic potential can be drawn up which identifies both positive and negative economic influences. These apply especially, though not exclusively, to states such as Indonesia and Thailand which fared worst during the crisis. This table may offer a guide to economic growth and sustainability for developing countries elsewhere.

---

62 See, for example, Leslie Boyd, "My Word", *Sunday Times Business Times*, 10 June 2001, p.11.

An Asian Guide to Economic Potential and Stability

Positives	Negatives
Political and social stability	Ethnic business links and practices
Small and medium-size enterprise development	Pegged currencies
Sound macroeconomic fundamentals, low inflation	Absence of the rule of law and legal provisions
Potential for economic growth	Weak banking and stock-market regulations and institutions
Available and cheap business infrastructure	Corruption and lack of transparency
Positive continental/regional perceptions and rates of growth	Absence of political freedoms
Competitive tax structure and rates	Lack of media freedom, independence and investigative capacity
Low rates of crime, and comparative absence of socially destabilising factors such as HIV/Aids	
	Dubious business ethics and auditing practices
Ability to repatriate profits	Corrupt and ineffective policing and public service institutions
Labour costs and investor-friendly regulations	Weak bankruptcy practices and laws
Availability of skilled workers	

Effective and responsive governments and efficient markets are critical if globalisation is to work positively for developing countries. Democracy is necessary, not only for the protection of basic human values, but also to make governments more accountable. And given the mobility of private capital, the ability to attract investment crucial for economic growth is linked to levels of corruption, because it creates problems of uncertainty, delays and cost. The regulatory environment has to maintain a careful balance between excessive controls, which could prove a barrier to investment, and regulations sufficiently strict to protect investors, the consumer, labour and the environment alike.[63] In this

---

63 See UK Department of International Development, *Eliminating World Poverty: Making Globalisation Work for the Poor.* Presented to parliament by the Secretary of State for International Development, December 2000, pp.23-25.

way, globalisation also has clear implications for corporate governance. As Morris Chang, the founder of Taiwan Semiconductor
Manufacturing Co. Ltd, argued in June 1998:[64]

> So-called Asia-style corporate management has to change fun-
> damentally. . . . The world cannot wait for us to change very slow-
> ly. There are very good Asian values, such as closeness of families
> and emphasis on education. . . . Companies used to grow on the
> ground of their connections with the government. That model
> has crashed.

If Asia is to retain its technical advantage and employ this to best effect, it will have to continue to make a substantial investment in social
"software" (the judiciary, education, administrative excellence, scientific research centres) as opposed to the physical "hardware" (infrastructure, factories, machinery). The critical input here has to come from
the political institutions and, more specifically, from leadership. The
longer-term competitiveness of Asia rests, as Sachs and Woo note, "as
much on getting the institutions right" as on "getting the prices right".[65]
   A *second* lesson is the need to implement policies appropriate for
national success. In Malaysia, for example, there is a requirement for
social equity and redistribution alongside economic growth. In Taiwan, the external environment has been, and is, critical: the threat of
the PRC made national development a priority, but access to global
assistance (from the US, in particular) and global markets has facilitated its development. In the case of both Taiwan and Malaysia, infrastructure development has been used as a spur for development.
In all cases, political stability and government leadership is key. This
has been critical, in particular, in creating a sense of a *national* project
for economic success, where the state has played a leading developmental role. This involves more than just setting the parameters for
growth: it has been deterministic, interventionist and leading. It has
had a positive impact on domestic investor confidence and thus foreign investment flows.
   Third, the relationship between government and business has to be

64 Cited in Riés, *op cit*, pp.258-9.
65 "Understanding the Asian Financial Crisis", *op cit*, p.42.

carefully and productively managed, with a clear need for transparency and oversight. The nature of politics and political systems is also important in both the pattern of economic development and its sustainability, and, as Asia showed post-1997, in managing crisis and implementing reforms. Good governance and corporate governance is easier in democracies, too. Even though there was resistance to reforms in East Asian democracies, with governments sensitive about such changes, broad public and legislative support was easier to achieve. Democracy, far from slowing the pace of economic reform, proved more responsive than authoritarianism, and this advantage carried over to the depth of the reforms.[66]

Fourth, economic growth is ultimately a result of the effort of people, not governments. The success of Asia's economies raises questions about why African economies have performed so badly. In *Out of America*, Keith Richburg asks the same question, and challenges the simplistic excuses often offered by Africa's leaders. Granted, Africa had colonialism – but so did Malaysia and Singapore. It was destabilised by the Cold War – but not half as much as Korea and Vietnam. Asian states had as many (or as few) blessed or cursed natural resources. The nearest Richburg gets to an answer is quoted from Uganda's President Yoweri Museveni, who puts Asia's success and Africa's comparative failure down to "Discipline . . . The discipline of the Asians compared to the Africans".[67] Or as Dato Mohamed Jawhar Hassan of Malaysia's Institute for Strategic and International Studies (ISIS) has put it, "a good work ethic is sometimes taken for granted, but it is critical".[68]

Richburg's analysis distils to a single intangible essence a widespread African failure to build a stable environment. There may be something to be said about the Chinese entrepreneurial spirit and its ability to weather the "Asian contagion" after 1997. The four so-called "Chinese states" – the PRC, Taiwan, Hong Kong and Singapore – all fared better than any of the other Asian countries in terms of retaining their currency and stock-market value. However, the importance of growth with stability and good inter-ethnic ties is positively demonstrated by the Malaysian experience, and negatively by the

---

66 For a comparative discussion of this, see Stephen Haggard, *op cit.*
67 Keith Richburg, *Out of America: A Black Man Confronts Africa.* New York: Basic Books, 1997.
68 Interview, Institute for Strategic and International Studies (ISIS), Kuala Lumpur, 27 April 2001.

violent reaction of Indonesians towards the Indonesian-Chinese community during the 1998 upheavals.

Fifth, and finally, it is clear that the Asian crash and the international community's apparently slow reaction – or at least the limited impact of its policy medicine – raises questions about the role of the contemporary global financial architecture, both in terms of the overall (trade and aid) environment for growth in developing countries; and in terms of the legitimacy, speed and efficacy of external policy prescriptions. And there is another irony to this: these institutions were criticised both by their "patients" in Asia for the medicine handed out; and by an inward-looking US Congress for "distorting the markets".

Conclusions

If Asia's strategies for development do not provide a complete answer to the problems of developing states elsewhere, they may assist us to ask some of the right questions about what it took to effect the Asian economic and political renaissance – and in doing so provide an answer as to what aspects of governance can make states vulnerable to rapid reversals.

East Asia has, for all of its recent woes, been through a period of exceptional economic prosperity, averaging 5.4% real GDP growth between 1965 and 1997, compared to sub-Saharan Africa's corresponding decline of 0.2%. In spite of its failures and problems, East Asia's successes are enviable. As Leipziger and Thomas note:[69]

> No other group of developing countries has done as well in fostering growth, reducing poverty, integrating with world markets, or raising standards of living. Over the past 25 years, per capita incomes have almost quadrupled. Absolute poverty has fallen by two thirds on average, population growth rates have declined rapidly, and health and education levels have improved markedly.

The reasons for its comparative success include a focus on people-centred development, policies that have facilitated improvements in education and health standards and the rise of small- and medium-sized enterprises, and the use of infrastructure spending as a catalyst

---

69 Danny M Leipziger and Vinod Thomas, "An Overview of East Asian Experience", Leipziger, *op cit*, p.1.

for growth. Planning was important, but it was, to paraphrase the economist Paul Krugman, "one part inspiration and several parts perspiration" in the mobilisation of capital and human resources. While government interventions were important, they were not critical. This is the case even in those countries that have emerged worst from the crisis, such as Indonesia. As Adam Schwarz has observed:[70]

It is still not clear how history will remember Soeharto's rule. . . . In the mid-1960s, Indonesian society was convulsed with hatred and violence and its economy was nearly dysfunctional. In the three decades that followed, Soeharto's government oversaw rates of economic growth that were the envy of much of the developing world. He took an impoverished, agrarian nation unable to feed itself and brought it into the ranks of middle-income countries with a per capita income of over US$1,000. Soeharto's New Order government dramatically reduced the incidence of poverty while steadily raising education, literacy and health standards. But the negative side of the ledger is also full. Corruption, mismanagement and brutality were as much a part of Soeharto's government as economic development.

The 1997 and subsequent Asian crises illustrate, quite simply, the need for decisive action on issues of governance. Without it, economic prospects and political stability will inevitably suffer. As Camdessus has argued in this regard:[71]

Good governance is essential for all countries at all stages of development – from the poorest countries that are still in the process of building up domestic institutions and undertaking the basic reforms needed to accelerate economic growth to the advanced countries, both as regards their own internal governance and their dealings with developing countries.

Included within the broad framework of governance is the need to consider the careful sequencing of reforms, particularly where the institutions necessary for fiscal control and regulation should precede financial deregulation. Moreover, policies should reflect the impor-

70 *Op cit*, p.x.
71 *Ibid*, January 1998.

tance of matching reforms; so that, for example, the government does not try to defend its currency value with its capital account liberalised.

★ ★ ★

It is sometimes argued that, in the age of globalisation, the market is more powerful than leadership. The latitude of the latter is, according to this argument, seriously limited, and easily buffeted by market forces and even by individuals (in the form of speculators) in spite of sound domestic economic fundamentals. Yet Asia's 1997 crisis and subsequent developments have, in at least two ways, highlighted the role of leadership and its importance in maintaining stability and growth.

First, events have illustrated the importance of building the institutional foundations of development on democracy and consultation. Asia's economic successes led to a debate over the "benefits" of authoritarian government to developing economies, which questioned whether economic development was possible within a democracy, in the presence of high degrees of poverty and social inequality. But as Philippe Riés has observed, the Asian crisis showed how "democratic societies . . . had a greater capacity to withstand the shock than countries ruled by authoritarian regimes".[72] Although democracies (South Korea and Thailand) were hit hard, authoritarianism encouraged cronyism, exacerbated inefficiencies and distorted the market.

Democracy is in itself a necessary, but not necessarily a sufficient, condition for *sustained* economic progress and development. For example, the staging, in 1999, of Indonesia's first election in four decades has not brought stability. Nor, indeed, has this yet altered the web of cronyist military-business-familial linkages, which have for so long determined and dominated Indonesia's political economy. This emphasises, in turn, the importance of institutionalising more than just procedural forms of the democracy advanced by international donors, to provide the substance of public welfare, consultation and accountability.

Second, Asia's crisis has also illustrated how important it is not to take the competency of politicians (or their ethics, or those of their business compatriots) for granted. Conversely, it has demonstrated the importance of sound leadership, to identify core problems and devise solutions, and engage with external institutions in the search for stability.

---

72 "Asian Storm", *op cit.*

The key lesson to be learnt from Asia's economic growth and its emergence from the 1997 financial crisis is of the need to develop systems, institutions and practices of accountability and governance within a democratic framework if sustainable economic growth is to be achieved. The promotion of such appropriate standards, values and practices has to be the result of a collaborative effort between external agencies (through the application of both conditionalities and assistance programmes), local and international NGOs, and, critically, between business and government. Without such action, developing nations in Africa, Latin America and elsewhere will probably be doomed to repeat Asia's mistakes without enjoying its successes.

CHAPTER FOUR

LATIN AMERICA
Governance, Reform and Transition

> When God made Argentina, he gave it everything. Mountains, rivers, the best land and a fantastic climate. When other nations complained, God gave it the Argentinians to even things out.
>
> ARGENTINE MILITARY OFFICER, *November* 2001[1]
>
> Argentina, so rich at the start of the 20th century, has been ruined by Freud and Peron. It has a complex of being isolated and of self-identity. It suffers defects of national characters and a very corrupt political class.
>
> SPANISH BUSINESSMAN, *March* 2002[2]

Introduction

At the Museo Nacional de Bellas Artes in Buenos Aires hangs an oil painting by Ernesto de la Carcova. Entitled *Sin pan y sin trabajo* ("Neither Bread Nor Work") and painted in 1894, it portrays a man, woman and baby in grim domestic circumstances, the husband peering out of the window as if in search of employment. For many of the 12 million in the capital of Argentina, things look similarly bleak more than a century later.

One hundred years ago, the phrase "as rich as an Argentine" was common among Europeans. In December 2001, after four straight years of economic decline, and the successive appointment of five presidents in a fortnight, Argentina's capital, Buenos Aires, was engulfed in riots. The "golden age" of the early 20th century was scarcely recalled, as signs of disgruntlement and poverty became increasingly widespread, and not only confined within Argentina's borders. The regional trade grouping, Mercosur (Southern Cone Market), previously held up as a shining example of what can be achieved through co-operation, was plunged into difficulty as its two principal members, Argentina and Brazil, confronted economic difficulties in apparently incompatible ways.

---

1 This joke was told by a senior Argentine army officer when quizzed about why his country, once so wealthy, faced ongoing systemic economic crises.

2 Interview, Madrid, February 2002.

Analysts pondered how Argentina could have transformed so rapidly into a basket case, and what the role of the international community should be in trying to assist it out of its crisis.

Reforms, Parallels and Process: Latin America and Africa

Latin America and Africa share many similarities. But there are key differences, both between states within these regions and between the regions themselves, in terms of their economic reform policies and practices. Both face an agenda characterised by new issues and new players.[3] This has been, and is, changing the regional political and economic landscape as well as the nature of interaction necessary in the global context.

The 1980s and 1990s in both regions were characterised by the transition from military or undemocratic regimes to democracy; and by the shift from the travails of import substitution, burgeoning debt, economic uncertainty and crisis to market economics. These changes were to a great extent linked to international and regional political developments. The end of the Cold War, the emergence of a new consensus on economic orthodoxy, and the spread of democratic systems and values were influenced and reinforced by the pace and depth of globalisation.

The 1990s became, in Latin America, the era of so-called "neoliberal" reforms, characterised by privatisation, currency exchangeability, fiscal austerity and strict monetarist measures. These brought inflation under control, encouraged foreign direct investment, and increased regional co-operation and integration. In Latin America, regional integration took the form of the Mercosur trade agreement between Argentina, Bolivia, Brazil, Chile, Paraguay and Uruguay,[4] the North American Free Trade Agreement (NAFTA), the Andean Pact, and discussions preliminary to setting up a continent-wide Free Trade Area of the Americas (FTAA). In Africa, a similar drive has occurred through initiatives such as the Economic Community of West African States (ECOWAS), SADC, the East African Community (EAC) and the Common Market for Eastern and Southern Africa (COMESA).

3　For a good summary of the wider regional developments, see Julia Buxton and Nicola Phillips (eds.), *Developments in Latin American Political Economy*. Manchester: Manchester University Press, 1999.

4　Bolivia and Chile are associate members.

Much of this integration has been underpinned by strategic business-government co-operation and the end of state control, which has widened the role of the private sector in economic affairs.

At the start of the 21st century, both continents for the most part face the challenge of *consolidation* of economic and political reforms rather than fundamental *transition*. The introduction of the template of liberal market reforms – known in Latin America as the "Washington consensus" and in Africa as "structural adjustment" – has had its successes. But these policies are viewed by many as also having their costs, with notable failures, such as the emergence of serious social problems (including poverty and crime) and "jobless growth". While around 40% of sub-Saharan Africa's 600 million people live on less than US$1 per day, around 200 million of Latin America's 500 million inhabitants are similarly indigent.

While many countries have been able to set in motion the first two of the three stages of such reform (inflation and macroeconomic stabilisation and liberalisation leading to the emergence of a functioning market economy), they have been less successful in terms of the third stage, that of export-led growth. This may be because no one country in Latin America (even Chile, which arguably comes closest) or in Africa has implemented the full neo-liberal market orthodoxy, though this may be because the overall political environment has made it impossible.

In some Latin American countries, the democratisation process has been less than perfect, with the emergence of so-called *democraduras* ("democratorships"), dependent on presidential powers and exhibiting high levels of corruption. Unhappiness with this state of affairs has led to more frequent and more visible manifestations of popular discontent and civil society mobilisation. This would appear to be an increasing, not decreasing, aspect of political life in many Latin American and, indeed, African countries, such as in Argentina and Zimbabwe. It has also led to concerns over what should be on the agenda in planning "second generation" structural reforms, in areas such as labour policy. Domestically and transnationally, what should be the role of civil society in consolidating democracy – both within and between states? There are also critical questions to be asked about the nature of the relationship between democracy and economic reforms, and democracy and governance. Are unpopular reforms possible in democracies? Or are they impossible without democracy? Which is the better example: Chile, Mexico or Argentina?

This has led in both regions to a debate concerning the role of the state and its institutions, and their relationships with other sectors, including those regionally and further afield. The state remains at the eye of the developmental storm, arguably more after the events of September 11 than before. These caused a change in perception from notions of human security once more to state-centric security. The shift in the debate has also moved from one about "trickle-down" and "spill-over" theories of economic growth towards issues of public spending and social cost. How can the neo-liberal/SAP free-market reforms of the 1990s be "adjusted" to deliver social rather than just economic benefits? What are the limitations on the expansion of small- and medium-sized enterprises in developing economies, seen by many as the pistons in the engine of growth providing employment? What can be done to expand the activities of bigger business, the flywheel of prosperity? Also, how can these policies accommodate an increased focus on issues of human rights, accountability and transparency, judicial reform and the eradication of corruption?

In both Africa and Latin America there remains also the challenge of modernising societies and institutions such as the military, in which there has been a fundamental reappraisal of the "winner-takes-all" notion of the balance between military autonomy and civilian control. The move from the putative concept of a developmental role for the military has been raised in an environment of declining budgetary allocations, the exposing of vested institutional and personal interests, and indistinct security threats. In order to modernise, African and Latin American countries will have to look for guidance from both the micro- and macro-managerial theory and practice in this regard.

In many of these areas of transition and debate, Latin America has been ahead of Africa, and has provided a test case from which Africa can learn many lessons. This chapter examines the issues set out above, with a particular focus on (and comparison of) Argentina, Chile and Mexico.

★ ★ ★

Argentina's Apoplexy

My arrival at Ministro Pistarini Airport in Buenos Aires in November 2001 provided some idea of the challenges facing Argentina's economic reform and recovery. By international standards, the arrival hall is basic 1950s, and long overdue for refurbishment. But the airport was, more tellingly, the focus, during 2001, of a vitriolic battle between the unions and government over the difficulties experienced by *Aerolineas Argentinas*, the state carrier. The airline was privatised debt-free in 1990, but by 2001, was struggling under a debt of US$900 million. *Aerolineas* had been forced to cut back on its flights, retaining international routes only to Latin America, America, Australia and Spain. Most of its fleet of seven 747s were left parked on the runway, mothballed until the return of better days.

The national airline was one of the state-owned enterprises sold off during the economic reforms of the 1990s carried out under the leadership of President Carlos Menem. The reforms were designed to help Argentina adapt to the realities of the global economy, and return the country to its former glory. At the start of the 20th century, Argentina had the tenth largest economy in the world, with the sixth highest per capita income. Between 1900 and 1920, GDP doubled, inflation stood at just 1.5%, and the stable currency was pegged to the gold standard. But as the Great Depression bit in the 1930s, the demand for Argentine exports fell. The nation entered an era or protectionism and the nationalisation of some public services, including railroads and power generation and distribution. These were areas which had seen the first major foreign investment in the late 19th and early 20th century. During the 1950s and 1960s, the economy was once more opened up to foreign investors, particularly in the automotive, petroleum refining, chemical, and machinery industries. Put differently, whereas its GDP was twice that of Brazil's in 1910, by 2001 its northern neighbour had a GDP 2.5 times that of Argentina.

Menem, first elected in 1989, implemented a harsh structural adjustment programme. By moving away from the traditional Peronist dogma of state-centric welfare and price and wage control, he reversed six decades of economic decline, bringing down inflation from a record 200% per month in 1989 to 0.2% in 1996. His economic model centred on three principles: first, international reserves should match Argentina's monetary base, with the peso pegged to the US dollar. Second, all price-adjusted clauses in commercial, rental and employment contracts should be prohibited, which would reduce inflationary tendencies significantly. Third, the government should develop a set of liberal investment policies, reducing trade barriers, opening local financial and capital markets to foreign participation, abolishing exchange controls and implementing a radical privatisation programme. Whereas US$50 billion had flowed out of the economy in the 1980s, US$90 billion in portfolio and foreign investment flowed in between 1994 and 2000. Argentina's economy grew at an annual average of 7.6% between 1991 and 1994, peaking at 8.2% in 1997. This made a difference to the lives of Argentinians all over the country: for example, prior to the privatisation process, it took three to four years for a citizen to acquire a telephone connection, a procedure which cost between US$3,000 and US$6,000. At the end of 2001, this period had been reduced to just a week, owing to the impact of digital communications, but also to better services.

Four problems abbreviated Argentina's recovery, plunging the country into crisis at the start of the 21st century.[5] First, the government was unable to bring rampant public spending and corruption under control. This situation was exacerbated by the relationship between the federal government and the 23 provinces, some of which refused to toe the budgetary line. The consolidated fiscal deficit of around 3.5% (including that of the provinces) had to be financed by inward capital flows.

Second, the inability of the provinces to work with the federal government reflected far-reaching problems in the political domain, notably the weakness of the ruling Radical Party-led alliance and the restructuring of the Peronist opposition. The role of the latter was shaped by the jockeying for presidential candidature in the 2003 elections, while the power of the former was weakened by the fracturing of the ruling alliance. A confrontational relationship between the Radicals and business contributed to the conditions leading to the economic crisis. The response of the electorate to deepening economic travails was expectedly either to vote for the opposition or not vote at all, as a result of which the ruling party lost the October 2001 congressional elections, further eroding its already weak position.

Third, external shocks saw a significant drop in Argentina's terms of trade. In 1994, Argentina, Brazil, Paraguay and Uruguay had joined up to become members of Mercosur. Intra-Mercosur trade increased fourfold in the first five years, exceeding US$20 billion in 1997. Argentina's export trade doubled to US$26,2 billion from 1993 to 1997 in total, including that with Mercosur, which increased threefold to US$9,5 billion, with Brazil taking 31% of Argentina's total exports.

5 See also Manuel Pastor and Carol Wise, "From Poster Child to Basket Case", *Foreign Affairs*, 80, 6, November/December 2001, pp.60-72.

But the Brazilian currency crisis of 1998 saw the delinking of the Brazilian real from the US dollar, which instantly made many Argentine exports uncompetitive. Exports to Brazil fell from US$7,95 billion in 1997 to US$5,690 billion the following year. Although this picked up again in 2000 (to US$7 billion), the figures were expected to drop by around 15% in 2001.[6] These problems were compounded by the rise in the value of the US dollar at the same time, and by the relative failure of Argentina's manufacturing export sector to develop during this period.

Fourth, as noted above, Argentina's demand for capital saw it borrowing heavily in international markets. By 2001, public debt totalled over US$140 billion, 70% of which was denominated in dollars. Capital was too easy to access, and borrowing masked problems like manufacturing inefficiencies, market limitations, and the abandonment of fiscal rectitude. At the same time as inflation fell under Menem, Argentinians took on personal debt, much of which was denominated in dollars. Peso debt carried a higher inflation rate – signs of the trouble to come and a lingering lack of confidence. Capital outflow was exacerbated by the lack of confidence many Argentinians felt about the economy and the way in which it was being managed. Fearful of another devaluation, many preferred to invest in dollars or Euros outside. It is estimated that, by late 2001, more than US$50 billion in private Argentine wealth was lodged in the Uruguayan banking system. Exporters to Argentina were not paid, as local businesspeople hedged against the expected devaluation, further reducing confidence in what was already considered a difficult operating environment for business.

The outcome of all of this was simple: an overvalued exchange rate, an economic recession, and tightening budgetary controls against soaring foreign debt payments. In 1999, the Argentine economy shrunk by 3.4%, and in 2000 by 0.5%, with unemployment hovering at the 15% margins. GDP was expected to contract by between 4% and 6% in 2001 and again by at least a similar percentage in 2002.

---

6 These figures were supplied by the Argentine Foreign Ministry, November 2001.

Argentina's Economic Collapse

	1996	1998	2000
GDP Real Annual Change %	5.5	3.9	-0.5
Inflation CPI %	0.1	0.7	-0.7
Unemployment	17.2	12.9	14.7
Fiscal Balance % GDP	-2.2	-1.4	-2.4
Current Account Balance US$m	-6,285	-14,682	-8.973
External Debt US$m	93,841	141,923	146,172

President De la Rua, who took office in December 1999, promptly tightened fiscal policy in an attempt to win back the confidence of investors. The prices of export commodities fell to their lowest levels in more than a decade, and the economy moved, not upwards, but down into a deflationary trap.

With the economy in crisis, signs of public unrest increased throughout 2001. The social welfare and health system was bankrupt, and crime on the rise in major cities. Emigration of Argentina's young professionals to their ancestors' countries of origin (notably Italy and Spain) was on the rise, while homelessness had doubled over four years. Perhaps the social nadir was the arrest of former president Carlos Menem in June 2001 for illicit arms deals worth US$100 million. This was the first time an elected president had been arrested in democratic Argentina. Menem, who had planned to run for the presidency in 2003 after a five-year hiatus, stood accused of re-routing arms to Croatia in 1991 in contravention of a UN arms embargo, and selling arms to Ecuador in 1995 while attempting to mediate in its border war with Peru. Although he was later cleared of these charges, Argentina and its leaders were both being dragged through the mud.

In an attempt to break out of this deflationary cycle, in April 2001 Finance Minister Domingo Cavallo, was brought into government by his economics archrival De la Rua to deal with the growing problems. Cavallo immediately introduced a parliamentary bill that effectively proposed the de-linking of the peso from the dollar by introducing the Euro into the equation, creating a basket of currencies to this peg. This proposal created the suspicion that the minister was attempting to create a "back door" to devaluation, making it impossible for Argentina to service its foreign debt. The peg with the dollar had been viewed as a bulwark against the hyperinflation which had

savaged the Argentine economy in the 1970s, but it was now proving a millstone to exports and, ultimately, economic performance.[7] Although these difficulties could not totally undermine the economic
logic of the Menem years – for the need to reduce government expenditure and stabilise prices – they fuelled uncertainty and anxiety in
an already nervous domestic electorate. In June 2001, the dollar peg
was undermined, fatally as it turned out, with the finance minister's
introduction of a 7% devaluation of the peso for exporters. This served
to create even more uncertainty about the Argentine economy, and
failed to address what many saw as its fundamental problem – its inherent rigidities and macro weaknesses, including "a chronic current
account and budget deficit"[8] – rather than the fixed exchange rate
mechanism, which was often cast as the sole villain. The dollar peg
was formally abandoned in January 2002, but not before Argentina
had reneged on its foreign debt payments.

It is remarkable that a country which had a GDP/per capita touching US$8,000 per annum should have found itself in recurrent eco-
nomic crises of this sort. In looking for reasons for Argentina's economic fragility, some analysts have pointed to the impact of Argentina's
history and its social and cultural make-up as the most significant contributory factors.

One answer argues that the country "had experienced a long process
of decadence, especially in the second half of the 20th century [which
left] Argentine society with not enough strength to deal with these
problems".[9] Officials and private sector representatives from Spain,
the second largest investor in Latin America, have singled out four
related issues as contributing to the crisis:[10]

• First, there is an inability to alter an economic model of "the early
  20th century which is no longer sustainable". Argentina still has an
  income tax to GDP ratio (15%) that is too low, and high fiscal expenditure, compounded by widespread corruption.
• Second, there is little evidence of real state reform, a result of the

7 For details on the pros and cons of pegging, see Ramon Moreno, "Pegging
   and Stabilisation in Developing Countries", on *http://www.frbsf.org/publica-
   tions/economics/review/2001/article2.pdf*.
8 See "Latin American Economies on the Brink", *International Herald Tribune*, 23 June 2001 on *http://www.iht.com/articles/23763.html*.
9 Interview, Dr Rosendo Fraga, Buenos Aires, 27 November 2001.
10 These views were gathered during a series of meetings and interviews in
   Madrid and Barcelona during February-March 2002.

populist stance taken by political parties and their consequent unwillingness to "present policies that do not have the support of the
population".

- Third, there are "more profound problems", which go to the heart
of how Argentinians view themselves as a nation. A "change in political and social culture" is thus needed to address the necessary
reforms with any hope of success.
- Fourth, attempts to marry a "European welfare state" with a "US
capitalist, free-market model" have failed. Political and social cohesion, particularly among the middle class, is under threat from
globalisation when it is represented by lower tariffs, greater competition from outside and therefore lower job and individual security. One economist summed it up thus: "Argentina coped well with
hyperinflation, but has not been able to make the adjustments necessary for globalisation."

Whatever the combination of causes, in a time of weak political leadership, most Argentinians hoped, at the end of 2001, that the political
economy would "muddle through" by adopting a stability package
that would hold until the 2003 presidential elections. However, the
political crisis took a turn for the worse, with street demonstrations
and soaring unemployment, coupled with harsh banking restrictions
on personal withdrawals. The public outcry forced, first, the resig-
nation of Cavallo and, in quick succession, De la Rua and his cabinet.
This was followed by the election of two caretaker presidents: first,
Adolfo Rodriguez Saa, and a fortnight later, Eduardo Dulhade, who
had lost to De la Rua in the 1999 presidential election. Before resigning, Saa announced a debt repayment moratorium – the biggest public debt default in history; and, almost on taking office, Duhalde de-
creed the devaluation of the peso. The country faced two challenges:
The first was to address its short-term economic transitional difficulties, including moving from a pegged to a free-floating currency, dealing with foreign and domestic debt, avoiding hyperinflation, and cutting government spending.

The second, longer-term, more fundamental problem demanded
the Argentinians evolving an economy, system of government and way
of thinking that was compatible with the contemporary requirements
of globalisation. Here their relationship with the international community was critical to assist Buenos Aires out of the crisis. The country needed, in the words of one observer, "to be taught a lesson – that

you cannot simply run the country badly and expect the international community to bail you out, again".[11] Conversely, for some analysts, such as Paul Krugman, Argentina's crisis served to highlight, once more, the failure of the Bretton Woods institutions to provide guidance and the necessary package of reforms to enable it to steer itself out of the crisis. Although Argentina's mix of fiscal policy, debt levels and exchange rate regime was widely seen as unsustainable, critics argued that the IMF's attempts to maintain the dollar-peso currency peg and adopt a "one size fits all" approach to emerging market reform (in which loans were tied to tight fiscal policies) simply worsened a situation that might have been saved by tax cuts to stimulate economic growth.[12]

Argentina's difficulties serve to confirm two factors of significance for developing nations in reforming their economies. First is the political vulnerability of governments to special interest sectors when attempting far-reaching liberal reforms. Second is the fragility of the economy if these reforms are badly or incorrectly managed.

In Argentina's case, poor management was the result of a combined failure of political will and the inability of the population to adjust their expectations and living standards. As a result, Argentina was left exposed when its sources of (especially external) capital contracted – and when, for political reasons, it had simply not made the requisite fiscal adjustments. This may eventually result in the emergence of a new political order, one breaking with the Radicals and Peronists with their vulnerability to populist pressures, tendency towards corruption, and common inability to implement deep, sustained economic reforms. As one Spanish politician argued derisively in 2002: "Radicals don't know what is government; Peronists don't know decency in government."[13] Although globalisation was frequently blamed for Argentina's economic woes by Buenos Aires' famously fretting middle class, in reality the fault lay principally with the indecision, corruption and weaknesses of the politicians. As Cavallo put it in 2001:[14]

---

11 Interview, Madrid, 5 March 2002.
12 See, for example, "IMF blamed as Argentina goes from boom to bust", *Weekend Argus*, 5 January 2002.
13 Discussion, Ministry of Foreign Affairs, Madrid, 5 March 2002.
14 See "Economic plunge exacts social toll in Argentina", *Washington Post*, 9 November 2001.

Nobody should fool themselves . . . Argentina's loss of credit has to do with excessive spending . . . and the nation still has prolonged and unresolved problems. Poor administration of the social security and PAMI [health insurance for the aged] systems, oversized [government] organisations, excessive bureaucracy and high political costs – these are the problems shared by both the nation and the provinces . . . problems that we have to set straight.

And the crisis and the response of the electorate reflected, too, the changing rules of the political game and the more visible role of civil society. As one government official sagely noted:[15]

Government can today only obtain political power by identifying with social issues and demands. Society is today demanding much better systems of government, a much lower cost government, cleaner politics, a working justice system and end of the culture of impunity for politicians, and focused delivery on issues of insecurity, crime, unemployment, health, education and income distribution. They also want an end to austerity programmes, wanting the government to spend more and cut taxes more.

The collapse of De la Rua's government and – in spite of the subsequent appointment of the Peronist Duhalde as president – of Menem's liberal reform legacy, has been interpreted by some analysts as a signal event for Latin America's economies, heralding the failure of so-called "neo-liberal" reform policies. But if the Argentine political economy has failed to make the necessary transition to longer-term recovery, the economy is still, in 2002, even with its difficulties, arguably better off than it was before Menem's original reforms were instituted.

The Chilean Story

Ricardo Ffrench-Davis[16] has provided a useful time series in which to examine the changes in the Chilean economy. The first period is the rule of Salvador Allende (1971-73); the second, the first stage of the

---

15 Interview, Dr Guillermo Mondino, Secretary of Economic Policy, Ministry of the Economy, Buenos Aires, 26 November 2001.
16 These insights were gained from a conference focusing on Chile and South Africa held in Santiago, 20-21 November 2001.

military junta under Augusto Pinochet (1973-82); third is the second half of Pinochet's government (1982-89); and finally, the civilian governments of Patricio Aylwin (1990-93), Eduardo Frei (1994-99) and Ricardo Lagos (2000-).

Variable	Allende	Pinochet	Aylwin	Frei	Lagos
GDP Growth	1.2	2.9	7.7	5.6	5.4
Growth of Exports	-4.2	10.6	9.6	9.4	7.5
Inflation	293.8	79.9	17.7	6.1	4.5
Unemployment	4.7	18.1	7.3	7.4	10.0
Real Wages (1970=100)	89.7	81.9	99.8	123.4	134.4
Investment %GDP, 1977 pesos	15.9	15.6	19.9	24.1	22.3
Government surplus %GDP	-11.5	0.3	1.7	1.2	0.1

Chile's economic growth over the past decade has been nothing short of remarkable. During the 1990s, it averaged an annual rate of GDP growth of over 7%, income per person doubled, and annual inflation was brought down from 30% to under 5%.

This success was built on three pillars.
The first pillar was the institution of free-market economic reforms in the mid-1980s by Pinochet's team of bright young economists – the so-called "Chicago boys". These included the promotion of a high domestic savings rate, the introduction of government policies guaranteeing the remittance of profits and capital, privatisation, free choice as to the percentage of foreign ownership and non-discrimination with local investors, and tariff liberalisation.

But these reforms were not, contrary to some impressions, based on purely market-driven state policies and behaviour. In 1973, the junta dealt with its socialist inheritance from Allende (which had included widespread nationalisation), by implementing radical market-driven liberalisation. This involved the privatisation of banks, the freeing of interest rates, and tariff reductions. However, these moves resulted, by 1982, in very high interest rates (touching 40%), high unemployment (over 30%), and a 15% economic *contraction* as dollar-denominated borrowings threatened to cripple the economy as the peso fell.

The second period of Pinochet's rule (1982-89) was characterised by different policies, *inter alia* by the introduction of price controls and subsidies on exports, and the strict regulation of interest rates. The second pillar of economic reform was a cyclical upswing in commodity prices (especially those of copper and wood pulp), on which the economy is heavily dependent. Copper, of which Chile holds 40% of the world's supply, accounts for two-fifths of export revenue. Investment in this area was, in turn, facilitated by low income tax, identical treatment of foreign and local companies under Chilean tax laws, the establishment of free trade zones, progressive foreign investment incentives and transparent regulations. Critically, Chile kept corruption down to a minimum, and not just by Latin American standards. Its police force, while accused of human rights abuses, is still regarded as the best in Latin America today. Chile is the third ranking developing economy (behind Singapore and Hong Kong) in Transparency International's *Corruption Perception Index*, ahead of countries such as Ireland, Spain, France and Japan.

This has not been without its problems, however. Chile's dependence on mining largely explains the economic problems the country experiences in the wake of the fall in the global copper price in 1998 to the lowest levels since the 1930s. This followed the collapse in Asia's demand, which previously accounted for 80% of Chile's exports. This economic setback was compounded by one of the worst droughts this century, caused by *La Niña*. Some analysts argue that government dithering worsened these problems, while higher government expenditures in 1998 had the effect of forcing up real interest rates, prompting a credit squeeze. In 1998, GDP growth slipped to 3.7%. In 1999, Chile recorded a 1.1% contraction, with a recovery to 5.45% recorded in 2000. Unemployment leapt up from 4.5% in 1997 to 9% in 1999, exacerbating already poor income distribution patterns. However, the effects were to some extent contained through a low inflation rate – around 4% in 2000.

Chile's over-dependence on copper as its single main export item and the mini-recession experienced at the start of the 21st century resulted in a number of calls for reform from economists. Ffrench-Davis, for example, argues for a number of strategies to be applied so that Chile can repeat the 7% growth achieved in the 1990s. These include:[17]

---

17 Ricardo Ffrench-Davis, *Economic Reforms in Chile: From Dictatorship to Democracy*. Ann Arbor: University of Michigan Press, 2001. See also his *Reforming the Reforms in Latin America*. London: Macmillan, 2000.

- the maintenance of a competitive exchange rate and stabilisation of interest rates;
- the matching of demand with productive capacity;
- the development of export incentives to add value to natural resources;
- more intense efforts at regional integration, given the importance of market access to export diversification;
- encouragement of additional long-term savings, and their channelling to local small- and medium-sized enterprises;
- greater investment in human capital which will improve productivity;
- the addressing of unequal income distribution, the stepping up of efforts at social expenditure, the fighting of tax evasion and the closing of tax loopholes; and
- improvement in the delivery of state services and public administration.

The third pillar has been, as is intimated above, the commitment of successive Chilean governments to trade openness and access. Chile now maintains a flat tariff rating of 7%, which has been decreasing every year since 1998 at 1% annually until it reaches 6%. The country has concluded free trade agreements with a wide range of partners, including Mercosur, the European Union, Canada, and Mexico. It is anticipated that an agreement with the US will be finalised by the end of 2002.[18]

Whatever his critics may say, Pinochet's lasting contribution to Chile's development was to establish a functioning market-driven economy, control over which he was prepared to cede to professionals. In stark contrast to the Latin American experience, the military under Pinochet was also comparatively corruption-free. Moreover, he was ultimately prepared to hand over power to a civilian government – again, hardly typical of military leadership in the region – through a democratic process.

Pinochet's role in Chile's economic reform and the comparative experience of Argentina and East Asian nations raises questions about

18 According to the Chilean government, trade agreements (*Tratados de Libre*) have been concluded with Canada, Central America, the EU, South Korea, the European Free Trade Area, the US and Mexico. See *http://www.direcon.cl.*

the conventional wisdom that economic reform is more, not less, successful and likely in authoritarian states. Although this issue is dealt with in detail in the Conclusion, here it suffices to say that the evidence is mixed. Responsive democratic government is arguably more necessary to the development and the implementation of sustainable reforms. Authoritarianism is more often than not used to excuse poor or autocratic leadership, to obscure poor management and to restrict accountability and transparency. Moreover, notions of democracy have to be carefully scrutinised, because the nature and "culture" of the democratic system and the relationships of key sectors (such as the ruling party, legislature, executive and civil society) are crucial to the success of economic reforms.

Mexico's Successes and Challenges

A former Mexican ambassador to South Africa was engaged in a drawn-out battle in the mid-1990s with the advertising standards authority and a local company for its use of a stereotype of a sleepy, simple sombrero-bedecked *Mexicano* in selling a local tortilla-based snack. Such derogatory impressions were arguably reinforced by the collapse of the Mexican economy in its 1994-95 financial crisis, leading economists to label the contagion to other emerging markets as the "Tequila effect".

Yet Mexico's economic performance has, since this crisis, been outstanding. The republic has "made foreign trade the engine of its economy", its success being underpinned by its relationship with the US through the North American Free Trade Agreement. At the time of the passing of NAFTA in 1993, bilateral trade with the US totalled US$81 billion. Today around 80% of Mexico's trade is with its giant neighbour. It hit US$233 billion in 2001, with Mexico becoming the US's second largest trading partner, exporting more to Mexico than to Britain, France, Germany and Italy combined. This is compounded by the annual southward flow of more than US$8 billion in workers' remittances.[19] During the 1990s, Mexico's exports increased from US$45 billion to US$165 billion, or 15% per annum, with the contribution of manufactured goods to Mexican exports doubling to reach 90%. While Brazil is the largest economy in the region, Mexico is the

---

19 Peter Hakin, "Two Ways to Go Global", *Foreign Affairs*, 81, 1, January/February 2002, pp.150-2.

largest exporter. The net result has been five years of solid growth, averaging 5.5% from 1996 to 2000 compared to the "virtual stagnation" of the economy during the 1980s.[20] Today Mexico is the world's 13th largest economy, the eighth largest exporter of goods and services, and the fourth largest oil producer.

Mexico's Revival

	1996	1999	2000
GDP Real Annual Change %	5.2	3.8	6.9
Inflation %	30.7	14.9	10.9
Unemployment %	—	2.5	2.2
Fiscal Balance % GDP	-0.2	-1.6	-1.8
FDI Inflows US$ bn	9.2	11.9	13.3
External Debt US$ bn	—	—	157

While economic reform has been facilitated by regional integration efforts and a close economic partnership with the United States, it has also been consolidated by political change. The election of President Vicente Fox and his Partido de Acción Nacional (PAN) in July 2000, ending 71 years of domination by the Partido Revolucionario Institucional (PRI) has assisted in changing the face of Mexico as a credible, investor-friendly emerging market with a positive future. As President George W Bush put it in September 2001,[21] "The United States has no more important relationship in the world than our relationship with Mexico. Each of our countries is proud of our independence, our freedom and our democracy. We are united by values and carried forward by common hopes." Although Mexico's economic and political problems were in the past summed up in the slogan "So far from God and so close to the United States", today its geography is proving a distinct economic advantage, with 2,600 American companies having operations in Mexico and a US FDI stock of US$35.4 billion by 2000, a 70% rise since 1993.

This has not been without its challenges, not least in terms of social problems, including spending on social infrastructure (such as health and education) and the observation of human rights by the police and military, and more widely regarding its cultural identity: eco-

---

20 World Bank Country Brief on *http://www.worldbank.org*.
21 See *http://www.state.gov/e/rls/rm/2002/9438.htm*.

nomically it is tied into North America, culturally it is a Latin American country. Just around 5% of its trade is with Latin America, with Brazil representing under 1%. Poverty also persists, with nearly 30% – 27 million – of the country's people classified as poor, though unemployment is (officially) low at just 2.2% in 2000. Corruption remains problematic. In Transparency International's 2001 "Corruption Perception Index"[22] Mexico was 51st (with South Africa 38th, Brazil 46th, Argentina 57th and Bangladesh 91st). The public sector had to absorb a huge non-performing loan portfolio after the 1994-95 financial crisis, one of the causes of which was the poorly supervised and regulated banking system. Mexico is vulnerable to the fickle international tourism market and oil revenues for the health of its external accounts but most importantly to the health of the US economy.

While problems remain, overall Mexico's economic turnaround illustrates the importance of political stability, market access, trade agreements, currency characteristics, export competitiveness and the ability to adapt to new technologies and products. Economic growth has also been expedited by a business-friendly contract and legal regime (at least when compared to much of Latin America) and by the impact of privatisation, especially of its port system.

While Latin America is arguably more exposed to external risk than any other region globally, given its dependency on commodity exports and high levels of foreign indebtedness, Mexico, like Chile, has been able to escape the effect of Argentina's and Brazil's earlier economic difficulties, given its trade ties (and thus investor perceptions of its linking) with North America and the European Union. Mexico enjoys free trade agreements with 35 countries (the greatest number worldwide),[23] granting virtually barrier-free access to 75% of the global economy. Access has been facilitated, too, by the competitiveness of the Mexican peso.

---

22 Where 1 is least corrupt.
23 US and Canada (under NAFTA), the 15 countries of the EU, the G3 (Colombia and Venezuela), Chile, Costa Rica, Panama, Israel, Bolivia, Nicaragua, the Central American Pact (Guatemala, El Salvador, Honduras), and Brazil. Mexico also has a partial accord with the full Mercosur members, and is exploring agreements with Japan, Switzerland, Iceland, Norway, Lichtenstein and Singapore. See *http://tendencias.infoamericas.com.*

Assessing and Reforming the Reforms

The table below summarises the policy reform processes described above.

Neo-Liberalism and Economic Adjustment

Case Study	Successes	Failures
Chile	Political stability and transition	Initially (1973-82) high interest rates, unemployment and inflation resulting from lack of prudential controls and quick-fix liberalisation
	Necessary balance between free market economic reform, political stability and investor confidence	Reliance on one product (copper)
	Fiscal and monetary control	
	Internal conditionalities	Slow development of services and manufacturing sectors
	Privatisation	
	Low, flat taxation	Income distribution inequity
	Low tariffs	
	Limited government regulatory intervention	
	Strict prudential control post-1982	
	Avoidance of recessionary cycles	
	High FDI flows, and high domestic investor confidence	
Argentina	Monetary control and currency stabilisation	Brazilian devaluation
		Poor prudential supervision
	Inflation control	
	Privatisation	Provincial federal political and economic control and fiscal recklessness

Mexico	Market access, especially to North American and EU markets	Failure to reduce debt
		Weak political leadership
		Failure to achieve political transition, stability and compromise
		Linked currency affected by the rising value of dollar
		High rates of poverty and poor social infrastructure
	Political stability and transition	Underdeveloped transport infrastructure
	Banking reform	
	Low production costs and improving integration of technology	High levels of corruption
	Growing domestic market	

Ten Steps for Sustained Reform: Applying Latin America to Africa?

The above comparison of select Latin American economic transitions produces a number of lessons.

First, macroeconomic stability is a necessary but not sufficient condition for economic growth. While there is a need to balance the fiscus, there is also a need to take care over how this is managed. For example, one cannot simply cut public sector wages or prune the budget of the health or education sectors.

Second, changes in the external environment may have serious effects on longer-term growth prospects. This is true both in terms of deep engagement with global trade and investment markets, and also in terms of the overall "rules of the global game" by developing nations in particular. (This is examined in Chapter Five.)

Third, in spite of the point made above, there are interventions that states can make without external assistance: examples are prudentiality, fiscal reforms and corruption fighting.

Fourth, the role of the state is critical in three respects: one, the promotion of efficiency in the management of resources; two, the reduction of public sector deficit; and three, in maintaining the necessary balance between economic reform and social welfare. The economy clearly cannot function on the basis of pure Darwinism. There is also a critical difference between policies that simply aim to sustain livelihoods and those that build businesses: that is, between addressing poverty and creating the conditions for prosperity.

Fifth, there is a need for urgency in restructuring and reforming the economy.

Sixth, the regional environment is of crucial importance in providing a positive trade, investment and security environment (or, paradoxically, in raising the costs of entry through poor investor perceptions). Trade agreements are a pillar for export growth.

Seventh, FDI brings technology, market access and confidence. Though most investment will be domestic, local investment is important to inspire confidence in foreign investors.

Eighth, good corporate and political governance rest on similar tenets: the need for oversight of and checks and balances on the executive, and a keen awareness of minority interests. Transparency, disclosure and accountability are equally necessary to both.

Ninth, over the longer term, education and skills enhancement are key to sustained export growth.

Tenth, and perhaps most important, there is a need for a political compact which ensures that the business sector does not push for those things which are politically impossible, and that the politicians do not push for those things which are economically impracticable.

Conclusion

This study of Chile, Mexico and Argentina shows that, like Africa, Latin America is not a homogeneous region. They are countries with different histories and different political cultures; they have contrasting levels of state capacity, respect for institutions, and norms of governance. They illustrate both the importance of sound policy, and the limits of policy in the absence of political will. They demonstrate the importance of leadership and of the policy choices made by government.

The experience of the countries examined here also demonstrates the necessity of providing the right environment in which businesses can develop. Argentina's recovery path depends on the extent to which government can separate itself from the survival of businesses. There, the role of government is not to protect or save inefficient industries and cover their debts. Equally misguided were the import restrictions and subsidised industry of an earlier era.[24] Debtors and creditors in business have to be allowed to work out survival plans themselves, transferring the cost of reviving industry to the corporate sector according to rates determined by global markets, not by domestic government. To do otherwise is just another form of Asian-style crony capitalism. The protection of jobs and of company owners, the guarding of political interests, and doing what is best for the economy are not necessarily all the same thing, as the case of Argentina shows all too clearly.

---

24 See "Crony capitalism is deeply entrenched in Argentina", *Financial Times*, 1 March 2002.

CHAPTER FIVE

PORTO ALEGRE MEETS DAVOS?
Globalisation and Global Governance

> I cannot stress enough the importance of partnerships. The task ahead is too formidable for any single institution or set of institutions to tackle. Every one of us has a role to play: private sector, public sector, civil society, nongovernmental organisations, academia, religious groups, multilateral and bilateral donors, and development organisations.
>
> JAMES WOLFENSOHN, 2000[1]

> The United Nations remains the only organisation still vaguely capable of articulating the notion of one world, a sort of symphony of humanity.
> BEN OKRI

Introduction

In his controversial thesis, the "Clash of Civilisations", Samuel Huntington argues that the world has not, with the end of the Cold War, reached the end of history, but is entering a new, non-Western phase, where, he says:[2]

> ... its centrepiece becomes the interaction between West and non-Western civilisation, and *among* non-Western civilisations. In the politics of civilisations, the people and governments of non-Western civilisations no longer remain the objects of history as targets of Western colonialism, but join the West as movers and shapers of history.

Huntington has been criticised on a number of fronts. His thesis stands accused of (over)simplifying the complex make-up of societies and factions, and the divisions and differences within and between

---

1 Foreword to the World Bank's Annual Report 2000 on *http://wbln0018. worldbank.org/news/pressrelease.nsf/673fa6c5a2d50a67852565e200692a79/ b1df0200ff835e5f85256963004bc298?OpenDocument.*

2 See Samuel P Huntington, *The Clash of Civilisations and the Remaking of World Order.* Sydney: Simon & Schuster, 1998, esp. pp.56-78. For commentary, see Greg Sheridan, *Asian Values, Western Dreams.* Australia: Allen & Unwin, 1999, pp.4-5 and 301; and Daniel P Bell, *East Meets West: Human Rights and Democracy in East Asia.* Princeton: PUP, 2000, esp. pp.4-5.

them. These groups – or civilisations – are not homogeneous, and are fraught with tensions within and between religions, between modernity and traditionalism, and between ideologies. Although Huntington argues that Western civilisation is not universal, and should give up this pretension, this is because of cultural limitations in those societies rather than the content and strength of Western values.

The way in which the West has pursued its interest at the expense of non-Western civilisations is noted by Huntington: "The West is in effect using international institutions, military power and economic resources to run the world in ways that will maintain Western predominance, protect Western interests and promote Western political and economic values." This, as Kishore Mahbubani argues, "is a prescription for disaster" where 15% of the world's population is attempting to legislate for the remaining 85%.[3] The events of September 11 gave Huntington's arguments a boost. As Allan Little has observed, the attacks on the United States seem "to represent a dramatic polarisation of aspiration", in which "the values around which our societies seek to cohere are more sharply defined than they were before September 11".[4]

What is required to make the attributes of the "Western way" – democracy, personal freedoms and liberties; the separation of party, church and state; and observing the rule of law – globally accepted? Differences in culture need not imply that values must collide. Is it reasonable to propose that providing improved global governance will spur development and prevent the differences between states from manifesting themselves in radical, violent action?

★ ★ ★

The New Partnership for Africa's Development has set its sights on creating a "rules-based" international system, in an attempt to level the global playing fields between rich and poor states, and to effect a "resource transfer" from the developed North to the developing South. Thabo Mbeki, as one of NEPAD's key proponents, has argued: [5]

3 Kishore Mahbubani, "The Dangers of Decadence: What the Rest Can Teach the West", *Can Asians Think?* Singapore: Times Books International, 1998, p.85.
4 Allan Little, "A New World Order?", in Jenny Baxter and Malcolm Downing, *The Day that Shook the World*. Sydney: BBC with ABC, p.222.
5 "Africa calls on fortress Europe", *Business Day*, 5 April 2000.

Most of our countries [in Africa] are trapped in a vicious cycle of
poverty and lack of capital. A good part of the required capital
must therefore come from abroad . . . We seek the agreement of
our European friends that extraordinary measures will have to
be taken to encourage larger foreign direct investment inflows
into Africa.

As Mbeki put it in his budget speech to South Africa's parliament in
June 2000:[6]

Globalisation . . . has a profound impact on the sovereignty of
states. The smaller the country, such as ours, the greater the loss
of sovereignty, as we get more and more integrated within the
global community. Globalisation means we cannot overcome our
inherited negatives except within the context of the global community of which we are an integral part.

Mbeki's calls for greater international equity with Africa and for equality for developing countries on the world stage have found resonance
in the manner in which some commentators have portrayed the challenges of globalisation. They note the "unfair" manner in which globalisation has impacted on developing societies – and the effect on
global affairs of these differences, particularly post September 11. At
the same time, a set of transnational bonds has emerged, which reflects the features of the information era (even though it is antithetical
to the changing patterns of social norms within states). These common features include recognition of:[7]
• the need to preserve the environment;
• the accelerated movement of people, capital, goods and services
  – and the management of this phenomenon;
• the emergence of pernicious influences in worse forms than before,
  notably terrorism and related issues of organised crime including
  people, drug and weapons smuggling, and money laundering;
• the search for new, relatively unpenetrated markets; and
• the importance of advances in knowledge.

---

6 "SA must put the focus on a better life for all its citizens", *Business Day*,
  14 June 2000.
7 For a detailed investigation of the impact of transnational influences, see Alan
  Dupont, *East Asia Imperilled: Transnational Challenges to Security*. Cambridge:
  CUP, 2001.

Just as new norms are emerging within states, new bonds and ways of doing business are developing within the broader global milieu. The twin concepts of good governance and democratisation have emerged as indispensable to economic and sociopolitical development. The question, however, remains: How can good governance and democracy be implemented at the same time as building an equitable global order that accommodates clashing nationalistic tendencies and varying developmental needs and circumstances?

The shift in the debate towards questions of "global governance" can be seen in the themes discussed by the Davos World Economic Forum. Whereas ten years ago debate concerned ways of taking advantage of globalisation, the Forum has altered its focus to a discussion of partnership. The following list of the WEF's annual conference themes illustrates this point:[8]

- 2002: Leadership in Fragile Times: A Vision for a Shared Future
- 2001: Sustaining Growth and Bridging the Divides: A Framework for Our Global Future
- 2000: New Beginnings: Making a Difference
- 1999: Responsible Globality: Managing the Impact of Globalisation
- 1998: Priorities for the 21st Century
- 1997: Building the Network Society
- 1996: Sustaining Globalisation
- 1995: Challenges Beyond Growth
- 1994: Redefining the Basic Assumptions of the World Economy
- 1993: Rallying all the Forces for Global Recovery
- 1992: Global Co-operation and Megacompetition
- 1991: The new Direction for Global Leadership

Or, as Kofi Annan put it to the 2002 WEF summit:[9]

> [Y]ou are sharing this small planet with well over a billion people who are denied the very minimum requirements of human dignity, and with four or five billion whose choices in life are narrow indeed compared to yours. In fact the planet seems to many of us more and more like a small boat driven by a fierce gale through dark and uncharted waters, with more and more people crowded on board, hoping desperately to survive. None of us, I

8 See *http://www.weforum.org.*
9 At *http://www.davos.org.*

suggest, can afford to ignore the condition of our fellow passengers on this little boat. If they are sick, all of us risk infection. And if they are angry, all of us can easily get hurt. Our problem is one of reality multiplied by perception. The reality is that power and wealth in this world are very, very unequally shared, and that far too many people are condemned to lives of extreme poverty and degradation. The perception, among many, is that this is the fault of globalisation, and that globalisation is driven by a global elite, composed of, or at least represented by, the people who attend this gathering. That perception is not universal, but it is widely shared especially in places like Argentina and East Asia, which have recent experience of severe financial crises, but also by an increasingly vocal section of public opinion in the developed world.

In 2001, the Swedish Foreign Ministry published the results of a working group on "formulating an integrated Swedish globalisation policy". It formulated a long list of what should be done in the world that was not unlike Mbeki's or Annan's. The group's recommendations included the need to secure global financial stability in order to bring about growth and development, sustainable development, respect for human rights and growth, fair distribution of wealth, effective measures against cross-border financial crime, prevention of the illegal trafficking in arms, growth through open unregulated trade, debt cancellation for poor countries, an increase in aid to developing nations, provision of food and necessary medicines to all, access to IT and the Internet for all, the strengthening of democracy and freedom of speech, an end to trafficking in women and children, and an increase in opportunities to study and work in other countries. To achieve all of the above, the report advocates solidarity on welfare issues at home, consensus in the EU on policy matters, including issues of trade, and improved global collaboration as "one step towards more vigorous action". On the IMF, the working group recommended that it should "adapt its recommendations to the special circumstances in each separate member country", though strengthening the global financial system "requires many interacting measures".[10] Like most of the calls for "global governance", however, this is hardly a blueprint for action. It is a statement of concerned interest rather than of intent.

---

10 *A More Equitable Globalisation.* Stockholm: Government Printer, 2001.

Taking Annan's and Mbeki's concerns and those raised by the WEF together with this rather naive and unrealistic wish list, we can identify a number of common and relevant questions. How can countries exploit international opportunities better, so as to spread and share the benefits of globalisation? What should be the role of international financial institutions in this process? How, related to this, can a balance be struck between aggressive liberalisation and preventing this from marginalising developing countries? What are the current strengths and weaknesses of the multilateral system? How might this be improved? What role has foreign policy to play in meeting these challenges?

Porto Alegre meets Davos?

When the WEF held its annual summit in January 2002, the World Social Forum (WSF) was meeting in Porto Alegre in Brazil. While the WEF is seen as the forum for the exponents of globalisation, the WSF brought together those (more vociferous) critics of globalisation who were concerned about its excesses, the growing divides in wealth, and the cost of economic growth to the environment. Highlighting the apparent contradiction between the summits in Porto Alegre and Davos, Annan noted:

> Do not underestimate the attraction of the rival gathering, timed to coincide with yours, that has just finished in Porto Alegre, Brazil. Its title, "World Social Forum" is intended as a criticism of yours, implying that you are interested only in economics, or in profit, and that you do not care about the social effects of your economic activities. And that criticism resonates around the world. I believe that perception is wrong and that globalisation, so far from being the cause of poverty and other social ills, offers the best hope of overcoming them.

These meetings occurred against a global milieu quite different to that of 12 months earlier. The events of September 11 had not only forced the WEF meeting off-piste to New York from Davos, but placed questions about global governance at the top of the agenda. These questions concerned the need to address the conditions which had given rise to the terrorist attacks. Both the Porto Alegre and Davos summits gave priority to the questions raised, sometimes violently, by the protests marring the 2001 Genoa G8 summit and earlier NATO, IMF

and WTO fora in Gothenburg, Prague and Seattle respectively during
the previous 24 months. Both also focused on the reasons behind the
Argentine crisis, where an economic and political impasse had been
broken by street protests, and discussed the probable consequences.

Although the January 2002 meetings sought to identify and deal with
the challenges of globalisation and global fragmentation, there was also
evidence to support the benefits of deeper integration.

On 1 January, the European Union's single currency – the Euro –
became a reality in 12 nations. It was touted as the "most dramatic
building-block so far in the making of a new Europe".[11] Many European leaders saw it as the instrument to achieve greater consolidation. In the words of German Foreign Minister Joschka Fischer, the
Euro would "make good the shortfall in political integration". The
WTO summit in Doha had ended a month earlier, having achieved
consensus on the need for a new global trade round. This represented encouraging compromise between developed and developing nations, positive evidence, too, of the benefits of globalisation.

Also, a new study by the World Bank (discussed briefly in Chapter
One) released at the end of 2001[12] shows that, contrary to the conventional wisdom, over the past two decades the number of those
living in conditions of absolute poverty have fallen, not risen, and that
economic integration has reduced poverty and global inequality. According to this study, the numbers living in extreme poverty peaked
at around 1.4 billion in 1980, although this was just 30% of the world's
population compared to the 85% who existed in similar conditions in
1820. Today, the figure is down to 1.2 billion people, or 20% of the
global population. Moreover, there is also evidence that a number of
developing countries have participated successfully in the global industrial economy, even though there has been rising income inequality within both developing nations (particularly in Latin America and
China) and developed ones. The percentage of manufactured goods
as exports of developing countries rose from one quarter in 1980 to
more than 80% by 1998, with much higher growth for those countries which had used this as a means to increase their participation

---

11 *The Economist*, 5 January 2002.
12 See the report *Globalization, Growth and Poverty: Building an Inclusive World
    Economy* on *http://lnweb18.worldbank.org/news/pressrelease.nsf*.
    See also "Globalisation is wrongly accused", *Business Day*, 7 January 2002.

in the global economy. The study showed that 24 developing countries which had followed this path over the two decades ending in the
late 1990s, had achieved higher growth in incomes, longer life expectancy and better education for their citizens. These countries, home
to some three billion people, enjoyed an average 5% growth rate in income per capita in the 1990s, compared to 2% in rich countries.

According to the Bank's 2000 report on developing countries, regions that saw the largest declines in trade barriers – East and South
Asia, and Latin America – also saw the largest acceleration in exports.
By contrast, growth in export volumes in sub-Saharan Africa averaged
only 2% annually, partly because world trade in the products they export grew at half the rate of trade in general. Countries in sub-Saharan
Africa and in the Middle East and North Africa also saw market share
in their traditional exports decline.[13]

The problem is, however, that while the group of 24 successfully
integrating countries described in the World Bank's 2001 study represent three billion people (or half the world's population), about two
billion people live in countries that are not globalising or developing,
and are facing global marginalisation. These countries faced negative
growth in the 1990s, and many of them are, unfortunately, in Africa.
In addition to the political hardships caused by poor policies, predatory leadership and collapsed or weak state structures, they face the
economic consequences of having narrow commodity bases. Added
to these constraints are the irremediable ills of poor climate and hos-
tile terrain, including a difficulty of access to global trade routes.

The question that arises next is: Are there any alternatives to playing
by the rules of globalisation? Or is there any way of shaping those rules
to the best advantage of developing countries?

Frankly, there appears to be little purpose in attempting to turn back
the clock and revert to protectionist measures, unless you are a French
farmer or North Carolina textile worker. The last time this happened,
between 1914 and 1945, governments responded to economic depression through protectionism. Over this period, controls were imposed
on the export of capital. Anti-immigrant sentiment rose. The decline
in poverty was pushed back to 19th century levels, to well below the

---

13 See *Global Economic Prospects and The Developing Economies 2001* on
    *http://wbln0018.worldbank.org/news/pressrelease.nsf/673fa6c5a2d50a67852565e
    200692a79/999119e933f6b6ca852569ac004c4bdf?OpenDocument.*

rate of population growth, increasing the absolute number of poor people by 25%. The world's rate of growth fell by about one third. In 1950, exports as a share of world income were back to 1870 levels at just 5%. As Angus Maddison has argued: "Between 1913 and 1950, the world economy grew much more slowly than in 1870-1913, world trade grew much less than world income, and the degree of inequality between regions increased substantially."[14]

Action is required on various fronts, however, to avoid growing global wealth divides. Not only should countries get their own houses in order and create an attractive investment climate; there is also a need to address a number of macro (or global) challenges if globalisation is to provide growth for all at a pace that meets expectations. These challenges include the following imperatives:

• to build consensus on the benefits of globalisation, and thus on the need for *integration* rather than *isolation*;
• to reduce trade protectionism and offer greater access to developing countries.
• to provide support for less developed countries, including technical and financial, developmental assistance along with debt relief; and
• to reduce the volatility of capital flows to emerging markets.

The remainder of this chapter examines the prospects of achieving the above, within the current global framework.

★ ★ ★

The Strengths and Weaknesses of Multilateralism

The weakness of the responses (or lack of them) to African and other developmental crises might be said to illustrate the most difficult contemporary international relations challenge. This is the collapse of multilateralism, the ethos behind multilateral interventions in the spirit of the UN Charter and the Universal Declaration of Human Rights. Chapter One of the UN Charter outlines the purpose of the UN:

> To maintain international peace and security, and to that end: to take effective collective measures for the prevention and the removal of threats to the peace, and for the suppression of acts of

---

14 See *http://econ.worldbank.org/files/2896_ch1.pdf.*

aggression or other breaches of the peace, and to bring about by peaceful means, and in conformity with the principles of justice and international law, adjustment or settlement of international disputes or situations which might lead to a breach of the peace.

Secretary-General Annan has said that:[15]

> As its Charter makes clear, the United Nations was intended to introduce new principles into international relations, making a qualitative difference to their day-to-day conduct. The Charter's very first Article defines our purposes: resolving disputes by peaceful means; devising co-operative solutions to economic, social, cultural and humanitarian problems; and broadly encouraging behaviour in conformity with the principles of justice and international law. In other words, quite apart from whatever practical tasks the United Nations is asked to perform, it has the avowed purpose of transforming relations among states, and the methods by which the world's affairs are managed.

Ironically, global governance, as epitomised by the UN, has been far from uniform and even-handed in its practice under the leadership of Mr Annan. When he was head of the UN's Department of Peacekeeping Operations, more than 500,000 people were massacred in Rwanda in the course of 100 days in 1994 and, although they could have, the world and the UN did not intervene. After he took over as UN Secretary-General, a conflict on the scale and geography of the First World War was allowed to range in an arc from Sudan across the Congo to Angola in Africa, yet the civil wars in Kosovo and Bosnia merited substantial international military intervention. While the answer to such apparent double standards, particularly as applied to African crises, lies in a combination of national/regional interests and the intractability of African conflicts rather than Mr Annan's leadership *per se*, it points to the uneven nature of the global playing field. It is also indicative of a lack of interest in a critical aspect of globalisation: that of the need for political standards, human rights and democracy.

This failure in global governance is not only limited to the UN and

---

15 See *http://www.un.org/News/ossg/sg/.*

its agencies, however. The WTO is at the centre of a drive towards a more liberal global trade environment, but this is obstructed by widespread economic crises (to which global institutions have responded weakly) and by resistance to liberalisation. This points to the need both for better and more democratic systems and institutions of global governance and for global leadership from the sole remaining superpower, the United States.

Herein rests a fundamental paradox. The modern age has rejected the notion that a balance of power is requisite for international peace. But the power of global institutions to address people-centred issues – and upholding a (Woodrow) Wilsonian consensus of peace – is linked to the consent of governments. Whereas Wilson's idealism foundered 80 years ago on its premise of the primacy of mankind before states and empires,[16] the effectiveness of the multilateral environment necessary to deal with the phenomenon of globalisation hinges on both the willingness and ability of states to participate in and to devolve responsibility to multilateral institutions, and on the corresponding ability in these institutions to accept and deal with these challenges. As William Pfaff has said, the UN is a human institution embodied in contemporary political history, sometimes useful, sometimes not. Its failures, he notes, are human failures.[17]

The UN System: *The Symphony of Humanity?*

Conway Henderson has identified three types of constraints facing the UN. First is the "lack of a dependable process for handling violation of the peace". Second is the absence of an efficient bureaucracy with a reliable budget. This relates to organisational inertia, empire-building on the part of its various agencies, and vested national interests in maintaining current structures. As President Bill Clinton noted: "The UN simply does not need a separate agency with its own acronym, stationery and bureaucracy for every problem." Third is "the distraction and division caused by different expectations for the world body".[18]

---

16 For an excellent, if provocative, discussion on the effects of Versailles and the impact of Wilson's 14 points, see David Sinclair, *Hall of Mirrors*. London: Arrow Books, 2001.

17 Cited in William Shawcross, *Deliver us from Evil: Warlords and Peacekeepers in a World of Endless Conflict*. London: Bloomsbury, 2001, p.201.

18 Conway W Henderson, *International Relations: Conflict and Co-operation at the Turn of the 21st Century*. Singapore: McGraw-Hill, 1998, p.417.

These weaknesses can be summed up by the argument that the UN, a body only as strong as the will of its membership, remains hamstrung by a lack of consensus among its members. As one UN official put it, "All members are in favour of reforms that don't matter to them. They have different starting positions determined by NIMBY – not in my backyard."[19] As Annan acknowledged in his Millennium Report delivered in 2000:[20]

> Clear answers are necessary to energise and focus the organisation's work in the decades ahead. . . . [T]he central challenge we face today is to ensure that globalisation becomes a positive force for all the world's people, instead of leaving billions of them behind in squalor. Inclusive globalisation must be built on the great enabling force of the market, but market forces alone will not achieve it. It requires a broader effort to create a shared future, based upon our common humanity in all its diversity. That in turn requires that we think afresh about how we manage our joint activities and our shared interests, for many challenges that we confront today are beyond the reach of any state to meet on its own. At the national level we must govern better, and at the international level we must learn to govern better together. Effective states are essential for both tasks, and their capacity for both needs strengthening. *We must also adapt international institutions, through which states govern together, to the realities of the new era.* We must form coalitions for change, often with partners well beyond the precincts of officialdom. [Emphasis added.]

Or as the Australian Foreign Policy White Paper observes, "International organisations can only accomplish what their member states enable them to accomplish."[21] Yet problems of capacity and political will are, unfortunately, replicated in many other multilateral agencies, of which the Non-Aligned Movement is another sad example.

However, as the attacks of September 11 showed, the cost of states controlling power by using counter-power and the absence of an effective international society as embodied by the UN system, is invariably high. When George W Bush put together his war on terrorism, he de-

19 SAIIA seminar, Johannesburg, November 1999.
20 See *http://www.un.org/News/ossg/sg/*.
21 On *http://www.dfat.gov.au/ini/wp.html*.

clared it would be a "new kind of war", involving diplomatic, police, legal, intelligence, and financial as well as military assets. It would freeze bank accounts, search out financial support networks, establish a Director of Homeland Security, draw in allies, and critically involve a military campaign for as long as it took. The so-called post September 11 "Bush Doctrine" has indeed been less unilateralist and one-dimensional and more multilateralist, collective and multidimensional than his presidency first hinted. It has by definition been global rather than isolationist, creating a coalition of international norms, methods and assets in the struggle against terrorism.

But while the war against terror might cripple Al-Queda and the Taliban, safeguarding populations against similar attacks and dealing with the roots of developmental, often transnational, problems such as over-population, trade access, pollution, and small arms proliferation has to involve co-operative ties and solutions. International organisations such as the UN could – and should – play an important role in establishing agreements on norms and policies, a step towards common cultural and moral bonds. Without this, conflict will invariably hold primacy over co-operation in defining international relations. Again, September 11 has highlighted the areas in which such co-operation is needed, and the costs of not doing so. As Henderson has argued:[22]

> A major and deepening trend for the 21st century is likely to be an intensifying interdependence that propels states to co-operate for mutual benefits. Actors are realising that in order for "us" to have peace, more wealth, better health, and a sustainable environment, "all" must enjoy these values as indivisible interests.

The Bretton Woods Institutions
The need for reform of institutions of global governance before they can be said to be truly multilateral extends beyond the political and security domain, however. Globalisation has occurred simultaneously with the introduction of a "rules-based" global trading regime and the application of strict conditionalities on domestic economic policy reform. These multilateral and bilateral agreements and undertakings have internationalised and led, as noted in the previous section, to a congruence of domestic policy choices. At the same time, however, this system is seen to be uneven, tending to marginalise developing

---

22 *Op cit*, p.499.

countries and vulnerable sectors such as women and children within these societies. Some would argue that we now have a global economy which has outstripped its systems of governance, partly because the Cold War polarised and stunted the development of such institutions of global governance, but also because of the dramatic pace of integration. Others might also argue that reform has been delayed because these institutions as they stand today serve the financial interests of the developed world. This would explain why the focus of restructuring efforts in global financial institutions is on issues of competition and market efficiency rather than on social and welfare policy.[23]

Much of this focus on reform has dwelt on the role of the IMF and the World Bank. Both were created in July 1944 to play different, if complementary, roles, with the overall aim of creating a world free of poverty. The IMF was established to provide stability in the international monetary system by assisting governments to overcome balance-of-payments problems. The World Bank was to set up programmes to promote post-war reconstruction, particularly in the immediate post-war period in Europe. This is a role indicated by its full name, the International Bank for Reconstruction and Development (IBRD). In simple terms, the Fund's job is ensuring macroeconomic stability; the Bank's development.

Concerns about the role of these institutions were heightened by the Asian and subsequent Russian and Brazilian financial crises in the late 1990s. And, as noted in Chapter Four, Argentina's economic problems at the start of the 21st century once again raised questions about the role of the Fund in providing guidance and the necessary package of reforms to help steer Argentina out of its crisis. Critics argued that the IMF's attempts to maintain the US$-peso currency peg and its adoption of a "one size fits all" approach to emerging market reform in which loans were tied to tight fiscal policies, simply worsened the situation, while its failure to insist on a devaluation earlier simply postponed the inevitable.

There are generally two related concerns expressed with regard to the IMF. One is about the soundness of the architecture, personnel and decision-making processes within the Fund, particularly the influence of shareholders. The second has to do with the efficacy of poli-

---

23 For an elucidation of the problems facing global economic institutions such as the World Bank and the IMF, see Robert J Samuelson, "Response to Fukuyama", *The National Interest*, 56, Summer 1999, p.42.

icy advice handed out, the nature of its delivery, and its impact.[24] The second area involves macro-tenets such as capital account liberalisation, debt dynamics and the longer-term impact of financial rescue packages, as well as micro-remedies. But the advice does not always take into consideration local conditions in its delivery. For example, at one point in Indonesia's collapse in 1997-8, the IMF negotiated a programme that involved 50 simultaneous structural reforms in a country that lacked financial management.[25]

The Bank has faced criticisms on a number of fronts. There are overall concerns about the efficacy of development aid generally. Questions are raised about the centrality of the Bank in a world increasingly dominated by private capital flows; the relative benefits of spending on poverty alleviation, education and health care as opposed to bricks and mortar projects; dangers of "mission creep"; the relationship between the Bank and private sector borrowers; and its role (or not) in providing policy advice as a so-called "knowledge bank". More specifically, critics discuss the Bank's alleged failure to take proper account of human and environmental needs in its projects, and the nature of its own evaluation process (where it is seen to be the judge and jury of its own projects).

Both organisations face three central problems. The first concerns the "fungibility" of aid flows – whether they end up in the right hands, or whether they are diverted, either directly or indirectly (especially where there are weak conditionalities), enabling countries to avoid necessary economic reforms. The more aid is directed towards balance-of-payments support and software initiatives such as health and education through local central government, the easier it is to steal or divert these funds. Second, there is a critical relationship between the nature of the aid environment and the role of the Fund and Bank – that they have a vested interest in perpetuating their role. The third and most central concern is whether aid promotes development or whether it may instead be counterproductive.[26]

---

24 See, for example, Lael Brainhard, "Capitalism Unhinged: The IMF and the Lessons of the Last Financial Crisis", *Foreign Affairs*, 81, 1, January/February 2002, pp.192-8; and Paul Blustein, *The Chastening: Inside the Crisis that Rocked the Global Financial System and Humbled the IMF*. New York: Public Affairs, 2001.

25 Sheridan, *op cit*, p.307.

26 See, for example, Helen Hughes, "Foreign aid offers a poor policy", *The Age*, 27 March 2002.

There are a number of arguments as to the possible nature and focus of the reforms of the Bretton Woods institutions. These include re-
ordering the global financial system so as to assist the less developed
countries in times of crisis; improving the standards of supervision of
threatened economies (for example, in their banking systems) to ensure that they can help themselves without getting into trouble in the
first instance; and transforming the nature of the global financial institutions to make them more democratic, responsive and equitable.

Both the Bank and the IMF have recognised the need to reform and
adjust to current realities. As the Fund put it in an April 2000 policy
brief:[27]

> The IMF's membership has grown fourfold since it was estab-
> lished, and it has become correspondingly more diverse. At the
> same time, the global economy has become increasingly inte-
> grated, and economic policy challenges have become more com-
> plex, often requiring more rapid responses. . . . It is only natural
> that the IMF should evolve to serve the needs of its changing
> membership in an evolving world economy.

But the organisation, unsurprisingly, sees a need for its continued existence:

> The IMF finds itself in such a central role in many different areas
> for two very broad reasons. First, macroeconomic and financial
> policies interact with virtually every other strand of countries'
> policy-making and national aspirations. For example, poverty re-
> duction requires economic growth, which requires macroeco-
> nomic and financial stability, including low inflation. The evi-
> dence is clear that low inflation helps the poor. Therefore, the
> IMF can make a vital contribution to poverty reduction. That
> role makes sense in the poorest countries, even if the detailed
> work on social policies is done by other agencies. Second, the
> IMF is the only international agency whose mandated activities
> routinely bring it into an active dialogue on economic policies
> with virtually every country. That makes it a natural vehicle for

---

27 See "Debt Relief, Globalisation and IMF Reform" on *http://www.imf.org/ex-
ternal/np/exr/ib/2000/041200b.htm#IV*.

discussing some of the key issues related to the stability of the international monetary and financial system, such as standards and codes, and consequences of rapid capital movements.

Views on the types of IMF reform necessary (which are equally applicable to the Bank in some areas) vary, largely according to political orientation. What is agreed is that reform is necessary, and that, as one reviewer put it, there is a need to convene a second Bretton Woods conference to ensure that the Fund is "correctly structured for the modern global economy".[28] For those who look for structural change, there are three broad areas of recommendation.

- First, the Fund should be eliminated, either as a waste of public funds (for those on the right) or as a constraint on the freedom of developmental policy (for those on the left).
- Second, the institution should be redirected, altering its role to focus primarily on the promotion of financial stability and the reduction of inequalities.
- Third, Fund operations should be scaled down, becoming a lender only of last resort.

For those that recommend the perpetuation of the Fund, suggested initiatives include the need for:[29]

- improved transparency and input in decision-making structures, including the provision of transcriptions of meetings;
- the elimination of loan subsidies on interest rates;
- the shift of financial onus to private investors and institutions, not taxpayers;
- the appointment of an independent advisory board to review IMF policies and recommendations;
- an end to successive rescue packages for chronically mismanaged economies;

---

28 See Bryan T Johnson and Brett D Schaefer, "A Checklist for IMF Reform", Heritage Foundation Backgrounder, 1204, 16 July 1998 on *http://www.heritage.org/library/backgrounder/bg1204.html*.

29 *Ibid*. See also The Halifax Initiative on *http://www.halifaxinitiative.org/hi.php/G-20/234*; Rainer Falk, "Reform of the IMF: A Provisional Appraisal and Perspective on the International Debate" on *http://www.weedbonn.org/finance/Falk_Reform_IMF.pdf*; and the Bretton Woods project on *http://www.brettonwoodsproject.org/*.

- audits on lending; and
- the linking of loans to economic and political freedom conditions.

The relevance of the Bank's role has been questioned by Western donors who see it as an ineffective aid organisation with a wasteful bureaucracy, incapable of delivering growth, and increasingly irrelevant in the face of the role of private business and capital flows. Developing countries and activists, on the other hand, challenge the Bank as representing a form of neo-colonial control and repression.[30]

Sachs and Woo[31] have expanded on the challenges faced by the Bretton Woods institutions in describing 30 reforms necessary to forestall future economic crises of the sort that wracked Asia in 1997. In terms of reforms within developing countries, these include:

- the adoption of international accounting standards;
- improved prudential supervision of financial institutions, taking into account the volatility caused by a high percentage of loan portfolios being denominated in foreign currencies;
- the diversification of bank ownership, thereby preventing the possibility of systemic banking collapse;
- the development of the non-bank financial sector as a source of credit, thereby reducing the possibility for panic;
- the clarification of corporate governance standards and rights;
- the introduction of modern bankruptcy law;
- more frequent reporting by financial institutions on their risk exposure; and
- the imposition of tight limits on short-term borrowing by financial institutions.

Necessary external reforms include:

- the establishment of a review commission of the IMF's functioning and handling of crises;
- greater transparency on IMF information and analytical materials;
- reform of IMF voting powers to give greater representivity to developing countries which "bear the burden of failed IMF strategies";

---

30 See *http://www.ifg.org/imf.html*.
31 "A Reform Agenda for a Resilient Asia" in Woo, Sachs and Schwab, *op cit*, pp.5-11.

- overhaul of the IMF's executive board and its activities, including the need to host regular outside hearings and invite greater participation of outside parties;
- the need for countries to pursue flexible exchange rates;
- an increase in support by regional monetary bodies for a reduction in the influence and role of the IMF;
- the establishment of an international bankruptcy system "to accelerate an orderly workout of international debts when a developing country falls into an extreme indebtedness crisis";
- the inclusion of debt relief as an integral part of rescue packages;
- making sure that IMF programmes do not defend pegged exchange rates, a practice that has either promoted recession or prevented currency collapse only temporarily;[32] and
- ensuring that rescue packages do not simply bail international private investors out, thereby shifting the responsibility for renegotiating payment terms from governments and intergovernmental organisations to the creditors.

It is important, however, to recognise that substantial policy innovation has taken place within these organisations, especially within the Fund. There is a trend towards lessening the Fund's role in ongoing balance-of-payments financing. To an extent this reflects the imperative to balance short-term stabilisation and prevention of collapse with necessary longer-term structural reform. Institutional changes have also been made, including the creation of a new developed/developing nations G20 steering group.

There is little doubt that improved international co-operation could help to stabilise global markets. The role of the Fund and the Bank should arguably intensify their focus on the creation of more stable systems with less focus on the distribution of aid and assistance. But the question is not so much about their role in reform, as about the type of reforms necessary in a global context. For example, the notion stemming speculative capital flows as the purported cause of financial and monetary crises is sometimes suggested as a fillip to the need for a re-engineered global financial architecture.

---

32 Although focused on the Asian crisis, these recommendations have relevance elsewhere, for example in Argentina.

Global Capital Flows[33]

There is a burgeoning international debate on the importance of foreign exchange controls – on both inflows and outflows.

In 1972, James Tobin, a Nobel economics laureate, first aired the notion of taxing international capital flows to reduce exchange rate volatility and promote the autonomy of macroeconomic policy. This gained currency following the 1997 Asian crisis and subsequent events in Russia and Brazil. Argentina's crisis at the start of 2002 once again raised the question of the desirability of instituting global capital controls to prevent, in particular, foreign denominated debt, and also the sometimes destabilising effect of short-term portfolio (or so-called "hot" money) currency inflows.

In the late 1990s, the Bank of International Settlements indicated that more than 10% of all foreign exchange transactions had a maturity of two days or less, with around 80% of all forex transactions involving so-called "round trips" of seven days or less. Many see these flows as politically, economically and socially destabilising, especially in developing states with fragile socioeconomic-political balances.[34] The Tobin Tax is promoted by many in the anti-globalisation movements as a means of reducing or eliminating the incentive to speculate, as it would help stabilise exchange rates by reducing the volume of speculation. The tax is set deliberately low – somewhere between 0.5% and 0.05% – so as not to have an adverse effect on trade in goods and services or long-term investments.[35] The tax is not just a developing country concern, however. It is still on the agenda of the EU as both an instrument to calm volatility in currency markets and a means to finance Third World development.[36]

Mahathir Mohamed has been among the foremost critics of the negative impact of the volatility of global capital flows on developing nations, likening global capital markets to "a jungle of ferocious beasts".

As was noted in Chapter Three, the Malaysian economy performed admirably for most of the 1990s, averaging over 8% annual real GDP

---

33 For coverage on the debate around capital controls, see
    http://www.stern.nyu.edu/globalmacro/acad_res/int_cap_flows_controls.html.

34 See Francisco Nadal-De Simone and Piritta Sorsa, "A Review of Capital Account Restrictions in Chile in the 1990s", *Working Paper of the IMF WP/99/52*, April 1999 on *http://www.imf.org/external/pubs/ft/wp/1999/wp9952.pdf.*

35 For the views of the anti-globalisation protestors on this measure, see
    http://www.twnside.org.sg/title/ pa2.htm.

36 See "Tobin tax back on the EU's agenda", *Financial Times*, 22 September 2001.

growth. But in 1998, Malaysia's 50% decline in its currency value was
second only to that of Indonesia. Given that the government viewed
external forces as the source of the country's economic problems,
Prime Minister Mahathir imposed partial restrictions on the repa-
triation of foreign capital.[37] With the aim of making offshore ringgit
transactions illegal, he introduced a series of measures at the beginning of September 1998. Domestic banks were prohibited from lending to non-residents and stockbrokers, or from engaging in any swap
or repurchase transactions with non-residents. This was designed to
eliminate non-resident ownership of ringgit balances held abroad.
In addition, the only permissible transactions in external ringgit accounts were for the sale and purchase of ringgit assets; balances could
not be transferred between non-residents. The import and export of
ringgit notes was strictly limited though Mahathir was probably less
attempting to protect Malaysia from external speculators than prevent
Malaysians from sending their money out. As a result, it became impossible to settle ringgit contracts unless through Malaysian banks in
Malaysia. These measures, designed to insulate domestic interest rates
from external conditions, were combined with a decision to peg the exchange rate. Longer-term flows and FDI were not regulated, and the
currency continued to be fully convertible for commercial transactions
so long as they were undertaken through Malaysian banks. As the currency stabilised, these controls were progressively dismantled from
February 1999.[38] Yet the Malaysian controls were a guard against capital outflows and flight and currency depreciation rather than preventing capital inflows, which was an unintended consequence.

In Chile, a Tobin-type inflow tax was imposed in the early 1990s on
certain inflows and short-term capital in the form of a non-interest-
paying, one-year unremunerated reserve requirement up to 30% of the
inflow.[39] This was later extended to certain portfolio and some FDI
inflows. The idea behind this measure was to "offset, or at least mod-
erate, the appreciation of the currency while keeping the [domestic]
interest rate differential required for reducing the excess of desired
expenditure over output". This tax, which was relaxed along with regulation affecting capital outflows in the late 1990s, had the following
mixed results. There is some evidence that it has been successful in
increasing domestic interest rates; weaker evidence that it has altered

---

37 See, for example, Ethan Kaplan and Dani Rodrik, "Did the Malaysian Cap-
    ital Controls Work?", *NBER Working Paper 8142*, February 2001.
38 See the South Centre, "Malaysia: Rationale and Effects of Currency Controls"
    on *http://www.southcentre.org/info/southbulletin/bulletin27/bulletin27-06.htm.*
39 See *http://www.imf.org/external/pubs/ft/wp/1999/wp9952.pdf.*

the composition of capital flows in favour of longer-term movements; mixed and weak evidence that the tax has reduced the magnitude of capital inflows; and no evidence that the tax has changed the level of real exchange rates.[40] As Krugman has argued: [41]

> Chilean-type capital inflow controls may do little good, even if they succeed in limiting the amount of short-term foreign currency denominated debt. The point is that as long as free capital mobility and convertibility are maintained, the absence of such debt offers scant protection against speculative attack.

In summary, capital controls are seen to have the following advantages for developing nations:
- they can guard against a decline in (and possibly even expand) monetary authority;
- they can improve welfare and reduce the potential for economic destabilisation by external agents;
- they can assist in maintaining economic equilibrium – particularly in providing for social welfare needs;
- they can encourage longer-term capital flows.

Such controls also potentially have a downside:
- they can raise the bar of entry for foreign investors to unacceptably high limits in a competitive market. It is easy to dodge them by moving investments to countries which do not impose such restrictions;
- they can create foreign exchange shortfalls, exacerbating negative balance-of-payments situations by preventing inflows;
- they do not solve the problem that the biggest sellers of local currencies have often been local firms trying to hedge or repay debts denominated in foreign exchange, not foreign speculators;
- they do not solve the macroeconomic weaknesses which such controls are sometimes designed to deflect attention from;
- they are difficult to enforce in practice.

More important, arguably, are the lessons from the economic collapse that has given rise to this debate, rather than discussion around the efficacy of such controls. Two key lessons can be identified.[42] First is

---

40 On *http://www.imf.org/external/pubs/ft/wp/1999/wp9952.pdf*.
41 "Curfews On Capital Flight: What Are The Options?" on
   http://web.mit.edu/krugman/www/curfews.html.
42 "Keeping the hot money out", *The Economist*, January 1998.

the need to sequence reforms carefully, opening up domestic financial systems before opening up to foreign capital. Without this, political
influence and crony capitalism can lead to unproductive investment and
currency exposure. Also, liberalisation requires strict bank regulation
and prudential supervision, to prevent either a reversal in capital flows
or a sharp rise in interest rates from breaking the banks. As Shailen-
dra Anjaria observes:[43]

> The opening-up must occur in proper sequence; this is the moral
> of the Asian story. Some Asian states chose, mistakenly, to stress
> short-term borrowing by domestic banks over longer-term for-
> eign investment. The sequence of these measures, not liberalisa-
> tion itself, compounded the suffering when the crisis erupted and
> confidence vanished.

Second, exchange-rate flexibility is imperative to keeping macroeconomic balances:[44]

> Free capital movement and pegged exchange rates are a danger-
> ous mix [as] not only does a fixed rate prevent a central bank from
> using interest rates to prevent an economy from overheating (be-
> cause higher interest rates would push up the value of the curren-
> cy), but it also encourages too much foreign-currency borrow-
> ing when foreign interest rates are lower than local ones.

Overall there are two omnipresent dangers to bear in mind in this debate on capital controls. First, exchange controls on inflows and outflows are often (perhaps deliberately) confused; and, second, such
measures are frequently used for political ends, to deflect attention
away from local economic conditions. In such cases they are utilised
as less of a financial remedy than an attempt to avoid the costs of liberalisation, while simultaneously enjoying its benefits. This is not to
discount the need for a strong global institutional supervisory framework to regulate the liberalisation of financial markets, and to provide
safeguards. But the benefit and cost of such flows is more a reflection
of domestic conditions of transparency, accountability and pruden-

---

43 "The Capital Truth: What works for commodities should work for cash",
   Foreign Affairs, November/December 1998 on
   http://www.imf.org/external/np/vc/1998/111098.htm.
44 *Ibid.*

tial controls than it is of the ability of the international global financial architecture to provide this environment. It is primarily a national rather than an international challenge.

Summing up the Challenges

A key issue that developing countries will have to deal with in the future relates to their ability to cope with the changes ushered in by the global political economy. Globalisation presents three particular challenges.

- First, the changing nature of the global economy and the advances made in e-commerce dilute (and possibly finally will remove altogether) the role played by the "middleman" in business. This is a role that the Chinese have played throughout East Asia. Technology – notably IT – offers major growth advantages to developing nations. It should be recognised, though, that IT also presents social and political challenges, altering the norms that tend towards hierarchy and conformity which pertain in many developing nations, and can offer more pernicious opportunities for nepotism, for example in the licensing of telecommunications.
- Second, international governance standards and expectations are being harmonised, especially with regard to auditing, the role of the media, public accountability, banking and stockmarket regulations, and public scrutiny. This includes allowing a more active political role to local and international NGOs and businesses.
- Third, there is a role to be played by international institutions in promoting and institutionalising the standards referred to above.

After the events of September 11, there is a growing awareness that the nations of the world face shared challenges, including the absence of stable, ordered societies in large areas of the world. These territories are characterised instead by criminalised governments and weak (or non-existent) borders with little control over their territories, yet are empowered by information technology and the digital age. Poverty, refugee flows, and death from curable disease and neglect (some of these the result of state weakness) are even more prominent on the international agenda today than before.

The belief that improvements in global governance will assist in ending the cycle of underdevelopment and conflict assumes, however, that the relative absence of this governance is responsible for these conflicts in the first instance. It also presupposes the link between poverty/underdevelopment and conflict, whereas there are stable poor countries and unstable rich ones. There is a need, when considering the risk of conflict, to distinguish poverty from other causes of instability. Not all of the factors that predispose societies to conflict are susceptible to simple political or economic solutions. It is unclear how global governance can change persistent forms of social culture and leadership practices, or, for that matter, religious and ethnic differences. But it is clearer that poorer countries are more likely to suffer conflict, and that poverty can often act as a "trigger" for conflicts that in turn can serve to worsen poverty.

To state the obvious, the responses to these problems depend entirely on the situation in which states find themselves. An important point to be made with regard to the future we face is that the identification of challenges has differed enormously between developing and developed countries. Though there are also clear differences between the circumstances of developing nations, the debate for this group is largely about ending conflict; providing, even inventing, state capacity; managing change; and improving governance within their states and regions. For more stable, generally developed states – with a few exceptions, such as in Bosnia/Kosovo – it is about doing this within *regions other than their own* and in doing so, to leverage technology to develop an appropriate security response.

What more can the multilateral environment do with its current resources? Can intervention or mediation be useful in conflict which is not civil, not interstate but rather transnational in nature, particularly where there is no central authority to treat? Can conflict be ended in the absence of alternative survival strategies for people, and without creating local security networks? How can nongovernmental and first-track security-building efforts be linked? These raise in turn questions about the cycle of conflict prevention, peacekeeping and peace-building. How are these best pursued? How can a positive cycle between prosperity, investment, stable government and security be created, breaking the vicious trap of corruption, crime, Aids, war and poverty in which too many developing nations find themselves? Some of these issues are the subject of the following chapter.

Conclusion: *Towards Global Governance?*

September 11 has highlighted the relationship between governance, poverty and terrorism, and the need for state modernity including democracy and respect for human rights, in order to remove the conditions that foment radicalism. Importantly, the US-led response has emphasised the link between domestic politics and foreign relations in two ways – one is that domestic political values and actions shape foreign policy. The other is the use of military means to change domestic regimes. September 11 has linked transnational threats to the outcomes of bad domestic politics and a failure to adopt modern state and social norms.

In a speech to the Lord Mayor's Banquet in London in April 2002, British Foreign Secretary Jack Straw outlined four principles "to underpin the modern idea of global community" and a "more peaceful and prosperous" world.[45]

- First, international relations should be founded on the principle that every nation has an obligation properly to meet its global responsibilities.
- Second, the global community has the right to make judgements about countries' internal affairs, where they flout or fail to abide by global values.
- Third, given the nature of interdependence between states, the international community must make renewed efforts to resolve persistent conflicts threatening global security.
- Fourth, the global community must play a more active role in dealing with conflicts within states, which in the past have been overlooked until too late and irretrievable damage has been done.

Mr Straw's elucidation of such principles is, however, nothing new. From the 1990s until the early part of the 21st century, responses to the idea of the reform of multilateral institutions through the adoption of a "global governance" agenda have generally followed the same "formula".[46]

- The UN, including the permanent and rotating membership of the Security Council, should be reformed. An overarching UN econom-

---

45 "Principles of a Modern Global Community". Speech given by the Foreign Secretary, Jack Straw, at the Lord Mayor's Banquet, Mansion House, London, Wednesday 10 April 2002.
46 See for example the recommendations of the Commission for Global Governance on *http://www.cgg.ch/welcome2.html*; and "Time for a New Order in World Affairs", lecture given by Ingvar Carlsson at the Center for International and Comparative Studies, Northwestern University, Chicago, 23 October 1996.

ics body, sometimes proposed as an Economic Security Council, should be created.

- An International Criminal Court should be established (This has, of course, now happened, though without US participation.)
- Global aid should increase, not decrease.
- So-called "smart" partnerships between developed and developing nations should be created, facilitating technology transfer.
- The Bretton Woods institutions should be reformed or disestablished.
- The WTO and the global trading system should be reformed.
- Capital volatility should be reduced, especially in developing economies.

How might this affect Africa?

In NEPAD, Africa has called for improved systems of, and an architecture for, global governance, and fairer global trade terms, with less volatile capital access. Yet *the continent's failure and inability to manage, act on and reduce perceptions of risk* largely explains why sub-Saharan states have been able to attract on average only 4% of private global capital flows, despite the fact that, in 1999 for example, rates of return on investment in Africa were the highest worldwide. It is also the reason why the continent remains so reliant on public development assistance, which accounts for 70% of the inward capital flows, as against 10% for the developing world as a whole.

The management of both economic and political risk is to a large extent in the hands of Africans themselves, notwithstanding the sometimes negative effects of portfolio flows. Here there is a need for the harmonisation of policies, more strenuous efforts to end conflict, improve cross-country connectivity, and retain people with skills. In this regard, it is important to recognise the sometimes unheralded upsides to globalisation. For example, currency trading, which aims to exploit price differentials, is often singled out as an enemy of developing markets. But as Bundesbank President Ernst Welteke has argued, a tax on currency trades would jeopardise the role of such trading and undermine market stability.[47] As the experience of the Asian tigers and cubs illustrates, globalisation also reduces, not increases, corruption. The less corruption, the less likely is a financial crisis of the sort that afflicted Asia in 1997. But as Asia also showed in 1997, where there are

---

47 *Financial Times*, 27 September 2001.

national weaknesses, these can be greatly magnified by a flawed financial system.

It is also clear, however, that the international community will have to come to the party if Africa is to realise rates of growth sufficient to achieve political stability through economic prosperity. It is not enough for African states to achieve the current levels of between 2% and 3% growth given their poverty backlog. There is a need to reward performing and reforming states in order to provide a normative – if not institutional – global political economy in the longer term.

While there is no doubt that the role of international financial institutions and other aspects of the global architecture will continuously demand adjustment and refocus, the best way for the international community to assist the attainment of stability and prosperity in Africa – and in other developing states – in the long term has to be through improved trade access.

According to Mike Moore, then director-general of the WTO, if developed countries drop domestic agricultural subsidies, developing countries stand to earn at least three times more in exports than the amount they currently receive in international aid. Allowing developing countries to export agricultural goods to Western countries that currently subsidise their farmers is the quickest way to increase employment and reduce poverty in Africa. Moore has argued that: [48]

> If we removed those agricultural subsidies, that would return maybe three to five times more than all the overseas development assistance put together. This would return eight times more than all the debt relief . . . So the [anti-globalisation] protesters should be protesting about agricultural subsidies not just about debt relief.

Or as Belgian Prime Minister Guy Verhofstadt argued in his aforementioned letter (see Chapter One): "If all world markets were fully opened up to competition, the total income of developing countries would be boosted by US$700 billion per year or 14 times the total development aid that they currently receive."[49]

If the "Western way" – democracy, personal freedoms and liberties, the separation of party, church and state, and observance of the rule

48 "WTO Boss Urges End to Subsidies", *The Nation* (Nairobi), 8 February 2002.
49 *New Straits Times*, 27 September 2001.

of law – is adopted worldwide, this cannot be the responsibility of states alone. Better trade access, more aid, and a more tightly managed, more dependable multilateral process for handling violations of peace are all beyond the scope of developing states acting alone. The events of September 11 have shown, if nothing else, that globalisation is a two-way street. The problem is not too much globalisation, but not enough for those who most need it and its benefits – modernity, democracy, good governance and growth.

If developing countries want to avoid crises and benefit from globalisation, they have to ensure sound economic and financial policies, including a stable domestic financial architecture. This requires dependable institutions and financial systems that ensure banking and financial market supervision. The role that the international community can play to assist is in opening up trade markets and reducing subsidies, thereby encouraging market reforms and competitiveness – if this is their goal. It has been estimated that a new global trade round could lift 320 million people out of poverty, and that such a process would be five times more effective than aid.[50] As Moore has argued, "Development is trade and trade is development."[51] This, more than grandstanding on global governance, points the way forward. There is, put differently, a need for more Dohas and fewer Genoas. The success of the AGOA in Africa shows that, given the right (fair) conditions, African manufacturing industries can compete in the global market.

Africa, like the developing world elsewhere, needs more globalisation, not less.

50 Mike Moore interviewed on BBC TV, 21 March 2002.
51 *Business Day*, 12 February 2002.

CHAPTER SIX

A NEW INTERVENTIONIST DISCOURSE?
Governance, Aid, Conditionality & Sanctions

> I have eliminated the words "foreign aid" from our vocabulary. These two words don't seem to excite a lot of people.
>
> US SECRETARY OF STATE MADELINE ALBRIGHT, 1999[1]

> Developing countries receive approximately US$50 billion every year in aid. That is compared to foreign investment of almost US$200 billion in annual earnings from exports of US$2.4 trillion. So, to be serious about fighting poverty, we must be serious about expanding trade.
>
> US PRESIDENT GEORGE W BUSH, *Monterrey, Mexico,* 22 March 2002

Aid: *Poison or Saviour?*

Robert Mugabe's apparently fraudulent victory in the March 2002 Zimbabwean presidential election coincided with the staging of the UN conference on development finance held in Monterrey the same month. Both raised concerns about the role to be played by external agents in promoting political and economic reforms, and of the relationship between aid and governance. There was a fear in the case of Mugabe's Zimbabwe that additional humanitarian assistance could both be utilised by the regime to secure its grip on power, and portrayed and interpreted by it as a "reward" for its political (mis)behaviour. The Monterrey conference again highlighted the differences between increased aid volumes, improved aid effectiveness, and the different developmental impacts of increased trade access and aid flows.

★ ★ ★

The World Bank, the UN and 189 countries committed themselves at the UN's 2000 Millennium Assembly to cutting poverty in half, reducing child mortality by two thirds and ensuring universal primary education by 2015. It is argued that these goals are not only morally

---

1 See *Time,* 11 October 1999.

correct, but also essential if the growing divides between peoples are not to become security threats to richer nations. For this reason, both Kofi Annan and James Wolfensohn have urged the doubling of international aid (to US$100 billion annually).

But does aid work? Although the World Bank claims that the success rate of its projects has increased from 60% in the late 1980s to 80% by 2002, much of this analysis is conducted by the Bank's own Operations Evaluation Department. As Adam Lerrick has put it: "[W]hen the auditors are captive, when the timing of the judgement is premature, when the criteria are faulty and then the numbers are selectively chosen – how credible are the conclusions?"[2] The reliability, transparency and objectivity of the evaluation of other aid programmes such as those of the European Union have also been questioned.[3]

Current research examined here suggests that aid works – or at least works better – when good, reasonable policies are in place. But which comes first – aid or good policies? And how can the latter be achieved? What is the synergy between making aid more effective, and improving national governance?

The *paradox of aid* remains that those countries in greatest need of assistance are, by definition, unable to use it in the manner intended. And states unwilling – or unable – to adhere to conditions on aid distribution opt instead for taking out loans, which pile up as debt when invested in sectors of the economy that do not generate revenue, or not invested at all.[4]

Strategic political considerations have often outweighed the need to ensure that the countries assisted have sound policies and institutions that are able to make full use of the aid given. Much of the aid given during the Cold War was used to bankroll regimes considered to be allies of the US or Soviet causes. While it is true that much assistance given to Africa's dysfunctional states has been stolen or wasted, most of what has been stolen was taken by regimes that the international community knew in advance could and would steal it.

There is, moreover, a perverse logic to the argument that if conditions were right, no humanitarian assistance (or development aid

---

2 "Audit the World Bank", *Financial Times*, 6 March 2002.
3 See "Rattling Europe's skeletons", *The Economist*, 16 March 2002.
4 This has, in part, motivated the Bush administration's call for more grants and fewer loans. See, for example, Cameron Hume, "Grants instead of loans are way to development", *Business Day*, 19 March 2002.

for that matter) would be needed; therefore it is given only where it cannot work. Much of the time, such assistance appears to have been used to buy influence or give business to nongovernmental organisations (NGOs) or multilateral agencies, ignoring the problems of ordinary people, which are barely understood by the international community. This is also a product of an environment where humanitarian relief is mobilised by the shock "CNN factor" rather than by any policy of providing more effective preventative action. It is difficult for the West to idly watch when scenes of desperation flood the television screens of their local constituents, and especially difficult when it is blackmailed into intervening by African governments who cry racism and global hypocrisy if little or no assistance is forthcoming.

Three ongoing African debates – NEPAD's commitment to governance; the means available to resolve present and prevent future conflicts; and the role of the World Bank and the IMF (along with other multilateral and bilateral donors) in economic stabilisation and development initiatives – have one critical feature in common. That is the relationship between external and internal actors and the means whereby they can encourage, cajole, persuade and, if necessary, force states to adhere to core conditions of good governance, democracy and respect for human rights. At a more primitive level, this also means fostering a willingness to engage in political negotiations.

Discourse on the use of sanctions and conditionalities has become commonplace in international relations, as other measures of encouragement or alternatively limited diplomatic coercion have failed to persuade states to adhere to the rule of law, observe human rights and honour previous agreements. Sanctions have also emerged, mostly through multilateral agencies, as leverage in the imposition of political and economic conditionalities. In particular, they are used as a means to pressurise and isolate states until they undertake political reform. In the current discourse, economic and political interventions made in search of state security and capacity, are labelled as means to achieve a goal of "structural stability". As the EU document on conflict prevention argues in this respect:[5]

> Given the fact that (i) experience shows that lack of development is not the only major source of violent conflict; that (ii) the EU

5 See Communication from the Commission to the Council, "The EU and the issue of conflicts in Africa: peace-building, conflict prevention and beyond". Brussels, 6 March 1996, SEC(96) 332.

policy aims concerning Africa might be summarised as *helping* to *foster peace and stability, development, democracy and the respect of human rights;* that (iii) those aims are interdependent/mutually reenforcing; and that (iv) sustained development is often interpreted in a narrow economic sense, the ultimate policy goal could be summarised under the term structural stability.

Structural stability could thus be defined as a situation involving sustainable economic development, democracy and respect for human rights, viable political structures, and healthy social and environmental conditions, with the capacity to manage change without having to resort to violent conflict. Working towards structural stability would mean the targeted reinforcement of those factors that enable peaceful change.

Clearly, different situations – ranging from situations of tension, to open conflict, to a post-conflict environment – will require different approaches and solutions, including: support for training and political dialogue; the use of peace-building instruments, sanctions, peace enforcement measures and humanitarian aid; support for confidence-building initiatives, and so on. To understand the efficacy of economic provisos and sanctions in this context, one has to consider, first, the reasons for the apparent failure of past attempts to reform African economies and, second, the impact of similar programmes elsewhere, such as in Asia.

★ ★ ★

Reforming the Recalcitrant? *The African Context*

As has been described in previous chapters, Africa's share of the global economy has declined, in spite of massive aid transfers and numerous attempts at reform. Although Africa's percentage of world development assistance rose from 17% in 1970 to just under 40% twenty years later, its percentage of global trade has reduced from around 5% by the end of colonisation to less than 2% today; and its share of global GDP is now under 1%, even though African countries remain highly trade dependent.[6] The continent has also not been a beneficiary of

---

6 The share of GDP/trade in Africa was 15.8% and 18.9% in 1986 and 1996 respectively. For Latin America this was 7.9% and 17.3% and East Asia 9.1% and 13.1%. See World Bank, *African Development Indicators*, 1998. CD Rom version.

foreign capital inflows – at least on the scale of Asia and Latin America – and has instead suffered the downside of this aspect of globalisation, capital flight. Of the global FDI total of US$800 billion of which developing countries received 25%, just US$10 billion flowed to the continent in 1999.

Two stages of reform attempts of African economies, in which a remedy to post-colonial collapse was sought, can be identified. The first was to arrest the slide that began precipitously after the 1973 oil shock. The decline was especially pronounced when measured against the performance of other developing regions, and took the form of an increasing dependence on external actors, notably the IMF and the World Bank. These assisted in terms of financing and policies. This saw continental debt increase from US$15 billion in 1974 to more than US$150 billion in 1992, and US$250 billion by the end of the decade. The extent of international financial institution borrowing as a percentage of debt stock increased from 19% of the total in 1980 to 28% in 1992 and 32% in 1998.[7] Much of this was bilateral or multilateral in origin rather than privately held (as was the case in Asia and Latin America), though the total of African private debt was estimated to amount to US$100 billion at the end of 1990.[8] As a result, as Thomas Callaghy points out, the number of African countries indebted to the IMF rose from two in 1978 to 28 in 1990, or 41% of all IMF agreements by 1999.

However, in spite of the leverage granted to the Bretton Woods institutions as a result, many African countries resisted the thoroughgoing implementation of structural adjustment programmes, given their political cost. Most went through only the motions of reform, which in any case were subject to external (Cold War) and internal political whims on the part of the donors.

Second, the period from the early 1990s onwards illustrated the divisions in the relationship between the Bretton Woods institutions and the African countries dependent on their aid. These were exacerbated by Africa's ongoing difficulties in attracting foreign investment and the often half-hearted efforts of governments to initiate the necessary reforms. The Bank and the Fund also acknowledged failures in their formulation and management of programmes whose implemen-

---

7 Callaghy, *op cit*, p.48.
8 See the paper by Percy Mistry on debt on
   http://www.fondad.org/publications/afridebt1_preface.htm.

tation often proved politically untenable. This led to a reassessment of the economic reforms proposed, the nature of their micro-management, and of the necessity of democratic political reforms under the notion of "good governance". In the economic domain, the result of the change has included the Heavily Indebted Poor Country (HIPC) initiative, in the terms of which 41 designated countries (33 of which were in sub-Saharan Africa) qualified for debt relief conditional on the acceptance of poverty relief strategies. This initiative has been built on the regular Paris Club debt re-scheduling.

According to HIPC reduction initiatives, the debt burden should be reduced in countries that have a record over several years of solid economic policy and a carefully planned poverty reduction strategy that shows how debt relief can assist in the fight against poverty. Under HIPC strategies launched at the behest of the G7 in 1999, debt relief to these countries could be worth as much as US$30 billion. Some NGOs continue, however, to lobby for faster and greater relief.

While there is clear evidence that debt relief does assist in poverty-alleviation especially in the provision of primary education and health care, the longer-term benefits are less clear.[9] Additionally, debt relief might result in less aid coming from individual donors for countries massively dependent on external largesse. Second, if the relief comes in the form of loans, then the HIPCs[10] risk returning to unsustainable levels of debt. Third, there is also the danger that the process is motivated less by the existence of good governance structures and better policies in the recipient states than by political pressure on the donors. Finally, related to the last point, the pace of debt relief might not be accompanied by a similar acceleration in the development of governance structures both to ensure the same situation is not reached again and that poverty alleviation is a sustained rather than a once-off process. Put crudely, as with aid, debt relief may indeed devolve responsibility away from government towards external actors, slimming the link between the ruling elites and their constituents.

---

9 See "Can debt relief make a difference?", *Business Times*, 19 November 2000.
10 This section draws on a number of sources, including the Africa Debt Background paper on *http://www.africaaction.org/docs99/dbt9903b.htm*.

Has External Intervention Helped?

According to the World Bank, aid has helped in Africa when the policy environment has been "good" or receptive. A recent Bank report, *Aid and Reform in Africa: Lessons from Ten Case Studies*,[11] found that the quantity of aid that countries received has "no effect on the quality of their macroeconomic policies".[12] A number of reasons are suggested, including the political context, especially the health of the democratic system (or not), and the length of the tenure of the incumbent government. Growth rates reflect the success (or not) of reforms. Many of the better reformers were those countries that had few options and were mired in crisis – had their "backs against the wall". In those judged to be mixed reformers, backsliding occurred as reforms became tougher and (politically) more intrusive (and expensive). Examples are those in Tanzania during the 1980s, which involved civil service reform, privatisation and budget management. Losers in reform, the report acknowledged, tend to "block" both the process and the policy changes required.

David Dollar, in an earlier World Bank study assessing the efficacy of aid,[13] highlights the link – also suggested by NEPAD – between aid flows and governance. Dollar focused his study on a number of countries ranging from Botswana to El Salvador, Ghana, Vietnam and Zambia. He concluded with six observations.

- Financial aid works in a good policy environment.
- Improvements in economic institutions and policies in the developing world are key to a quantum leap in poverty reduction.
- Effective aid can complement private investment.
- Development projects should aim to strengthen institutions and policies to ensure delivery of services.
- An active civil society can improve public services.
- Aid can nurture reform, but it requires patience and a focus on ideas, not money.

---

11 On *http://www.worldbank.org/research/aid/africa/release/aid.htm*.
12 Policy was seen in terms of a range of areas: macroeconomic policies (including fiscal, monetary and exchange rate policies), structural policy (such as tax and trade), public sector management (including the rule of law, judiciary and social services), and social inclusion/participation.
13 David Dollar, *Assessing Aid: What Works, What Doesn't, and Why*. Washington DC: World Bank, 1998.

In stressing the somewhat pointless developmental purpose of aid not connected with governance conditions, it is important to understand in empirical terms the comparative position of Africa with respect to both aid and governance. Africa is already receiving a higher percentage of aid relative to GDP than did Europe between 1949 and 1952. By 1996, as noted in Chapter One, African countries (excluding South Africa and Nigeria) received on average more than 12% of GDP in aid. In Mozambique, for example, in 1997 the GNP-aid ratio was 43%; in São Tomé and Principe 117%; in Guinea-Bissau 71%; and in Rwanda 49%. By comparison, total flows to Europe under the Marshall Plan never exceeded 2.5% of Europe's GDP.[14]

This problem is recognised by the international community through the declining flow of aid as a percentage of GNP, down from 0.34% in 1990 to 0.24% in 1999. While FDI flows have increased globally to more than US$860 billion by 1999, around 15 times the level in real terms of that in the 1970s, aid transfers have declined. This reflects both a change in attitude towards aid as a means of upliftment and, arguably, a weakening in post-colonial ties. Although the figure of US$51.5 billion in Official Development Assistance (ODA) from the 29 donor countries given in 1998 was up 9% on that of the previous year, this was still down from the highest level of US$60.8 billion given in 1992.[15] Donor fatigue has played its part in this shift, though to a degree this has been offset by the events of September 11 and the fear that increasing poverty will provide an even more fertile breeding ground for terrorism than already exists. Hence the Bush administration's 2002 pledge to increase foreign aid by 50% by 2006. Yet this is no panacea for development problems. It is estimated that rich nations have already given more than US$1 trillion in aid to poor ones over the past 50 years.

---

15 World Bank's Global Development Finance Report, cited in *Business Day*.

Select Global Aid Flows, 1999[16]

Country	Total US$m (% of GNP)
Japan	15,323 (0.35)
United States	9,145 (0.10)
France	5,637 (0.39)
Germany	5,515 (0.26)
United Kingdom	3,401 (0.23)
Netherlands	3,124 (0.79)
Italy	1,806 (0.15)
Denmark	1,733 (1.01)
Canada	1,699 (0.28)
Sweden	1,630 (0.70)
Norway	1,370 (0.91)
Spain	1,363 (0.23)
TOTAL	56,378 (0.24)

One study has found that, in 1990, US$1 billion in aid lifted 105,000 people above the absolute poverty line of US$1 per day. By 1997, the same amount of money had helped another 284,000 people out of poverty. Put differently, when measured in terms of delivering people from absolute poverty, in 1990, US$9,523 (or US$3,521 in 1997) was spent in order to lift each beneficiary by US$365 per year. As Ross Herbert has argued, "Given that success rate, would it not be more efficient and effective just to fly planes over Africa and push money out of the doors?"[17]

Aid is seen to have failed not only in empirical terms, but also in terms of its distortion of the relationship between government and those governed. For example, aid flows remove those with entrepreneurial skills from the productive and into the aid "sectors" of the economy, where the opportunities are greater (and payment is in hard currency). Aid is also accused of serving as a cushion, enabling Africa to postpone, hijack or avoid altogether reforms that market forces

16 UNDP, *Human Development Report*, 2001. New York: OUP/UNDP, 2001.
17 "The New Partnership for Africa's Development: Origins, Challenges and the Road Ahead", Unpublished Research Paper for the Canadian International Development Agency, 2002.

should have forced it to undertake years before. In this way, aid is seen to work as a powerful disincentive to reform. Although the relationship between donors and recipient nations tends to be a turbulent on-off, love-hate affair, with continuous loan condition reassessments and goal renegotiation, the incentives of the donors to give or lend money would appear ultimately to outweigh any failure to meet the original terms set.

Thus many view aid as a humanitarian "band-aid" – a means of salving Western consciences by appearing to deal with poverty issues, but from a safe distance. But can aid solve *development* problems? Does it provide an avenue and vehicle for prosperity?

According to the IMF, independent studies show that Structural Adjustment Programmes (SAPs) supported by the Enhanced Structural Adjustment Fund (ESAF – now replaced by the Poverty Reduction and Growth Facility – PRGF) have led to a marked turnaround in growth in recipient countries. Statistics indicate that in the late 1990s, per capita income growth in these countries, at 2.5% annually, was twice as high as in other developing countries.[18] Programmes supported by the IMF's concessional lending, the Fund argues, have had the effect of raising output and reducing inflation.

The Overseas Development Institute (ODI), a proponent of an increase in aid, has offered the following reasons for using aid as a developmental tool, to counter four commonly cited arguments to the contrary.[19]

• Aid is not wasted money, as "most recent evidence shows that, in general, aid makes a positive contribution to economic performance".

• Even though finance for investment is more productive in "countries with good economic policies", aid can still "make a positive contribution even where policies are weak".

• Aid conditionality can work in "supporting and encouraging reforms", even though it is "an insufficient lever to force recalcitrant governments to implement reform".

• Aid does not necessarily support bad governments, particularly as it is "now common for donors to suspend aid if government behaviour is unacceptable".

---

18 On *http://www.imf.org/external/np/exr/ib/2000/041200b.htm#II*.
19 Oliver Morrissey, "Aid Effectiveness for Growth and Development" on *http://www.odi.org.uk/opinions/2_aid_effectiveness.html*.

Bearing in mind the point that the aid relationship is two-way, between donor and recipient nation, the ODI briefing argues that:

> It is fair to say that aid has not achieved as much as might have been hoped by donors. Many countries are, in real terms, poorer now than they were in the 1960s. It is a moot point whether they would be any better off had they not received aid, but evidently aid has not benefited them much. Aid has often been misused and abused.

The reason most commonly given for a failure of African states to meet aid conditions is to blame the conditions themselves. Critics of SAPs have argued, first, that like other developing economies, the African states concerned are being made to pay for problems which are not of their making, and which are a result of both colonial policies and dependencies, and the decline in the value of commodities. Second, they claim that SAPs are neo-liberal programmes which weaken the ability of states to intervene in, and to manage, their own affairs, and which allow foreign companies to repatriate capital and to acquire assets at bargain prices through privatisation and deregulation. Third, they point out that the SAP requirements (public spending cuts, financial probity in the balancing of budgets, and the increase in interest rates to keep inflation down and revitalise the credit system) have a deleterious effect on women and the poor in particular, given their dependence on public institutions. Fourth, they hold that the tenet of convertibility, which in practice requires devaluation, leads to heavy increases in capital goods costs, with a negative effect on domestic industrialisation. Fifth, they maintain that SAPs are designed to make it possible for countries to repay debt by taking away finances from public spending, which amounts to a tax on the poor imposed by the international banking system. Finally, they contend that SAPs have failed because things have been getting worse and not better.

The response to these criticisms is that there are severe limitations on the capability of international financial institutions; that without SAPs, poverty would have got significantly worse in Africa; and that where there are problems with the programmes, they have usually occurred because the SAPs have not been implemented properly. It is not that they have been implemented and have failed.

But a few home truths concerning the economic performance of African states and the reasons for having SAPs in the first instance should be repeated.

First, as is often argued, the contemporary weakness of African economies can be traced back to the 1973 oil crisis, which imposed unacceptably high costs, particularly on African states which were dependent on imported energy. But it is also abundantly clear that those African countries that might have benefited from the oil price increase (such as Nigeria) were unable to take advantage of the opportunity. Second, governments go to the IMF and the World Bank because they have to, and they are in a pretty bad shape when they do. Third, much of the criticism of SAPs comes from African elites, who have gained much from overvalued exchange rates (which subsidise consumer imports while penalising exports and handicapping the promotion of local industry). Indeed, an overvalued exchange rate is far more destructive to local industrial development than is tariff dismantlement. Fourth, in the case of those states in Africa which have failed or are failing, there are few alternatives to SAPs and the discipline entailed, which includes clamping down on corruption in the interests of stabilisation.

Here the Asian crisis had a number of implications for Africa. In general, it cast doubt on emerging markets, even though the contagion effect of Asia's financial collapse was limited due to the continent's relative lack of global financial integration (although this did not apply to South Africa). More dramatic for African countries was the cost of a global downturn in the trade of commodities and their pricing, falling by more than 10% in the aftermath of the crisis. But, most important, it gave notice of a tightening of governmental and financial conditions on aid, loans and investment to the continent. This was due to pressure on international lending institutions to provide for an Asian bailout, but also, critically, because the evidence of financial impropriety in Asia had globalised issues of governance. A diversion of aid flows to Asia meant a reduction in aid to other destinations. More pressure was placed on those African countries which maintained continuous (aid-supported) fiscal and balance-of-payments deficits. This provided the donor community with leverage to force adherence to what Van der Walle describes as "the logic of international markets".[20] Put simply, Asia reminded the world that economic conditionality is a global fact of life, whether it is imposed by donors or investors.[21]

---

20 *Ibid*, p.281.
21 See Callaghy, *op cit*, p.52.

To reiterate, the problem with aid is not that donors have not given generously enough (which might be true), but that aid offers a perverse disincentive for countries to reform and make the long-term adjustments necessary for successful economic transitions. Understanding the reasons why African states avoid making these decisions is more complex. It relates both to the knowledge that there are donors willing to bankroll their failures and to the fragile political condition that African states and leaders find themselves in.

In summary, in the external domain, the nature and scale of foreign financial assistance is deemed by some to have considerable bearing on state performance, collapse and survival. But here it is important to make three observations that may possibly run contrary to conventional wisdom.

First, there is a debate concerning the link between aid and economic growth. As was noted above, as a share of GDP, levels of African aid are on average five times higher than expenditure on European states under the Marshall Plan. This raises important questions about the inter-relationship between the effectiveness of aid with state capacity, development and governance. At best, the picture is mixed. According to Dollar:

> Foreign aid has also transformed entire sectors. . . . Hundreds of millions of people have had their lives touched, if not transformed, by access to schools, clean water, sanitation, electric power, health clinics, roads and irrigation – all financed by foreign aid. On the flip side, foreign aid has also been, at times, an unmitigated disaster.

Second, SAPs have not weakened state capacity in Africa, nor worsened its prospects for growth. In fact the opposite may be true. There was no massive state retrenchment in many African bureaucracies. Nor does conditionality and structural adjustment appear to have been bad for those African states which followed its precepts closely, such as Ghana and Uganda, at least comparing their "before" and "after" situations. And even though civil service salaries comprise a relatively high percentage of overall government expenditures, state personnel in Africa represent a much lower percentage of the population than they do in OECD states (2% versus 7.7%).[22] This is arguably due more

---

22 *Ibid.*

to under-investment and high degrees of bureaucratic politicisation than to foreign policy interventions.

Third, while donor policies have not necessarily brought about the growth rates required (or in some cases, any growth at all), and may have undermined leadership through limiting patronage and rent-seeking opportunities, bad internal policies, weak state capacity and tenuous institutional and state formations provide unstable foundations on which to construct a more orderly dispensation.

Whatever the debates, aid, or more generally "external intervention", has not achieved a widespread positive impact, either in terms of creating sustainable peace or in delivering economic growth.

External Intervention, Democracy and Conflict Resolution

The creation of a sustainable peace remains a critical stumbling block. As Michel Camdessus put it in January 2000,[23] "The armed conflicts directly or indirectly affecting a full third of the sub-Saharan countries are today the greatest obstacle to development." This is not to blame the UN and other bodies for a failure to mount military operations to enforce a peace agreement, but rather it is to point out their default in not intervening proactively to bring about the conditions for political negotiations to occur and, in the longer term, for post-conflict peace-building. The latter was partly the focus of the Report of the Panel on UN Peace Operations[24] (Brahimi Report) published in 2000. As Sir Jeremy Greenstock, the UK Permanent Representative to the UN, has noted with respect to the challenges facing peace operations:[25]

> [T]he politics of conflict management is the main stumbling block. Political problems can only be resolved through a partnership between the willing and the able. The new sense of initiative and renewal in Africa, including the wish to develop such a partnership, is a hopeful example of this. In this respect above all, the roles of the regions are vital.

Here South Africa's democratic transition and its experience in African conflict mediation illustrates that successful resolution of inter-

---

23 On *http://www.imf.org/external/np/vc/2000/011700.htm.*
24 For the full report, go to
   http://www.un.org/peace/reports/peace_operations/report.htm.
25 On *http://www.ipacademy.org/Publications/Reports.*

communal problems rests on the need for communities to recognise the rewards of co-operating – and, conversely, the costs of not doing so.

From South African and other experiences *ten ingredients for successful mediation* can be identified. First, there has to be a real basis for an internal settlement. The parties should want peace rather than war, and be prepared to compromise rather than continue the conflict. Thus peace settlements should not be viewed as a *zero-sum* game. A way has to be found by which the major conflicting parties can both achieve essential elements of what they want. If the settlement merely puts off the day of reckoning (as it did in Angola), then mediation efforts are not going to progress far; nor will any agreement stick for a prolonged period. In South Africa, it could be argued that while the African National Congress (ANC) wanted to be in government, it recognised, too, that it required the co-operation of the white governmental and business establishment if it was going to make a success of things. At the same time, that white establishment wanted to preserve its position in South Africa, but needed the involvement and support of the ANC government in order to prosper and achieve this goal. Solutions emerging in this way are more likely to bring about a relatively peaceful transition, in which a critical mass of the skills necessary for economic transition are retained (as in South Africa) rather than scared off (as in Mozambique and Angola).

Thus there is an important link between the population and the negotiators. Civil society can play a significant role in creating this middle ground, providing the wider context – or normative values – in which leadership can be nudged towards compromise, as well as assisting in the development of democratic practices and institutions. This factor in turn affects the relationship between foreign funding and the development of civil society.

Second, there has to be a reasonably united international community in which different outside parties can bring pressure to bear on the rival domestic parties in favour of settlement. As Thomas Ohlson has argued, it is power-related factors such as military, diplomatic and economic pressures that tend to bring about peace settlements.[26] Apart from South Africa itself, the only post-Cold War case in which a negotiated solution to a Southern African conflict situation has thus far

26 See Thomas Ohlson, *Power Politics and Peace Policies.* Sweden: Uppsala University, 1998. See also Chester Crocker, "The Varieties of Intervention" in Chester Crocker and Fen Osler Hampson with Pamela Aall (eds.), *Managing Global Chaos.* Washington DC: US Institute of Peace, 1996, pp.183-197.

worked successfully, is Mozambique. There, as in the transfer from Rhodesia to Zimbabwe in 1979, the amount of leverage that the external mediators could exert on the domestic combatants was critical. The same could be said of the Namibian side in the Angolan-Namibian accords in 1988 which held fast, even if the Angolan part of that deal did not. By contrast, in the turbulent transition from the rule of Mobutu in the former Zaire in 1997 to that of Laurent Kabila (another unsuccessful attempt), Washington and Paris had their own (sometimes competing) agendas. It is clear, too, that Southern African leaders were also not in agreement over what to do in Zaire, often for reasons of personality and jealousies rather than policy substance.

Third, there is a need for prescient leadership and timing. Nelson Mandela and FW de Klerk played crucial roles in South Africa's transition, in recognising the need for compromise and being prepared to seize the moment.

Fourth, the external community has to offer the necessary resources, particularly in the peacekeeping and post-conflict peace-building phases. A critical factor in this external engagement is the requirement that the parties should be given the tools to do the job properly. For example, the 350 UN military peacekeepers in Angola were not sufficient for UNAVEM II's mandate between May 1991 and February 1995 – leading Margaret Anstee to comment, "I have been given a 747 to fly with only enough fuel for a DC-3." This was in joking reference to the UN Security Council Resolution 747, which formed the mandate for UNAVEM II.[27] Nor were 4,220 military personnel for UNAVEM III (1995-97) enough. But 8,000 UN forces for UNTAG (including 4,500 military observers) were sufficient to do the job necessary in Namibia from April 1989 to March 1990, as were some 10,000 personnel for ONUMOZ (with 6,625 troops) in Mozambique between December 1992 and 1994.[28] This reluctance to commit sufficient resources is a result of the end of the strategic imperatives that drove Cold War engagement; pressing domestic political and regional economic integration initiatives; doubts about the efficacy of UN peacekeeping; and a weariness of Africa's seemingly insoluble problems. All have contributed in compounding fashion to an increasing unwillingness in the West to offer forces to such African missions.

---

27 Cited in Judith Matloff, *Fragments of a Forgotten War*. Penguin: London, 1997, p.75. See also Dennis Jett, *Why Peacekeeping Fails*. St Martin's Press: New York, 2000.

28 See *http://www.un.org/Depts/dpko/dpko/ops.htm*.

While the provision of external facilitators or mediators may be important, this should not obscure the importance of developing local talent. There is a need, in this regard, to distinguish between the use of prominent personalities as *patrons* of a peace process and the use of *facilitators* to actually do the job. There is a danger also of expecting external agencies to take up the job of government, whether by design (as in Sierra Leone) or by default (as in Angola) through a reliance on humanitarian assistance.

Fifth, there is a need to lay the foundations to enable the peace agreements to hold, for instance in knowing one's negotiating opponent well enough to inculcate a sufficient degree of trust. In South Africa's example, the period between 1985 and 1990, when feelers were sent out between the ANC and Pretoria, was crucial in building the personal relationships and understanding necessary to make the move to the negotiating table possible.

Sixth, proper analysis is necessary to understand the causes of conflict and the possible means of resolution.

Seventh, trust-building and the need for dialogue never end.

Eighth, there is a need to follow the broad principle of inclusivity rather than exclusivity in devising democratic solutions. There is, however, a need to make a clear distinction between the use of a government of national unity (GNU) as a means to a political end, and its use as an end in itself, because the latter might be taken to legitimate fraudulent elections and outcomes rather than as a conduit for reconciliation.

Ninth, political programmes have to be accompanied by explicit plans and processes in government, including specifically the reorganisation of the armed forces through demobilisation and integration.

Tenth, elections should be seen as the conclusion rather than the start of a process of democratisation. There is a need for a deepening of the "culture" of democracy that goes beyond the creation of formal democracies through elections. Until this forms part of the essence of African polities, the potential for political reversal remains, as does the danger of programmes such as NEPAD faltering. This can happen when elite and local political interests are threatened by the implementation and operation of international norms, standards and, indeed, conditionalities. The setting and monitoring of such governance standards and establishment of such a culture has to be a bottom-up, civil society-oriented process, rather than one that is only leadership-driven.

These ten points outline the role to be played by external powers in exerting pressure on developing countries to change. The section that follows discusses the use of interventionist tools – including sanctions – as a means of doing so.

Sanctions as a Compliance Tool

In addition to arguments about the efficacy of aid and the application of attached governance conditions, questions can also be raised about the role played by external organisations in implementing so-called "political" conditionalities – at one extreme, "facilitating" political settlements through pressure and intervention, and, at the other, ensuring adherence to basic democratic principles, including respect for both human rights and the rule of law.

In February 2002, the European Union contemplated the imposition of sanctions against Robert Mugabe's regime in Harare, on account of the expulsion of the head of its election observing team. This event and the allegations of poll rigging by Mugabe raised, once more, a debate as to the utility of sanctions as a means of ensuring good governance.

Considerable data and literature are available on the course and possible types of sanctions. The material includes reports of the so-called "Interlaken process" which since 1997 has examined the range and impact of targeted sanctions, including the freezing of assets, the blocking of financial transactions, and travel bans.[29] Such occurrences have increased in the 1990s with the imposition of new sanctions, such as those against Liberia and UNITA in Angola.[30] Sanctions were used only twice during the Cold War, against Rhodesia (1968) and South Africa (1977). Since the end of the Cold War, no fewer than 15 sanctions regimes were adopted by the Security Council between 1990 and 2000: against Iraq (1990), the former Yugoslavia (1991), the Federal Republic of Yugoslavia (1992), Libya (1992), Somalia (1992), Haiti

---

29 See, for example, *www.smartsanctions.ch* which details the Swiss-led debate around smart or targeted sanctions. This section draws in part on research conducted at SAIIA with the support of a British Council grant in 2002.

30 See, for example, the Human Rights Watch report of April 2000 on *http://www.hrw.org/press/2000/04/brif-angola.htm*; also *http://www.globalpolicy.org/security/sanction/indexang.htm*; and the full text of the March 2000 "Fowler" UN report on *http://www.globalpolicy.org/security/sanction/angola/report.htm*. For details on the UN's monitoring mechanism, see *http://www.un.org/Depts/dpa/docs/monitoringmechanism.htm*.

(1993), UNITA (1993), Rwanda (1994), Liberia (1994), the Bosnian Serbs (1994), Sudan (1996), Sierra Leone (1997), the Federal Republic of Yugoslavia (1998), the Taliban (1999), and Eritrea and Ethiopia (2000). The sanctions against Haiti were lifted in 1994 and against the FRY in 1996. A new arms embargo against the FRY was imposed in 1998. Air sanctions against Sudan were never enforced. The sanctions against Libya were suspended in April 2000, but had not been formally lifted by 2002. The arms embargo against Eritrea and Ethiopia ended in May 2001, and sanctions were lifted against the FRY and Sudan in September 2001. However, sanctions against UNITA, Liberia and the Taliban were gradually stepped up by the Security Council.[31]

Sanctions have been used as both an important signal from the international community and as a tool for ensuring compliance with international norms. They are recognised, too, as a critical element in forcing negotiated political change, notably in the case of South Africa and Rhodesia, and in ensuring adherence to agreements struck, such as in the case of Angola.

But there are also cases where sanctions have been less than successful, as in Iraq, and in dealing with military regimes in Africa, Latin America and Asia. There are a number of difficulties in applying sanctions that should be acknowledged.

- There is a need to limit the damage done to populations by sanctions and instead target regimes.
- To a great extent, political regimes which come under the threat of sanctions often have already self-imposed financial and travel restrictions.
- Most intergovernmental initiatives, with the notable exception of a physical (oil, travel and electricity) blockade, take time to bite.
- Any immediate impact of sanctions would, to a degree, be offset by the flow of humanitarian aid.
- The uneven application of measures by different states can undermine their efficacy to some extent. Sanctions have to be carefully sequenced, and have to involve a number of key states along with multilateral institutions.
- Public and private sanctions – the two broad types identifiable – involve different types of action. The public, intergovernmental category includes "smart" personal sanctions, financial actions, and

---

31 For details, see   *http://www.un.int/france/frame_anglais/france_and_un/ sanctions_regime/sanctions.htm.*

physical sanctions. Private sanctions include financial and material actions.

• There is a need for identification of, support for and close co-ordination with internal, civil society elements alongside the imposition of measures against the regime targeted.

It is accepted that for sanctions to be effective, they should be:[32]

• closely monitored, limited in duration and regularly assessed;
• clearly targeted to avoid collateral impact on civilians;
• imposed with clear political objectives in mind, and accompanied by detailed criteria for their lifting; and
• an exceptional measure, being imposed under Chapter VII (in response to a threat to the peace, a breach of peace or an act of aggression so determined by the Security Council).

A background paper from the December 2000 UN working group on sanctions[33] concluded that: "Smart sanctions offer the possibility of concentrating coercive pressure on decision-making elites, while minimising humanitarian and third party damage. . . . The challenge is now to identify the means to effectively implement and strengthen [their] focus." These means could include closer monitoring by member-states, better co-ordination between the UN, other multilateral bodies and member-states, and the deployment of international observers.

Sanctions have emerged in the post-Cold War context as a more regularly used and increasingly targeted tool against both state and non-state entities. Not only is their application more attractive as a shared action by external actors, but they can be used beyond the restoration of peace and security to compel governments to "repel aggression, restore democracy and human rights, and pressure non-compliant regimes".[34] Along with the use of military intervention and criminal prosecutions, sanctions are increasingly important in the context of NEPAD and the development of the African Union (AU) as the successor to the Organisation of African Unity (OAU). Although NEPAD is to rely on voluntary "peer review" as a basis for adher-

---

32 *Ibid.*
33 See *http://www.un.org/sc/committees/sanctions/initiatives.htm*; and the latest report on smart sanctions on
  http://www.un.org/sc/committees/sanctions/background.pdf.
34 *Ibid.*

ence to good governance norms, its success hinges on the creation of conditions of peace and security. And the need for a new, more interventionist approach is apparent in the AU's Constitutive Act, its apparent intolerance of unconstitutional changes of African government and its call for the creation of an African stand-by military force. Article 4(h) of the Constitutive Act of the AU provides for "the right to intervene in a Member State pursuant to a decision of the Assembly in respect of grave circumstances, namely: war crimes, genocide and crimes against humanity". Article 4(j) provides for "the right of Member States to request intervention from the Union in order to restore peace and security". And Article 23(2) provides that "any Member State that fails to comply with the decisions and policies of the Union may be subjected to other sanctions, such as the denial of transport and communications links with other Member States, and other measures of a political and economic nature to be determined by the Assembly".[35] Indeed, Thabo Mbeki has noted that the political and economic integration of Africa would raise the question of the sovereignty of states: "[B]ecause we share a common destiny and need all of us to succeed . . . national sovereignty should be impacted on by the things that we do . . . [and] . . . in the process of implementing the integration of the African continent that this matter of boundaries will arise."[36] Sovereignty no longer affords protection to abusive governments and leadership. Instead the debate has shifted to the means to ensure compliance with international norms and the protection of citizens in the face of excessive leadership.

A Formula for External Intervention and Partnership?

The World Bank has called for a doubling of international aid from the current level of US$57 billion a year (in 2002), in order to meet the development goals under the United Nations' Millennium Development Goals. These are estimated as likely to cost US$40-60 billion in additional aid annually for the next 15 years. These goals are directed towards a halving of extreme poverty and making substantial improvements in health and education in developing countries by 2015.[37]

---

35 Cited in Jakkie Cilliers and Kathryn Sturman, "The Right Intervention: Enforcement Challenges for the African Union", *African Security Review*, 11, 3, 2002, p.29.
36 "Africa could redraw map – Mbeki", *The Citizen*, 30 May 2002.
37 UN IRIN, 21 February 2002.

But will an increase in aid solve the problems? Or will it simply forestall the inevitable – a collapse or, at best, stuttering along of African states?

David Dollar has concluded that five public policy reforms are necessary to make aid more effective.

- First, financial assistance must be targeted more effectively towards low-income countries with sound economic management. Until the 1990s, aid was evenly distributed both to poor and good policy environments, with mixed results. Before this time, it was distributed for reasons of strategic (Cold War) logic, with pernicious results, as in the case of the former Zaire.
- Second, aid should be provided to "nurture policy reform in credible reformers". Lasting change in African countries is dependent on their meeting conditionalities and showing strong leadership.
- Third, aid has to be tailored to the specific needs of countries and sectors.
- Fourth, there has to be a focus on "creating and transmitting knowledge and capacity".
- Fifth, there is a need for "alternative approaches" in those cases where there is the greatest distortion caused by aid, and where aid has failed.

Dollar notes that:

> The evaluation of development aid should focus instead on the extent to which financial resources have contributed to sound policy environments. It should focus on the extent to which agencies have used their resources to stimulate the policy reforms and institutional changes that lead to better outcomes.

International aid agencies have also been unable to establish conditions for sustainable economic reforms in the face of political pressures exerted by elements of African society on their governments for unpopular reforms to be abandoned. Undertaking and then giving up such reforms has invariably worsened rather than improved conditions for the poorest segments of the societies involved. This failing is implicitly admitted by the adoption of the HIPC initiative, designed to address poverty by using the leverage of debt relief.

The reasons for these failures in external interventions centre round a number of factors.

• First, a sustained presence by international institutions is needed.
There is apparently only one thing worse than a compromised role,
which is no role at all. As one official noted in 1987:[38]

> The alternative – a series of failed programmes in Africa – is not
> worth thinking about, and not only because of the human suf-
> fering . . . The basic idea of moving to a market economy, shifting
> policies out of grandiosity to step-by-step solid progress, will be
> discredited. If they fail in a series of countries . . . then it is a fail-
> ure of our approach to the economy, a failure of our institutions,
> a failure of our political will, and there's no way that we'll be able
> to say that it is just the failure of Africa! So we have a very, very
> big stake in this.

• Second, aid strategies at times appear to be focused more on the
need to appease vested interests (both within the donor nations, and
in terms of the international financial institutions' own roles), than
to effect long-term change.
• Third, there is a failure to co-ordinate donor actions; each tends to
follow their own agenda.
• Fourth, aid agencies fail to link with business, particularly domestic businesses. In some cases, donor agencies distort the local employment market by luring the best and brightest of local talent
away from the entrepreneurial sector.

Can Africans move from dependence on global charity to engagement on the basis of mutual interest as proposed under NEPAD?

Government co-operation and support, within and outside Africa,
are necessary for legitimacy and funding. The process to a great degree
depends, as NEPAD suggests, on Africans themselves identifying
their strengths and weaknesses. It also hinges on Africans singing from
the same hymn book to a greater extent than hitherto, subsuming narrow regional, racial and ethnic rivalries and even business-government
suspicions in a concerted search for prosperity. Without this, divided
Africa will make little progress.

Another critical prerequisite is the need for continent-wide standards of governance and democracy, and the policing of these criteria
by African states and external agents operating in tandem. These are
things that African states can do something about with little outside

---

38 Cited in Callaghy, *op cit*, p.53.

intervention. These are the conditions that, once established, will inspire external aid and investor engagement that goes beyond poverty alleviation strategies, humanitarian assistance and crisis management.

The achievement of such a desirable outcome suggests an increase in the application of politically sensitive aid conditionalities. In this regard, NEPAD proposed the establishment, through peer review, of a "club" of African states committed to good governance and ending conflict. This club will benefit from increased aid and trade access. But this is problematic, given that African support for the initiative hinges on membership inclusivity, though its effectiveness and international support is dependent on the strict application of entrance standards for this club. There has thus far been no evidence of an African willingness to apply governance and democracy conditions on others, preferring to close ranks, such as with Robert Mugabe's Zimbabwe. But as Mbeki has argued, "[A]ll of us must be subject to peer review on the basis of detailed, clear and agreed guidelines as to what constitutes good behaviour and what constitutes bad behaviour."[39]

This stance also reflects the paradox inherent in continent-wide schemes such as the African Union and NEPAD: *that unity and agreement are perceived as fundamentally necessary to establish these programmes.* Yet if they are to be effective, they should *be premised on a set of elitist and potentially divisive goals.* Put differently, political support is currently seen as a precondition for reforms which, if they are to work, have to be designed to exclude states failing to meet specific economic and governance criteria. Moreover, without commitments to governance and economic restructuring, aid and even preferential trade access is wasted as developmental tools, as Africa's history has shown. In spite of their privileged non-tariff entrée to the EU, the 71-strong African, Caribbean and Pacific (ACP) grouping's share of world trade and the European market has been steadily falling.

How can the conundrum of the need for simultaneous economic convergence and political solidarity be solved?

Consensus between African states on the application of governance conditionalities will be difficult to achieve for a number of reasons. These include the political and socioeconomic differences and disparities that exist between African regimes, the suspicion of the hegemonic behaviour of its larger states such as South Africa and Nigeria invariably involved in such actions, and the implicit overturning of the

39 SAPA, 12 February 2002.

principles of sovereign non-intervention that lies behind such schemes. However, these concerns could be outweighed by the benefits on offer and, simply, by the increasing willingness of democracies to adhere. As noted earlier, there were just four democracies in Africa in 1980; by the early 1990s, 42 sub-Saharan states had held multiparty presidential or parliamentary elections.

The Importance of Differentiation and Democracy

Africa's regional organisations – like those in Asia during the 1980s and 1990s – have an irreducible value in providing a framework by which to manage the differences between member-states. Regional differences – due in part to apartheid, the colonial legacy of development, and personality and policy disagreements today – are deep, and clearly need to be addressed. There does not have to be a contradiction between seeking excellence, deepening integration and providing such a framework, or (put differently) between moving the region forward at the pace that globalisation demands and not at the tempo that the slowest, most recalcitrant member is prepared to accept. The answer to the conundrum of achieving political solidarity and economic convergence lies, in part, in doing the easy things first with those that want to. This is to accept the need to encourage a variable regional geometry by which some states integrate faster than others. For example, many of the 14 member-states of the Southern African Development Community[40] are radically different in both economic and political terms. A failure to adopt a differentiated approach in the past also explains why the gains of African states are too often overlooked in sweeping dismissals of Africa as "A Hopeless Continent" by foreign analysts. Such gains as have been made reflect the freeing up of African financial and state sectors, including the implementation of radical privatisation programmes (where the similarity in positive market-related reforms far overshadows any differences) and the deepening of regional integration between states.

A policy of differentiation is arguably essential to developing successful strategies of external engagement. African states range in capacity, as noted in Chapter Two, from South Africa's modern, in-

---

40 Comprising Angola, Botswana, the Democratic Republic of Congo, Lesotho, Malawi, Mauritius, Mozambique, Namibia, Seychelles, South Africa, Swaziland, Tanzania, Zambia and Zimbabwe.

dustrialised economy to the devastation of Sierra Leone, from sprawl-
ing urban centres to rural agrarian societies. Hence it makes sense that
no one aid strategy should fit all types, where the nature of external
engagement has to range from aid to investment, from humanitarian
relief to humanitarian intervention to peacekeeping to joint investment ventures.

There is a need, however, for the birth and fostering of a "culture"
of democracy that goes beyond the creation of formal democracies
through elections. Until this forms part of the essence of African polities, the potential for political reversal remains. There is also the danger of NEPAD faltering when elite interests are threatened by the implementation and operation of international norms, standards and,
indeed, conditionalities. The setting and monitoring of democratic
governance standards and the establishment of such a culture has
to be a bottom-up, civil society-oriented process, rather than one that
is leadership-driven, as has been the case until now.

A third prerequisite is for aid to be focused on developing a closer,
more productive partnership between government and business, which
must form the basis for Africa's development. The single most important ingredient for Africa's success in both political and economic terms is the creation of wealth through employment across the broad
spectrum of its populations. This can only be achieved by sustainable growth which, in turn, is predicated on improving conditions for
commercial activity. As Robert Fowler commented following a G8
NEPAD preparatory meeting in Cape Town in February 2002:[41]

> Of course it's about money, but it's not just about money. In fact,
> its even not primarily about money . . . it's about putting in place
> the conditions that will allow investment to come to Africa, be-
> cause private investment is going to bring Africa far, far more
> than any foreseeable amount of global assistance could bring.

The reflation of Africa's economies through state intervention is not
advisable or possible in this era of globalisation. History has shown that
state corporations have failed to provide adequate returns to support
the growth rates that Africa now requires. Africa's governments will
have to shoulder the responsibility of creating an environment that
will encourage and attract the capital from domestic and global sources

---

41 *Weekend Argus*, 16 February 2002.

necessary to drive growth. There are many possibilities, including the establishment of preferential tax regimes, greater certainty in the investment environment, region-wide marketing initiatives, faster privatisation, and so on. These conditions will increase the likelihood of infrastructure investments, thereby reducing business transaction costs, long a principal deterrent to investors entering the African market.

An excellent example of this type of programme is to be found in Botswana, the world's fastest-expanding economy during the 1990s. Its success has been founded on sound and sensible leadership and good policies involving a close relationship with business, most notably through the Debswana diamond-mining entity. Today, the former British protectorate is the world's largest diamond producer. The industry accounts for two thirds of state income, and is the second largest employer after government. The annual per capita income of US$3,300 is more than six times the sub-Saharan African average. Yet diamonds were discovered there only in 1969.

The importance of government-business partnerships is underscored by the successful turnaround of other African economies, including that of Tanzania and Mozambique. The development of the Maputo Corridor and the Mozal smelter in Mozambique are testament to improving relations between the former Portuguese colony and South African-based business. This approach has seen the Mozambican economy average 3.8% real GDP growth in the 1990s, rising from 1% in 1990 to 11.9% in 1998 – albeit from a low base.

Conclusion: *Caveat Emptor?*

Africa is extraordinarily unimportant in the world economy, even though it may be increasingly relevant politically. African leaders have continually sought a quick fix to their problems for obvious domestic political reasons, but the reality is that undoing 40 years of economic collapse is going to be both painful and time-consuming. It is going to require more than spin-doctoring to correct structural deficiencies and to improve those perceptions which matter – those of bankers and investors. That is an unstated economic conditionality of a sort that developmental initiatives have until now largely avoided – the type that is not subject to intergovernmental whim but is a key element of the developmental bargain. For NEPAD or any similar programme to work, conditionalities have to be tougher and more fiercely applied, and not just by Africans. As one foreign donor put it: "Give

Africa more aid with fewer conditionalities, then it will only be frittered away. And aid only distorts the market, slows liberalisation, and makes governments less, not more, responsive."[42]

The problems that currently exist in the relationship between external aid flows and improved economic development can be summarised as follows:

- *An absence of detail:* The mechanisms and programmes for translating the aid into development are vague. Aid and the role of external agencies also run the risk of overlooking the more simple policy issues that states can do something about in isolation – notably those concerning good governance.
- *Money is not enough:* Although resource transfers are important, these will only occur on a sufficient scale to be of benefit after the establishment of the right conditions in which business can prosper. Globalisation presents opportunities for the flow of capital, but also focuses attention on the need for skills, good governance and management. The same applies to the benefits accruing from debt relief.
- *No single case fits all:* Aid has to be tailored to specific situations.
- *Top-down rather than bottom-up:* There is, for the most part, an absence of business and civil society from the debates over aid and its flows. Unless the debate concerning governance standards and project content is widened and bought into beyond political leadership, aid transfers will not achieve much.
- *An absence of conditionality:* This raises the point as to whether the approach of tying aid to strict conditions failed because of the nature of the conditions themselves, or because of the lack of will and capacity on the part of the donors. This suggests the importance of tagging aid to conditions that are likely to deliver visible, immediate benefits, and also to those areas that can offer longer-term structural change. The latter includes, for example, the linking of donor aid to a set of conditions based on improving fiscal administration, particularly the collection of revenue. This does not mean increasing taxes on honest business, but ensuring that it is paid and that it does go to national treasuries.

There are other donor-related problems. One is the special interests (and interference) of politicians with other (non-developmental) agendas. Another is a lack of political gumption on the part of the Bretton Woods institutions (fearful of offending their political masters, and fearful, too, of undercutting the role of their institutions), which have a big stake – perhaps too large – in maintaining a presence.

The most difficult thing of all to accept is that even the most successful reforms will not address the problems or Africa's marginality to the world economy. Indeed, "structural adjustment" in the form of the need for economic reform and state vitalisation has been required since the time of independence – not just since the term was invented in the mid-1980s. And structural adjustment will be required in the future as well. After all, other countries do it all the time. Again, this comes back to the political pressure for instant solutions for Africa. Yet successful reforms cannot be a one-off event, but require ongoing, sustained and necessary processes of adjustment and reform.

The solution to the aid-development dilemma rests in trying to instil conditions conducive to the creation of an effective state in Africa. The basis for this future lies in the combination of a law-abiding society, a strong governmental system, a functioning economy, an absence of conflict, sound infrastructure, and an honest, limited and effective government. In the short-term this must involve linking the allocation of aid to governance and transparency. But this means that donors will have to get their hands dirty and become more engaged in at times messy, and highly politicised arguments and debates. It demands improved inter-donor co-ordination. As is described in greater detail below, it means mobilising technical assistance to boost local expertise so as to ensure the imparting of skills and effective implementation of programmes. Essentially it means imposing the very kinds of SAPs that were lambasted by recipient nations as intrusive and destructive during the 1990s.

It could be argued that the past decades have demonstrated not so much a failure of aid in Africa as a consistent failure both of conditionality and of the institutions that were supposed to have enforced them. Spending aid constructively has to avoid its potentially distortive impact on the relationship between the government and the governed. It should support good governance, including respect for the rule of law and justice systems, and cultivate economic freedoms. For example, as a general rule, aid to Africa could be productive when spent:

- on Africans – for example, it is estimated that 85% of US aid goes to American citizens and firms;

- on institutions in civil society which promote good governance, such as the media (traditionally an under-resourced sector in Africa with little investigative capacity), and chambers of business and commerce;
- on education, particularly in the use of media and other technology in distance learning;
- in a carefully phased basis, with clear short-, medium- and long-term objectives, utilising continuous sustainability assessment exercises and through-life project costing and evaluation.
- on high-tech inputs into agriculture;
- in the form of differentiated spending: loans for economically remunerative projects and grants for social spending;
- on creating a local enabling environment, utilising, wherever possible, local technical and auditing capacity, and assisting in creating this environment through mentoring programmes;
- in close consultation and with the involvement of the local private sector, delivering aid under its supervision wherever possible;
- on public management and bureaucratic technical assistance programmes which mentor government institutions, particularly in the field of auditing, thereby creating greater capacity for delivery;
- on the creation, retention and return of African skills.

In summary, for long-term prosperity to take root, states need to develop an environment that encourages capital investment by the business community, both local and foreign. Unless civil servants are sufficiently well rewarded, the necessary infrastructure provided, and scarce resources transferred from parasitic importers to poor exporters, then investment will not be forthcoming.

It is difficult to assess whether the aid and governance conditionality medicine has been working. This is because it is difficult to know exactly what situation these states might be in otherwise, and also because governance conditions have not been strictly enforced. It is also difficult to see where the counter-argument (of greater amounts of aid in the pursuit of "development with a human face") might have taken these states, since there are no resources available to put this strategy to the test. Aid, put simply, is not much good in the absence of governance; and may, indeed, devolve governmental responsibility even further away from the people. In the longer term, any effective reform process has to build effective state bodies which can assist African development. These are institutions that can enhance the quality of governance and do not try to intervene in, or distort, the markets as a way of distributing political favours, as happened in East Asia in the late 1990s.

Making Africa a continent safe to do business in by practising transparency and accountability has short-term costs, not only for African elites. Western companies and governments perpetuate these conditions through their own business practices, in much the same way that aid agencies perversely thrive in disaster and conflict situations. Unaccompanied by thoughtful policy interventions, unconditional aid is part of the longer-term problem for Africa, though it remains a balm for Western consciences. As George Soros has warned:[43]

> Current foreign aid programmes are rarely effective and often counterproductive. Generally speaking, they are designed to serve the interests of donor countries, which like to channel aid through their own nationals. International institutions prefer to send foreign experts rather than cultivate domestic expertise. Donor countries insist on retaining control, resulting in a lack of co-ordination. Recipient governments often divert resources for their own purposes. There must be a better way.

In this respect, globalisation has significantly reduced the latitude for economic policies – the markets punish poor choices. Aid can provide more latitude, but it should instead be used to reduce the space to pursue alternative economic policies. Sanctions, similarly, can be used to pressure regimes into compromise and conditions of good governance, including respect for human rights and the observation of democratic standards. To achieve this, however, much more stringent monitoring regimes and greater resources will be necessary.

---

43 "The Free Market Hope", *Newsweek*, 29 October 2001.

CONCLUSION

THE BOTTOM LINE:
No Quick Fixes

> Every country has responsibility for its own destiny, and the main source
> of its future prosperity lies in its own efforts. Foreign investment and
> other assistance can only supplement the actions of the country itself . . .
>
> MICHEL CAMDESSUS, *IMF Managing Director*
> March 1990[1]
>
> Culture is not necessarily destiny. Democracy is.
>
> KIM DAE JUNG, 1994

Australia has a population of just 20 million people but a gross domestic product of over US$400 billion, 30% greater than all sub-Saharan
African countries combined. It ranks second of 174 countries on the
UN Development Programme's *Human Development Index*, which
measures quality of living worldwide. In 2001, the value of Australian
exports of cars and car parts alone exceeded US$2.5 billion, a 20%
increase on the previous year, and more than the GDP of 20 of 48 sub-
Saharan African states. Economic growth jumped to 4.1% in 2002, well
ahead of expectations, and in spite of the post-September 11 slowdown.

Why is it that Australia – no more resource-rich than African competitors – can apparently get things so right, while African states seem
to lurch from crisis to crisis in a state of perpetual underdevelopment,
on the periphery of the global economy? How has this young state,
which has just celebrated the centenary of its commonwealth, created
such an apparently strong sense of national purpose and identity? More
importantly, what can Africa do to change the situation, to learn the
lessons offered by other countries?

★ ★ ★

Four critical observations about African development stand out.[2]

First, the continent's economic situation has degenerated to the
point that Africans are less well off today than they were 30 years

---

1 *IMF Survey*, 19, 7, 1990, pp.108-111, in Callaghy, *op cit*, p.49.
2 This section is, in part, based on an article jointly authored with Jeff Herbst,
   which appeared in *The Sunday Independent*, 14 April 2002.

ago. In particular, as noted earlier, Africa's largest states – notably Nigeria, Sudan, Congo and Ethiopia – have done consistently badly in the post-independence period. Rather than act as engines of growth and sources of stability, these states have constituted the core problems of their respective regions.

Second, there is a need to acknowledge differences within and between African states, not only in terms of their performance records but also taking their size, and cultural and religious make-up into account.

Third, the history of Western engagement with Africa has been characterised by failure and by apparently inappropriate policies and institutions. In response, Africa has to develop its own concepts of aid, conditionality, democracy and governance, but, importantly, it also needs to show how these will both differ from past efforts and succeed if outsiders are to be persuaded to buy into them over the long term. While there is a broad consensus today on the ideological level about the economic model African countries should pursue, there remain questions about its implementation and Africa's means of integration with the global economy.

Fourth, Africa has received an extraordinary amount of attention despite its global economic marginalisation. This raises the question as to whether the West engages with Africa because of the possible transnational threats from widespread conflict and poverty it represents, or because of its potential to offer economic benefit. More positively, such attention provides an opportunity for Africa to air and specify its views. Of course, the events of September 11 were not caused solely by widespread poverty: 15 of the 19 hijackers were from Saudi Arabia, hardly a poor state. Nor are they solely caused by state weakness: many of the hijackers were trained in the United States and operated from cells in Germany, not your average dysfunctional state units. But there is a link with both an absence of modern state structures, which are free from divisive societal influences, and with the presence of globalisation, which raises tensions between states and groups and which offers the means to express this disaffection violently.

In moving from the general to the specific, three sets of questions arise.

- First, in an age of globalisation, what is the formula for creating sustainable socioeconomic prosperity and growth in developing states?
- Second, what can be done for those states – the Congos and An-

golas of Africa (and possibly elsewhere) – which suffer from state dysfunction and, in some cases, collapse?
- Third, what can be gained from internal qualitative policy alterations?

These questions are examined in the outline below, which details ten requirements for successful reform and prosperity.

★ ★ ★

A Formula for Developing Nation Success?

Requirement One: Plurality not Brutality – The Unbearable Essence of Democracy

The job of politicians, Phillipe Riés argues,[3] "is to develop good institutions and make sure they work". He notes:

> Instead of resorting to inward-looking measures such as intervention and protectionism – cures that were worse than the [economic] illness itself – the best way out of the crisis would be to create institutional and legal frameworks enabling developing economies to hold on to their hats when the going got rough. The single ingredient was democracy.

There is still a debate, however, about whether it is easier to implement free-market reforms in a democratic or authoritarian environment. It has been widely accepted that democracies – especially new democracies in many developing countries – have more difficulty in implementing far-reaching economic reforms, given their vulnerable, fragile nature and the difficulty leaders have in carrying important constituencies with them in the process.[4] This assumption is misleading on a number of grounds. First, many of the costs of economic reform are transitional, mostly short-term, and affect (and are thus resisted by) politically important domestic sectors. However, there is

---

3 *Op cit*, p.273.
4 See Barbara Geddes, "Challenging the Conventional Wisdom", *Journal of Democracy*, 5, 4, October 1994, pp.104-118; also Stephen Haggard, "Democratic Institutions, Economic Policy, and Development" in Christopher Clague (ed.), *Institutions and Economic Development: Growth and Governance in Less-Developed and Post-Socialist Countries*. Baltimore: Johns Hopkins University Press, 1997, pp.121-149.

no evidence to suggest that non-democratic regimes are less inclined to protect these sectors. If anything, the opposite is true. Second, authoritarian regimes are also by definition less accountable and transparent than democracies, permitting, even encouraging, interest groups as a source of political support. This is certainly true of East Asia (see below) and the former Eastern bloc, where the *apparatchiks* have had a strong grip on central government and the organs of popular mobilisation. Third, the interests of ruling groups are a good indicator of the likelihood of the implementation and path of reforms. As Barbara Geddes notes: "The bottom line . . . is that although some authoritarian governments have carried out successful transitions to more market-oriented economies, there is little evidence that authoritarianism as such increases the likelihood of such transitions."[5] Nor is there any evidence that political liberalisation runs any higher risk that a reform process will be derailed.

More important, arguably, is the regime "type". This refers, in particular, to the relationship between the executive, the legislature and the judiciary, and the role of interest groups. The absence of a clear separation of powers and an excessive concentration of authority in the hands of the executive not only creates tensions in the legislature, but can lead to a lack of accountability and undue influence on decision-making by vested interests.

Over-centralised systems of government provide clear challenges to economic reform, particularly in those causes where the presidency is isolated from the legislature and reliant for political and institutional support on government agencies. As Geddes argues: "In many countries the biggest, and certainly the most articulate and politically influential, losers from the transition to more market-oriented economy are government officials, ruling-party cadres, cronies of rulers, and the close allies of all three."[6] Liberalisation is a threat, especially in Africa, to traditional, patrimonial systems of government; and the biggest challenge to it thus comes from the families, cadres and clients who have been the beneficiaries of this pork-barrel environment. Conversely, where co-operation between parliaments and the executive is too close, policy is more likely to be an outcome of party discipline and need to co-operate with the executive than a response to the wishes of the electorate.

---

5 *Ibid.*
6 *Ibid.*

The setting and monitoring of governance standards, and the establishment of a democratic culture should be a bottom-up, civil society-oriented process rather than one that is leadership-driven. Foreign donors have an important role to play in supporting nongovernmental institutions,[7] where the health of a society can be measured by the strength of these institutions and by the ideas that they can generate.

Conditionalities are inevitably resisted, but represent necessary disciplines, both for the donor and the recipient nation. Not only do they guard donor nations against the political repercussions following on accusations of misspent aid at home, but they guard Africans against their own (at times) voraciously venal governments. More importantly, conditions are fundamentally common sense. Those societies which are more likely to succeed in the 21st century are those which are democratic and show respect for human rights. In these societies there is free speech, a free press, a free market, and universal application of, and compliance with, the rule of law. These foundations of good governance, on which countries are able to prosper, are prerequisites for success.

Strengthened conditionalities should include a number of other features. Closer supervision and regular auditing are required in recipient countries, particularly those utilising debt relief for anti-poverty programmes. Closer collaboration should be sought between aid agencies and business in implementing infrastructure projects. This would circumvent government, thereby reducing the potential for such obstructions as aid diversion and delays. Technical assistance, which serves both a mentoring and monitoring function, should be provided.

Attempts to implement such measures are likely to be strongly resisted (even resented) by African leaders as intrusive and neo-colonialist, for they reduce their ability to divert aid to their own purposes, all-important to them in an environment where the scope for patronage is increasingly limited. But a new aid regime should not only focus on African nations. It should also include a closer inspection of the World Bank programmes, and a validation (or not) of their investment and development decisions.

Authoritarian governments are, in the short term, less likely to col-

---

7 In 1993, there were an estimated 30,000 NGOs worldwide; today there are more than 100,000, with more than ten times that number classified as "non-profit organisations". There are around 25,000 international NGOs, with more than 1,500 identified as international "think-tanks".

lapse in the face of the costs of implementing liberalisation programmes than democratic ones, but they are arguably at least as susceptible to promoting vested interests at the cost of long-term economic sustainability. Even in parliamentary democracies, state, party and personal loyalties rather than popular sentiment can be the primary shapers of policy responses. While this environment may not impede – and indeed might facilitate – economic adjustment in the short term, the lack of broad support could prove decisive if the government is to ride out policy reversals. In the longer term, the benefits of political and economic liberalisation can only accrue to popular movements and the working classes, while the costs largely fall on party and government officials and their allies.

Requirement Two: **The Imperative for Modernity**

The events of September 11 and the problems faced by Arab states were summed up by Fareed Zakaria as representing the need to meet the challenge of modernisation. As he argued:[8] "[Bin Laden] and his followers come out of a culture that reinforces their hostility, distrust and hatred of the West – and of America in particular. The problem", he argued, "is not that Osama bin Laden believes that this is a religious war against America. It's that millions of people across the Islamic world seem to agree." Addressing this perception means getting to grips with the root causes of such hatred: the existence of dysfunctional Islamic states and their failure to install democratic, accountable regimes and curb excesses. In simple terms, Arab nations have yet to adapt to globalisation, with all its modernising demands.

As Zakaria has eloquently pointed out: "[M]odernisation takes more than strongmen and oil money. Importing foreign stuff – Cadillacs, Gulfstreams and McDonalds – is easy. Importing the inner stuffings of modern society – a free market, political parties, accountability and the rule of law – is difficult and dangerous." The challenge of modernity is not, however, necessarily linked to aid or wealth, but it is linked to governance.

Saudi Arabia – the home of a number of Al-Queda terrorists and financial support for terrorist organisations – is hardly poor. There are thus now questions about the stability and tenability of the pillars on which Saudi Arabia is constructed: oil wealth, the authority of the ruling house of Saud, the championing of puritan Islam, and unques-

---

8 *Newsweek*, 15 October 2001.

tioning US backing.[9] Similar questions can be asked about African nations, particularly those with fragile social and political compacts, religious tensions and patrimonial regimes.

As Huntington argues, "Modernisation does not necessarily mean Westernisation."[10] But, in terms of state capacity, it does include the reform of regimes and institutions that implement policy, including bureaucracies generally and central banks specifically. Apropos the requirement for democratic regimes and norms, critical in this equation is the need to undo the practice of state economic intervention. This is undoubtedly a tall order for systems in which institutionalised party and bureaucratic interests have long held sway, and where access to government is equated with access to power, influence and wealth. An effective and modern state should not be confused with an interventionist, protectionist and loyalist state.

Modernisation and reform inevitably raises the question as to whether unique paths of development that are cognisant of local values, practices and beliefs – be they Islamic, Asian, Hispanic or African – should (and, indeed, can) be developed. While there is no doubting the contribution that can be made by specific cultural factors, whether in terms of Confucian work ethic or of African history, stressing difference is a double-edged sword, too often utilised to excuse undemocratic, unjust, self-serving or plainly inefficient policies and behaviour. Just as bio-cultural determinism has been criticised as an innate, neo-racist "barbarism"[11], and a rationale for conflict and underdevelopment in the Middle East, Balkans and Africa, so too should it not be made an excuse for governmental double standards. Cultures are different; a multicultural approach can add value, but should not be used as a reason to avoid reform. Nor should the propounding of sets of cultural values be allowed to obscure differences which exist at the sub-regional and regional levels. Diversity and difference should be stressed, particularly where growth and reform are patchy.

Modernisation is synonymous with the importation or inculcation of the substance rather than simply the procedural form of democracy. It is especially important in terms of government accountability to citizens and the protection of individual rights against group authority. Admittedly, a key challenge is to reduce the likelihood of demo-

---

9 "Awkward friends", *The Economist*, 20 October 2001.
10 "The Clash of Civilisations and the Remaking of World Order", *op cit*, p.78.
11 Duffield, *op cit*, esp. pp.109-113.

cratic failure in an environment of prolonged economic austerity. This raises key questions about the role of external engagement in promoting a good governance agenda, including democratisation, in recipient countries.

Requirement Three: Economic Policy Mixes – More than the Fundamentals

Asia's weaknesses and failures after 1997 can be put down to a number of factors, notably high levels of non-performing loans, nepotism, bad management in the corporate and governmental worlds, and (related to the last point) poor banking supervision and regulation. It also emphasises the importance of the "sequencing" of economic reforms – the stages of liberalisation that domestic financial systems must follow before the economy is opened up to foreign capital.

At the core of Asia's problems, however, was the nature of the relationship between government and business. This reflects two features of developing economies and societies. First, leaders face the difficulty of keeping potentially volatile constituencies together in societal compacts which can become fragile under pressure, especially if there are few resources (and thus limited patronage opportunities). Second, in some cases leaders fail not only to adhere to democratic norms and principles, but even to fully understand Western conceptualisations of these practices. As South Korea's Kim Dae Jung has argued: "I think Asia's economic crisis stems mainly from a lack of democracy. In democratic countries, there is not the same kind of collusion between businessmen and the government." The answer, he has proposed, lies in developing both a democratic culture and a market economy.[12] Rather than supporting the contention that economic reform and authoritarian governments are two sides of the same coin, these experiences tend to show that democratisation is necessary for meaningful and sustainable reform.

On a visit to Africa in May 2001, US Secretary of State Colin Powell observed:[13]

I cannot state strongly enough, however, that all over the world experience has shown that trade and private investment have to

---

12 Cited in *Time*, March 1998, in Riés, *op cit*, p.207.
13 SAIIA/Wits University speech, 25 May 2001.

go hand in hand with openness within a country. . . . Money, simply stated, is a coward. Capital will run from those countries which are closed, which are corrupt, which do not have open systems, which do not believe in the rule of law, which are callous or which are caught up in conflict. *Money loves security; money loves transparency, legality and stability.* . . . Only when societies embrace sound economic and trade policies, when they embrace the rule of law, when they practise good governance, and when they can give official assistance and private investment working together the opportunity to play effective roles in development, then we can see the kind of success that we need, the kind of opportunity that will draw in more private investment

As Powell intimates, there is a need, of course, for leaders to establish the basic macroeconomic fundamentals for success – notably a free-market economy, monetary stability and fiscal restraint, privatisation and deregulation, the removal of trade barriers, and the liberalisation of capital flows. That there are *short-term*, transitional political costs to this strategy is undeniable. Welfare services will invariably suffer because of fiscal restraint. The prices of imports will rise as a result of exchange rate reform; wages could be forced downwards as a result of declining protectionism (though in the longer term export growth should cause them to rise); and state reform and downsizing will lead to an increase in unemployment. These changes also give rise to further, ongoing demands for economic management and reform.

Large currency inflows, for example, entail the management of the inter-related effects of rapid monetary expansion, appreciating exchange rate values, overstretched banking capacity, widening current account deficits, capital mobility, and inflationary pressures. Without control there is a real danger of macroeconomic instability. In addition, there is a need to factor in the inevitably cyclical nature of FDI and portfolio flows. Yet the Argentine crisis of the late 1990s parallels that of the early 1980s, when periods of capital inflow contrasted with major capital outflows and economic contraction. Such cycles remain to an extent determined by local conditions, but are also influenced by the nature of the global market, including the impact of interest rates and economic conditions in developed markets, trends towards diversification (or not), and the positive or negative effects of regional contagion.

The stress has thus to be on policy mix and management rather

than on prescription. As Calvo, Leiderman and Reinhart have argued:[14]

> There are some important lessons in macroeconomic manage-
> ment that emerge from the surge of capital inflows to Asia and
> Latin America in the first half of the 1990s. . . . the countries
> that have been the most successful . . . have implemented a com-
> prehensive policy package and not relied on a single instrument.

It is also assumed that FDI will flow as a result of a basket of reforms,
thereby offsetting the disadvantages. But these fiscal and monetary
reforms are not enough, even with the advantages of cheap labour.
There is a related need to integrate Africa's burgeoning informal economies with the formal sector. Countries have to keep up with the needs
of competitors, with the challenges of globalisation.

Therefore domestic economic reforms have to move beyond the
fundamentals. They have to involve more than just the provision of
a macro-policy framework to the more difficult and problematic stage
of micro-level implementation. Government has to develop strategies for the industrial, agriculture, tourism and financial sectors, for
example. Then there is the need for services, skills development, and
public service sector reform, which includes the judiciary, police,
telecommunications, and electricity supply and transmission.[15] Reforms to the education and training sectors should be planned, bearing in mind that skills and technical training are today more important than cheap labour. Other reforms include the need for managerial
and labour discipline. On the economic front, legal protection for foreign investments is required, as is the removal of obstacles to entry,
including the removal of tax distortions, the provision of access to
hard currency, and the removal of trade barriers.[16]

Put simply, countries have to listen to the market.

---

14 Guillermo A Calvo, Leonardo Leiderman and Carmen M Reinhart, "Inflows
   of Capital to Developing Countries in the 1990s", *Journal of Economic Perspec-
   tives*, 10, 2, Spring 1996, pp.123-39.
15 See, for example, the comments made by Iraj Abedien, *Leadership*, September
   2001.
16 See, for example, Joel Bergsman and Xiaofang Shen, "Foreign Direct Investment in Developing Countries: Progress and Problems", *Finance and Development*, 32, 4, December 1995, pp.6-8.

Requirement Four: Competition, Openness and Best Practice

There is a need for business and government in Africa to concentrate their activities on what they do best – not only in terms of division of responsibility, but in terms of the sectors in which they become involved. A critical component is the nature of the relationship between business and government. In Africa (and, indeed, in most developing nations) this relationship is contested, ranging from being too close (with the associated problems of corruption, nepotism and the lack of distinction between private and public accounts) to being too distant.

Enterprises have to be able to operate free from government intervention or favour, whether their ventures take the form of hotels in Malawi or state-owned enterprises in China or *chaebols* in South Korea. As part of this regime, businesses also have to learn to operate according to commercial practices, *inter alia*, to raise capital. Companies should be allowed to go bankrupt – or to carry out restructuring to prevent them from doing so. It is not the role of government to rescue commercial enterprises that are not self-sustaining. The so-called "Source Book" of *Transparency International* provides a useful template for government action in this regard, which includes:[17]

- a clear commitment by political leaders to combat corruption and to open themselves to scrutiny;
- an emphasis on changing systems of operation to prevent future corruption, including the adoption of comprehensive anti-corruption legislation;
- an identification of those government agencies most prone to corruption and a review of legal and administrative aspects and procedures;
- a programme to ensure that the salaries of civil servants and political leaders reflect their responsibilities and are comparable to those in the private sector;
- the creation of a "social compact" – or partnership – between government and civil society which includes business.

The goal of such reforms would be, in summary, to make corruption, as Transparency International terms it, "a 'high-risk' and 'low-profit' undertaking", and to entrench good governance practices.

It is clear that business has a major part to play in the future success (or not) of Africa. Without the commercial sector, there will not be

---

17 See *http://www.transparency.de/documents/source-book/summary.html.*

enough jobs, and there will be little in the way of an economy for government to manage or derive benefit from. For business to flourish, however, it requires a favourable environment – one which places investor security before politics. This not only applies to the role of government in improving the overall economic environment, but also concerns the relationship between government and existing enterprises. Rather than steadfastly urging government to accommodate its demands, too often business has swayed with the wind, frightened or at least reluctant to "take government on". At times this has led to a seemingly accepting attitude towards some of the most odious regimes in Africa, for example in the case of the relationship between white business and the National Party apartheid government in South Africa.

While aware that it is but one constituency, business has arguably more to gain than to lose by taking a much tougher line with, and keeping its distance from, government. If it is too easily intimidated, it will lose the respect of government and of the international community: worse, business will lose its relevance as a force for both change and stability. The reaction to the crisis in Zimbabwe beginning in 2000 is a case in point. South African business had a tremendous amount to lose by following President Mbeki's handling of the land reform issue, but rather than challenge Pretoria on his response, the business community preferred to wait and see. By the time it realised that there was more to be gained by speaking out than by keeping quiet, the damage to foreign investor sentiment towards South Africa had been done. A more forthright and strident attitude over the effect of political decisions on investment would cause short-term political ripples, but would carry much greater longer-term benefits. Moral courage and vision, although crucial, are apparently always in short supply.

Africa's promise and prosperity lies in improving conditions for commercial activity throughout the region, thereby ensuring higher levels of economic growth and better living standards for its people. As Baroness Valerie Amos, the UK Minister for Africa, has argued: "African governments need to work . . . in creating an enabling business environment in which investors feel confident and comfortable, and that enables long-term stability".[18] There is thus a need for urgency, prioritisation and direction in those African development

---

18 "NEPAD and the G8: Kananaskis and Beyond". Speech given to the SAIIA, 31 July 2002.

CONCLUSION

strategies to which business is committed in alliance with government. Although the Asian crisis points to the dangers that can arise in such a close relationship, a distinction has to be made between Asian state sector intervention in industrial policy (which was generally beneficial) and in the allocation of financial resources (which was generally destructive). As Asia has shown, a beneficial policy environment can create a long-term commitment to economic growth and co-operation, reducing transaction costs, diminishing uncertainty, broadening and lengthening planning horizons and, in doing so, increasing investment.[19]

There is also a need for corporate governance, as distinct from good governance, a fundamental whose importance has been recently highlighted, not only by the corruption which has blighted development in emerging markets, but also by the collapse of Enron (referred to at the start of this volume). The issue of corporate governance is not solely a domestic concern. The link between money laundering, transnational threats and poor corporate governance is one that has been emphasised by the events of September 11.

Corporate governance can also promote (and be promoted by) governmental reform. According to US Trade Representative Robert Zoellick, "The Bush Administration continues to move forward to advance trade and free markets."[20] He notes that:

> By identifying barriers to trade, we can work with our trading partners, globally, regionally, and bilaterally, to eliminate these barriers, while further liberalising our market at home. Trade improves the economic wellbeing of Americans, advances freedom around the world, and promotes our nation's security.

In this respect, the US government's 2002 National Trade Estimate (NTE) Report on Foreign Trade Barriers contends that most African countries are introducing economic and political reforms, promoting economic growth and facilitating their integration into global markets. These steps aim to improve their investment climate, and are consistent with the provisions of the US African Growth and Opportunity Act (AGOA). As noted in the Introduction, under the AGOA,

19 See Stephen Haggard, *The Political Economy of the Asian Financial Crisis.* Washington DC: The Institute for International Economics, 2000, p.21.

20 See the 2002 US Trade Representative National Trade Estimate Report on Foreign Trade, on *http://ustr.gov.*

which came into effect on 1 October 2000, the US president designates those African countries to receive duty-free benefits to the US market on account of their commitment to "appropriate" domestic policies supportive of good governance, a free-market philosophy and democracy. The 2002 US NTE report argued that a number of African countries should take additional steps to make their economic climates more attractive for foreign investors. For example, while tariffs had been reduced, they remained high in certain sectors and countries. US exporters, the report noted, were also hampered by onerous customs delays, ineffective enforcement of intellectual property rights, and corruption.

While there is no doubt that increased trade assists growth, and improved access to markets stimulates trade, there is a chronic double standard at play. Setting aside the obvious hypocrisy of US domestic tariff implementation and subsidy utilisation (such as in the farming sector), and while the AGOA provides an indication of the preferences of the US (and, indeed, other Western governments) for economic reform as a definitive condition for trade access, America's zeal for good governance is, critically, not applied with the same vigour to those US companies operating in Africa. The same could be said for a number of European states. Take the oil sector in Angola.

The 2002 Global Witness report on the Angolan oil sector, *All the President's Men*, details the role played by international oil companies and banking interests in an environment distorted by war and the absence of democracy. Of an estimated US$3.8 billion transferred to the Angolan government in taxes by oil companies in 2000, 44% was paid by Chevron, 36% by the Angolan oil company Sonangol, just under 10% by TotalFinaElf, 8% by Italy's Agip, and 0.5% each by Braspetro and Texaco. Yet only one company, BP-Amoco, has made full voluntary disclosure of the amounts paid, a unilateral initiative for which it was censured by its competitors and the Angolan government alike.[21] Undoubtedly, to be more effective, companies will have to act in concert; yet there is a strong resistance by some to go the route of full disclosure.

For business to prosper in the African environment, a number of things will have to be put right. Among them are the implementation of corporate governance standards, including the timely provision of

---

21 See Global Witness, *All the President's Men: The Devastating Story of Oil and Banking in Angola's Privatised War*. London: Global Witness, March 2002.

information to investors; a clear separation of interests by executives; strongly enforced independent audit practices; and clear lines of responsibility for corporate leaders.[22] Corporate transparency has wider, political benefits, too. It forces greater openness in government dealings through disclosure. Companies will, in most environments, be reluctant to disclose, given the potential risks to their relationship with governments and the possible loss of strategic business advantage, but avoiding such practices will raise the cost of doing business in the long term.

There is a leading role to be played by multinational corporations in setting standards for both government and local businesses. In the case of Angola, transparency in the dealings of oil companies will arguably do more to "reconnect" Angola's people with its government, *deepen democracy* and *deliver good governance* than any form of external aid conditionality. To enable this to occur, multinational corporations have to be encouraged to adopt these practices. Universal standards have to be set. Applying the ethical norms embodied in the AGOA – transparency, accountability, disclosure, rule of law – on US and other international companies at home, would be a good place to start. To emphasise Zoellick's argument, such leadership would advance economic wellbeing and security in both Africa and in its OECD partners.

Requirement Five: The Need for a Regional Champion

"The wind", the saying goes, "always blows hardest for the tallest trees." The same could be said for regional leaders, whether they be in West Africa, South Asia, Latin America, Europe, ASEAN or Southern Africa. Certain responsibilities go with the position and role, and with them, too, the cost of leadership in terms of political and personal relationships. The region requires leaders who have both the right abilities and the political influence and intuition to act as role models for others. There are obvious benefits flowing from improved regional co-ordination and co-operation, not least the ending of conflict; the creation of larger, more attractive markets through the removal of

---

22 See, for example, Andrew Hill and Peter Speigel, "Feeling the Heat", *Financial Times*, 8 March 2002 on the implications of the Enron collapse. Such measures are encapsulated within the King Report on Corporate Governance in South Africa. See Deloitte and Touche, *Commentary on the Draft King Report on Corporate Governance in South Africa*, 2001. Johannesburg: Deloitte and Touche/Institute of Directors, 2001.

barriers to trade and investment; increased investment flows; and the development of much-needed infrastructure.

There remain, however, significant obstacles to this process in Africa, especially in the absence of a congruence of democratic and economic values within regions. In particular, the larger African states (such as Nigeria, Congo and Sudan) have, as noted earlier, done very badly in their respective regions. Rather than acting as an engine of growth and sources of stability, these states have been sources of insecurity and economic problems for their neighbours. They have also not provided the leadership solutions that Africa demands.

Another major challenge for African regional integration is simply that, whereas in Europe this process has been the outcome of a development of similar national systems, in Africa the regional integration ideal has been used to drive the process. Put crudely, it has been a case of putting the cart before the horse.

The arguments in favour of closer integration should thus not obscure the immense challenges facing regional units, as they strive to overcome political differences and economic insecurities. In Africa, region-building has been a difficult task: intra-regional trade accounted on average for just 6% of African trade in 1990, and grew to just 10% in 1999. In the case of the SADC region, for example, South Africa's market domination, coupled with differences concerning leadership style and respect for democratic values and human rights, has made the regional project both complex and problematic. Similar difficulties have, unfortunately, been replicated throughout Africa – though conversely, *these difficulties arguably make regionalism all the more necessary.* The table below helps to identify those factors promoting or, alternatively, working against a regional integration imperative, which may prove valuable in examining both African and other initiatives.[23]

---

23 See, for example, Antoinette Handley's Concluding Remarks in Claudia Mutschler, *South and Southern Africa: Lessons from Emerging Markets.* Johannesburg: SAIIA Report No. 4, 1997, p.29. This table is reproduced from Greg Mills, "Assessing Regional Integration in the Asia-Pacific and Southern Africa". Paper given at a conference on "APEC and the Asia-Pacific: Lessons for Southern Africa", Johannesburg, 1 February 2001.

The Push and Pull of Regional Integration

Positive Trends	Negative Trends
Geographic propinquity	Small economies, both in terms of population size and GDP
Cultural homogeneity	Relatively low level of trade within the region
Economic (trade and investment) and infrastructure integration and advantage, including: • The greater the proportion of goods imported from the region and from member states in particular, the smaller the proportion bought from outside this area • The larger the internal market • The lower the costs of transport among states • The greater the diversity of production structures among member states	Heavy dependency on imports and foreign trade, in particular with advanced industrialised countries
Common and related security concerns, and an absence of major political/security disagreements	Shortage of value-added products
Common political values	Low level of industrialisation

It should be acknowledged that there are often sound political reasons behind what appears to be over-rapid regional expansion. Most notable is the need for political inclusivity and dialogue in regions which have in the recent past experienced (and in some cases continue to suffer from) conflict and instability. These problems of divergence might (and arguably should) be addressed by the application of variable geometry membership criteria to encourage the incremental, centrifugal development of similar economic ideologies and trajectories among member states. These would also take into account their heterogeneous nature. A regional approach to economic development has explicit advantages, because:
• external perceptions – both positive and negative – are focused on regions and not necessarily their constitutive elements;
• technology provides an opportunity to leapfrog development stages

in an integrated manner, and operates as a catalyst for development;
- regionalism offers economies of scale;
- Africa's regional markets are comparatively untapped;
- a regional approach builds on the strengths and opportunities present – including the sense of regional identity, the natural resource base, the existence of formal regional organisational ties, however embryonic and weak, and infrastructure and people linkages; and
- regionalism can assist in diluting culturally specific values which work against co-operation, as nations become acculturated to adopting a common set of protocols and practices likely to smooth their entry into the mainstream of international relations and the global economy.[24]

Any effective regional development strategy must go beyond the general to the specific, however. There has to be a focus on the creation of cheaper and more effective communications and networks, and the development of an integrated trade and investment market. Levels of the knowledge and skills that drive modern economies must be improved – to which end a massive investment in education is required. Private sector expertise and resources should also be harnessed and tapped to assist in skills training. A regional strategy needs to concentrate especially on those issues that governments and business in partnership can do something about, both at home and in the region.

With this in mind, ten specific areas on which Africa should focus can be identified, with the strategies that need to be adopted.[25]
- *Information, Communications and Telecommunications*: There is an urgent need to improve both fixed-line and cellular expansion, through the removal of monopolies, the speeding up of privatisation and the establishment of independent regulatory bodies.
- *Transport and Infrastructure*: This includes support of spatial development initiatives and public-private partnerships, the provision of concessions on railway lines and toll roads, and the improvement of the frequency of air links between African states. It is imperative to standardise and computerise port and airport customs clearance under private management contracts, as a means of reducing both

---

24 Han Sung-Joo (ed.), *op cit*, p.9.
25 This section draws, in part, on the work prepared for the 2001 SADC summit in collaboration with colleagues Tim Hughes, Mark Shaw, Ross Herbert and Elizabeth Sidiropoulos.

corruption and delays, and also to remove border-crossing bottle-necks.

- *Energy Provision*: There is a need to replace import monopolies with market competition, and to boost technical expertise through personnel swaps. African government monopolies on fuel imports have been plagued by corruption, and several also sell fuel at a loss for political reasons, which drains the national budget and limits the government's ability to manage other sectors properly.
- *Mining*: Here it is important to bring about monetary and foreign exchange stability, to offer security of tenure, and create attractive investment codes. While mining and oil are Africa's most important foreign exchange earners, their high capital costs mean that production in these sectors can be inhibited by unstable economic policies and particularly unpredictable or restricted access to foreign exchange. The high capital costs of mining mean that international investors demand an unambiguous legal framework for exploration and extraction. These must include competitive tax and royalty rates, security of tenure, and objective criteria and minimum discretionary powers for politicians and officials.
- *Tourism and the Environment*: There is a need to encourage the development of these sectors through the use of a regional/continental tourism brand, regional marketing, and common regional visas and tourist routing.
- *Harmonisation and Improvement of the Banking, Finance, Insurance and Retail Sectors*: Improvements of standards of performance in the financial sectors can be facilitated through the use of secondments, training, certification, and the establishment of regional ethics and corporate governance bodies.
- *Health Care*: There is an urgent need to integrate regionally the health campaigns to prevent and treat HIV/Aids and malaria. This requires co-operation between businesses and governments, and between governments.
- *Agriculture and Rural Development*: There is a need for considerable intervention in the rural farming sector. This could involve the use of tax credits, the disbanding of state-run agricultural boards, the creation of African brands and brand awareness, and the extension of training and technical assistance programmes, especially to farmers and farmworkers.
- *Developing and Retaining Skills*: There is a urgent need to prevent Africa's best-trained and brightest nationals from leaving the con-

tinent. Solving this problem requires fiscal discipline, the righting of the distortions in the labour market caused by inflated aid agency salaries, aggressive curriculum reform (especially the incorporation of agriculture and more science-based programmes), and the use of media, including television and video, for training.

- *Investment*: Regional ways to make African countries more attractive to investors include: the use of region-wide macroeconomic congruence targets; high-level corruption prosecutions; offering security of tenure to investors; the removal of red tape, partly through the creation of "One-Stop Regional Investment Shops"; and the correction of tax distortions. Another strategy is the encouragement of multiplier investment activity by taking a "corporate" view of investments within and without regions, involving finance, insurance, construction and manufacturing in up- and down-stream activities.

Requirement Six: Obey and Shape the Global Rules of the Road

As former US Ambassador to the UN Richard Holbrooke has contended, "[I]f you want to be part of the international community, you have to play by international rules." In an environment of global rather than simply national competition, there is a need for states to take a global view. This means involvement in realising consensus, with the aim of:

- restructuring trade and investment tariffs to take advantage of global markets and flows;
- establishing and applying global (best) practices and standards of quality and prices; and
- actively participating in global regime formation.

However, the latter requires a focus on skills within government departments as well as on statistical and analytical information, the sharing of information with business, and the development of joint business-government strategies. On the wider stage, it requires working with partners in developed and developing nations in pursuit of these goals. The outcome of the Doha WTO meeting at the end of 2001 points the way forward in this regard. Developed nations appeared more willing to take a broader, less parochial view of development, while their developing country counterparts, accounting for three quarters of WTO membership, were better organised, less nationalistic in their views, and more assertive than they had been at Seattle two years previously. This positive outcome will have to be replicated and expanded on in the future, where developing nations will have to strive not for preferential, but rather equal trade access.

Requirement Seven: Encouraging Diversity and Excellence

Integration with the global economy and the opening up of markets and capital opportunities has a further implication. This is the importance of developing, attracting, and retaining those skills without which global economic participation is difficult, if not impossible.

Therefore developing countries need to avoid xenophobia and encourage the importation of foreign expertise. Local skills creation and retention are also critical. It could be argued that in an increasingly homogenised, globalised world, diversity is needed to add competitive advantage to nations. As G Pascal Zachary[26] has put it:

> Diversity defines the wealth and health of nations in a new century. Mighty is the mongrel. . . . In a world of deepening connections, individuals, corporations and entire nations draw strength and personality from as near as their local neighbourhood and as far away as a distant continent.

The Economic Commission for Africa (ECA) and the International Organisation for Migration (IOM) estimate that between 1960 and 1975 some 27,000 high-level skilled Africans left the continent for the West. Between 1975 and 1984, this number increased to around 40,000 and then almost doubled by 1987, representing 30% of the highly skilled stock of the continent. Africa lost 60,000 professionals (doctors, engineers, and so on) between 1985 and 1990, and has been losing an average of 20,000 per year since that time. By 2000, Africa's share of world scientific output had fallen from 0.5% to 0.3%, with just 20,000 scientists (or 3.6% of the world's scientific population) being African.[27] As noted in Chapter Two, this gap has had to be filled by expatriates. About 100,000 expatriates work in Africa, (a greater number than at independence), at an annual cost of US$4 billion.[28] There remains, conversely, the fear of a xenophobic reaction to an influx of highly trained foreigners.

26 G Pascal Zachary, *The Global Me: Why Nations will Succeed or Fail in the Next Generation.* Australia: Allen and Unwin, 2000.
27 See "Can Africa's Brain Drain be Stemmed?", UN IRIN, 17 February 2000.
28 See Alan Gelb and Rob Floyd, "The Challenge of Globalisation for Africa", *South African Journal of International Affairs*, 6, 2, Winter 1999, p.13.

One study has shown that between 1989 and 1997, 233,609 South Africans (of whom 10% were professionals) moved to the UK, Canada, Australia and New Zealand alone, though official statistics claim this figure is much lower (83,911). Analysis also suggests that between 1994 and 1998, emigration had cost the country R8.4 billion in lost income tax and R285 billion in lost contributions to GDP. By comparison, immigration is running at one sixth of the levels of the 1980s. Post-1994, one report has noted, the annual emigration of professionals from South Africa was over 50% higher than for the period between 1989 and 1994, with the result that between one eighth and one fifth of South Africans with a tertiary education now reside abroad.[29] In 1998, over 250,000 African professionals were working in the United States and Europe. Conversely, around 18,000 (mostly white) South Africans emigrated to Africa between 1988 and 1997.[30]

The loss of skills has wide economic implications, including the cumulative loss of knowledge. This has created a need to attract new skills from abroad, along with fostering them at home. Yet statistics show that entry into South Africa has, post-1994, become *more*, not *less*, difficult for skilled migrants.

For South Africa, the crux of the skills inflow argument is that many black South Africans who were denied employment and other opportunities over generations resist the importation of skilled labour (and the arguments supporting it) on the grounds that this takes away jobs rather than creating new ones. However, the reality is that if South Africa is to enjoy widespread, long-term growth, it has to open its doors to foreign skills, particularly given the higher-than-average rates of skills loss from the Republic. In 2000, South Africa experienced its highest net migrant loss (7,000) since 1940. While the overall skills deficiency is part of the legacy of apartheid education, it is exacerbated by the impact of emigration and factors such as HIV/Aids, which is most prevalent in the age groups that are, or should be, economically active.

It should be noted that skills creation and retention is not only an African problem. Migration from Latin America has accelerated since the late 1990s. The reasons appear to be less concerned with fleeing political oppression than with seeking economic opportunity. Some

---

29 See Michael Dynes, "New revelations show exodus is reaching flood level", *Business Report*, 12 November 1999.
30 "Trek of the White Tribe", *Business in Africa*, February 2000.

15 million people born in Latin America have settled in the United States, while 18% of Spain's foreigners are also from the continent. An estimated 600,000 Colombians and 500,000 Ecuadorians departed their countries between 1999 and 2001. While they do send money home (the World Bank estimates that remittances from Latin America and the Caribbean totalled over US$15 billion in 2002, ten times more than in 1980, and five times more than aid flows) and they can facilitate investment and trade between the adoptive countries and those of their birth, many of the region's most productive (and thus most mobile) citizens are moving abroad.[31]

Requirement Eight: Rebuilding Humpty Dumpty?

The above template raises questions about what to do with those states which have failed to function effectively, or which, for reasons of colonial inheritance and poor leadership, have failed ever to function at all.

The single, consistent theme that runs through the collapse of African states is the absence of a structure of authority, good or bad, internal or external. Hence any solutions would appear to have to address this deficiency.

There is a radical split in opinion between those who believe it necessary to resurrect the validity of the state unit in Africa in its current form, and those who believe that alternatives must be found, given that existing structures (such as those in Rwanda and Burundi) are simply not viable. Yet while many recognise that, as Boutros-Ghali put it, the theory of sovereignty no longer matches the political reality, as Herbst has argued in *States and Power in Africa*, "The attachment developed by Africans and others to the current state system is extraordinary."[32]

International relations literature assumes that states are both necessary and desirable. Both positions require careful scrutiny. Failed states might be said to be necessary, and may even prove to be a good thing. They are arguably inevitable. But when a state is dysfunctional or has failed altogether, what are the alternatives? In some cases, it may entail a retreat to pre-colonial entities, to small-scale local principalities or even warlordism.

One must be wary of interpreting the difficulties facing the African state as representing the end of the nation-state's function as a basic

---

31 See "Making the most of an exodus", *The Economist*, 23 February 2002.
32 *Op cit.*

building-block. The global system is fluid: states will continue to be important as international actors and will simultaneously face challenges to their authority. As Christopher Clapham has argued, this situation does not necessarily represent a calamity, given that state withdrawal can enhance conditions of economic management and activity. Even without the existence of formal state units, economic units and individuals will also inevitably be linked to the international system through familial, *diaspora*, business and other networks.

Although we face collapse of state functions in some areas, ironically this underscores the importance of the state and the role of national identity and democratic institutions. There is no universal or static definition of "statehood". Yet in an age of increasing homogenisation and globalisation, the state is increasingly (rather than decreasingly) recognised as the vehicle for both stability and development. We should expect a continuation of the paradox of simultaneous state integration and fragmentation.

Leaving aside the possibilities of decertifying existing state units and the creation of alternatives to, or substructures within, the sovereign state, it is necessary to consider the reasons for the fragmentation or failure of states, and possible means of prevention. Remedying the conditions that give rise to this challenge demands a subtle, nuanced approach, in which a clear distinction between those states which are fragile, collapsed or emerging needs to be made. The process of state resuscitation has to come from within. Inevitably this will require strong leadership, which will hopefully end conflict and provide better governance, although the African record is mixed in this regard.

Requirement Nine: The Power of Partnership and Governance, not Aid

The African developmental problem is often pinpointed as deriving from an absence of finances, especially aid. But why is it that vast sums in aid – probably more than US$500 billion – have, in the case of Africa and arguably also further afield, been counterproductive? The reason for this is partly that funds are fungible – that is, governments can successfully avoid donor conditionalities and divert aid to other purposes. Arguably, aid often enables states to avoid, not pursue, necessary reforms, and not just in Africa. (Argentina is a case in point.) Moreover, the "extent of aid" argument does not explain how South Korea changed from being on an economic par with Ghana in 1960 to being a world technological powerhouse today, with

a per capita GDP around 20 times greater than that of Ghana. Similarly, how did Malaysia, Singapore and other Asian nations which were
relatively backward, radically change their fortunes?

The external and internal dimensions to finding a formula for prosperity in African states and beyond are not necessarily mutually exclusive. Both require reform of the state and its organs to make it more
effective, accountable and efficient. Further answers lie, as noted
above, in the regional arena.

Anyone doubting the talent of Africans to succeed in the international community should examine closely the experience of South
African firms abroad post-1994. And this refers not only to the giant
multinationals which have shifted their focus (and sometimes their
listing) overseas. That one can purchase Nando's chicken outside East
Putney Tube Station in London, at Chinatown in Kuala Lumpur,
or in Melbourne, speaks volumes for the benefits of global engagement.

There are also many things African states can do to make small,
incremental internal changes in partnership with external agencies.
As the IMF has argued:[33]

> The broad elements of a strategy include efforts by the low-in-
> come countries [which] can: promote growth through domestic
> policies that encourage macroeconomic stability and market
> forces by freeing trading restrictions, reducing subsidies, im-
> proving the quality of government services, and strengthening
> legal and financial institutions; [and] reduce poverty through
> "country-owned" strategies that promote pro-poor policies that
> are properly budgeted – including health, education, and strong
> social safety nets. A participatory approach, including consulta-
> tion with civil society, will add greatly to their chances of success.

And the advanced economies, the IMF notes, can:

> Reform their own trade policies, opening new markets to exports
> from poor countries; reduce domestic subsidies in sectors such
> as agriculture and textiles where poor countries are most likely
> to benefit; [and] increase not only the debt relief they provide in
> support of good policies, but also their official development as-

33 On *http://www.imf.org/external/np/exr/ib/2000/041200b.htm#II.*

sistance . . . reversing the downward trend of the past two decades. They could also make that aid more effective by reducing the extent to which it is tied to their own exports, and by better co-ordinating their assistance and debt relief with poor countries' poverty reduction strategies.

A successful strategy to revitalise Africa's economies should, as a point of departure, reinforce the principles on which the NEPAD programme is founded: the practice of good governance, corporate governance and inclusive government, and the absence of conflict. The adoption of mechanisms to both encourage and sanction these qualities will enable the region to realise the creation of a logic of stability, security and prosperity. Addressing governance issues and promoting demo-cratic norms is a prerequisite for increased aid and local and foreign investment. Kofi Annan has noted in this regard that:[34]

> Since 1970, Africa has had more than 30 wars fought on its ter-ritory, the vast majority of which have been intra-state in origin. Fourteen of Africa's 53 countries were afflicted by armed conflicts in 1966 alone. This accounted for more than half of all war-related deaths worldwide, resulting in more than eight million refugees, returnees and displaced persons. The consequences of these con-flicts have seriously undermined Africa's efforts to ensure long-term stability, prosperity and peace for its people. No one – not the United Nations, not the international community, not Africa's leaders – can escape responsibility for the persistence of these conflicts.

As Thabo Mbeki has similarly acknowledged, "We all know that you cannot achieve development . . . in situations of conflict and war. We must, as Africans, make a commitment . . . that we shall end all wars on the African continent."[35] It is simply not enough to expect the UN to negotiate an end to any conflict, and when there is a breakdown in the peace process to accuse the West of insufficient commitment. At the very least, any effort to end conflict has to be a joint effort – the

---

34 Cited on *http://www.un.org/peace/africa/SECGEN.htm.*
35 These comments were made at the opening of a SA Department of Foreign Affairs Heads of Mission conference, 11 February 2000. Cited in *The Citi-zen*, 12 February 2001.

internal parties must want peace more than they want to continue fighting, and they have to see an advantage in ending rather than perpetuating the conflict. Where the international community can play a role is in creating the consensus towards peace, and by pressurising negotiating parties to compromise.

Taking a lesson out of Asia's book, African nations have to develop social compacts between government, opposition, business and (in places, an increasingly estranged) civil society. Such an approach could be a critical ingredient in the creation of a long, durable period of political stability and economic prosperity.

Globalisation is thus a two-way street. Economic integration offers protection against outside military threats: it offers benefits, exacts costs and demands performance, but largely it ensures that countries and leaders get the economies they deserve. As *The Economist* has noted,[36] "Markets have restricted the ability of politicians to promise paradise to their constituents and lead them to hell." But as Asia demonstrates, states are always vulnerable, particularly in the absence of internal dialogue or engagement by leaders.

Requirement Ten: No Quick Fixes . . . Globalise

Globalisation has become the target of a coalition of many and disparate international groupings – from those concerned with the environment, to the "anti-capitalists", to the stridently nationalistic. It stands accused of bringing with it a range of pernicious transnational influences, including crime, drugs, and corruption. On the other hand, globalisation opens up economies, demands transparency and with it better governance, and creates access to international markets, breaking local, expensive monopolies. It thus helps to remove corruption, not entrench it, and gives individuals access to the global economy. In this regard, it is important not to confuse criticism of globalisation with the self-serving arguments of those protecting vested local or special interests.

Being in favour of globalisation should not, however, presume complete, uncritical agreement with its ideological counterparts – liberal, neo-liberal or free-market policies.[37] Moreover, support of the opportunities presented by the rapid deepening and extension of global

---

36 Cited in Riés, *op cit.*
37 See Jomo KS and Shyamala Nagaraj (eds.), *Globalisation versus Development.* Hampshire: Palgrave, 2001.

markets should not be taken as unqualified: the uneven, sometimes contradictory impact of globalisation is both a cause for concern and a source of widening division. Nor should advocacy of the positive aspects be interpreted as endorsement of the current global policy regimes and institutional framework of the IMF, the World Bank and the WTO. But it is clear that the world is increasingly wealthy as a result of the improved trade and capital access facilitated by globalisation, and that it has had a positive impact on social conditions, including reducing poverty and improving gender equality and literacy. Its downsides, which include employment volatility and insecurity, and child labour, need to be identified and acted upon, though this is difficult to do when the debate is both cluttered and dominated by so many diverse special interest groups.

Asia's and Latin America's successes (and their dramatic collapses) paradoxically illustrate the ability of respective economies to operate according to these new global rules. As the UK Department for International Development (DFID) White Paper *Eliminating World Poverty: Making Globalisation Work for the Poor* argues:[38]

> [I]f well managed, the benefits of globalisation for poor countries can substantially outweigh the costs, especially in the longer term. The rapid integration of the global economy, combined with advances in technology and science, is creating unprecedented global prosperity. And this has helped to lift millions out of poverty. With the right policies, many millions more people can benefit in the years ahead. . . . If developing countries are to maximise the benefits of globalisation, they need effective systems of government and action against corruption; they need to ensure respect for human rights, and to promote security, safety and justice for all. They need to prevent violent conflict. And they need to make markets work better for poor people.

Africa's situation – like those of Asia and Latin America – is, of course, varied and heterogeneous, contrary to generally held stereotypes. Some African countries are mired in conflict; most are beset by poverty. They face different regional and health challenges. Some have liberalised their economies, some not. Some have inflation in the triple-digit margin, most have brought it down to single figures. And while

38 *Op cit*, p.19.

some have state-controlled banking sectors, most are increasingly deregulated.

These different situations demand different solutions – or at least different quantities of medicine (if, indeed, the prescription is the same).

One should focus, however, on the common factors. African states all face difficulty in attracting and retaining skills and capital. All have to deal with low growth figures and high inequalities in their societies. All contain large numbers of poor people, many without either formal education or access to health care. This is aggravated by the extreme burden placed on health services by the Aids epidemic. And all face endemic problems of low state capacity.

The Logic of State Recovery: A Virtuous Circle

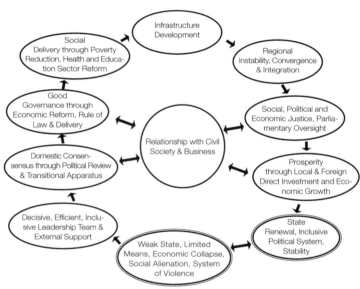

To address these common problems and to integrate prosperity, the following four-pronged formula for reform is necessary.

- Governance and state capacity should be improved, including better economic management, inclusive political participation, and strengthened institutions.
- Space should be made for private sector participation in both eco-

nomic decision-making and activity, thereby diversifying economies and improving the prospects for job creation.
• Aid conditionalities should be tightened up in the search for engagement and partnership, which should include an emphasis on local public-private infrastructure partnerships. Foreign technical assistance should be used as a monitoring mechanism.
• Government should invest in people and in civil society.

There is a critical need for two inter-related strategies: the need to modernise and the need to globalise. To achieve these mutually reinforcing goals, the costs of doing business have to be lowered, and standards of governance improved. The state has to be strengthened while, paradoxically, ceding power and shedding some of its functions. Political will and leadership are essential to bring this about. Also, the relationship with the external funding community has to be predicated on partnership and engagement, and informed by the maintenance of strict conditionalities and not by tautological self-interests.

★ ★ ★

Some might claim that Australia's treatment of its aboriginal population undermines the importance of its economic successes. This dark side of its history is today acknowledged by many Australians, both rhetorically and through financial compensation, though much remains to be done. It might also be suggested that Australia's diversity in natural resources gives it a huge developmental advantage. But the mineral-rich Congo is equally advantaged, with little of the benefit to show. And it is not that resources should necessarily benefit states. A case could in fact be made for the opposite, given that resource wealth is far less important at the end of the industrial era than it was before.

The first lesson to be derived from Australia's comparative success is, indeed, simply that natural resources are not enough; skills are required to exploit them. And if you don't have them, attract them in the form of trained workers. In Australia, immigrants make up over 20% of the population. In March 2002, Australia officially welcomed its sixth million migrant since the Second World War. The figures stood at around 70,000 annually in the 1990s. And the country is no longer an Anglo-Saxon entrepôt. Australia's cultural diversity is shown by the changing sources of migrants: 13% of Sydney's four million people were, by the mid-1990s, from Asia or the Middle East, more than twice the figure of 10 years earlier. "Number six million" is a systems analyst from the Philippines. But instead of openly welcoming such talent, African countries such as South Africa have been exporting it, to destinations including Australia. South Africans form the third largest group of business entrants to Australia, after Indonesians and Taiwanese. These migrants arrive on average with more than US$200,000 to invest, and employ on average more than four Australians.

This example demonstrates the importance to an economy of having a trained workforce (which need not be entirely local). But it also emphasises the importance of skills, and therefore the priority government should place on improving education and research.

Second, good policy, fostered within a competitive liberal democracy, is critical. There is no magic formula for success. This is as true for public services as it is for sport. Australia's admirable sporting success is the result of an enormous investment made since Australia returned virtually medal-less from the 1976 Montreal Olympic Games. Achieving success is about more than spending money, however. Australia's sporting success involves careful management of a talent identification programme, and the nurturing and support of selected athletes. Critical in all of this, too, is the need to encourage a mindset demanding excellence, not one that assumes that, for example, Africa has to take second place, and that it cannot compete with the world's best. The importance of managerial and leadership inputs into this process is crucial in sport as much as it is in business.

Third, a strong sense of national identity is another ingredient for Australia's success. While the Australian state has not had to extend its authority and define its borders through warfare, as happened in much of Europe, a national consciousness has emerged, partly as a result of the sacrifice made by more than 100,000 Australians in war (including the Anglo-Boer, First and Second World Wars, Korea and Vietnam) in the 20th century. The image of the Australian "digger" is, perhaps mythically, synonymous with national grit and determination.

Fourth, the regional environment is important. In Australia's case it is even more so, given its situation on the outskirts of the global trading routes. The success of Asia's economies from the 1970s onwards has seen a strong realignment in Australian trade and investment links towards that area. Paradoxically, its comparative international isolation meant that Australia had to develop global trade linkages well before globalisation took its current shape. Since the mid-1980s, the share of manufactures of Australia's total export of goods and services has increased from 15% to 25%, and services from 18%

to 22%. By comparison, the export of rural (farming) commodities has fallen from 31% to 21%, and of minerals and fuels from 36% to 32%. While the US share of Australia's total exports has remained more or less static at 11%, Europe's at 15%, and New Zealand's at 6%, Japan's percentage has fallen from 25% to 18% and the Middle East, Latin America and Africa from 21% to 17%. In contrast, the share of developing Asia (including China, Hong Kong, Taiwan, South Korea and the ASEAN states[39]) has leapt from 20% to 33%.[40]

Fifth, notwithstanding the above, Australia has pegged its diplomatic and security fortunes closely to those of the United States. This stems from the decision taken by then prime minister John Curtin to seek American assistance as the "keystone" of its security policy in the face of Japanese aggression 60 years ago. Australia's more recent participation in the Gulf War and its strong diplomatic and military support for US-led actions against terrorism in Afghanistan have reinforced this relationship.

Can these lessons be applied to Africa?
There is no argument to suggest why they should not. Of course African states face a more challenging regional environment, where contiguous effects cannot be shielded by geographic isolation. This emphasises, in turn, the need in Africa for engagement and diplomacy of the sort that was largely lacking in dealing with President Mugabe's disregard for the rule of law in Zimbabwe in 2002.

There is also no reason why South African, or African, business should not be as competitive, if not more competitive, than their Australian counterparts. This has already been demonstrated by South Africa's auto and mining sectors. Similarly, while political sensitivities to the importation of skills into Africa might still exist, any policy impediments can be addressed relatively easily. (Arguably it would be easier to address them than to try to get systems analysts and computer scientists to migrate to Africa.)

NEPAD's – and the West's – critics argue that there is not enough on reward for Africa's states to undertake the difficult and politically risky

---

39 Made up of Singapore, Brunei, Laos, Malaysia, Thailand, the Philippines, Indonesia, Myanmar, Cambodia and Vietnam. See also Keith Henry's Fourth Asia-Pacific Economic Co-operation (APEC) lecture, Monash University, 19 March 2002.
40 See Ross Gittins, "Are we throwing all our eggs in an East Asian basket case?", *The Age*, 23 March 2002.

business of economic and political reform. But as a formula for good governance, reform and democratisation, NEPAD makes good sense even without additional external aid and reward.

The big imponderable, however, is the nature of the state in Africa – and the response of leaders to this challenge. Many African states do not share a uniform sense of identity within their borders. Their populations are fragmented by combinations of ethnic, regional and religious differences that are, in turn, exacerbated by poverty. Yet indigence is a symptom of wider malaise in Africa, where states lack the capacity to extend authority beyond their borders. In many cases, the artificiality of borders is arguably less of a burden to African states than an asset to leadership, which has used the OAU's moratorium on their discussion to consolidate national rule.

The inability of African states to manage complex developmental challenges without conflict reflects, as this volume has shown, a core problem in the African state itself. This is that the state and its leadership are weak and insecure; its response to challenges is often through patronage, and the crowding out of private investment, divide-and-rule tactics, and external aggression. Breaking this pernicious cycle has to start with strong, single-minded leadership, and a clear, competitive policy framework within a liberal democracy.

The bottom line is simply that there are no quick fixes.

GLOSSARY

ACN	Andean Community of Nations
AGOA	African Growth and Opportunity Act
AFTA	Asian Free Trade Area
ANC	African National Congress
APEC	Asia-Pacific Economic Co-operation Forum
ASEAN	Association of Southeast Asian Nations
AU	African Union
COMESA	Common Market for Eastern and Southern Africa
CPI	Consumer Price Index
DFA	(SA) Department of Foreign Affairs
DFAT	(Australian) Department of Foreign Affairs and Trade
DFID	(UK) Department for International Development
DRC	Democratic Republic of Congo
DTI	(SA) Department of Trade and Industry
EAC	East African Community
ECA	Economic Commission for Africa
ECOWAS	Economic Community of West African States
ESAF	Enhanced Structural Adjustment Fund
ESCAP	UN Economic and Social Commission on Asia
EU	European Union
FCO	(UK) Foreign and Commonwealth Office
FDI	Foreign Direct Investment
FTAA	Free Trade Area of the Americas
FTA	Free Trade Agreements
GATT	General Agreement on Tariffs and Trade
GDP	Gross Domestic Product
GNP	Gross National Product
HDI	Human Development Index
HIPC	Heavily Indebted Poor Country
IBRD	International Bank for Reconstruction and Development
ICC	International Criminal Court
IMF	International Monetary Fund
IRIN	(UN) Integrated Regional Information Network

KMT	Kuomintang Party
MAP	Millennium Africa Recovery Plan
MERCOSUR	Southern Cone Common Market
MPLA	Popular Movement for the Liberation of Angola
NAFTA	North American Free Trade Agreement
NAI	New African Initiative
NAM	Non-Aligned Movement
NATO	North Atlantic Treaty Organisation
NEP	(Malaysian) New Economic Policy
NEPAD	New Partnership for Africa's Development
NIC	National Intelligence Council
NGO	Non-Governmental organisation
NTE	National Trade Estimate
OAU	Organisation of African Unity
ODA	Official Development Assistance
ODI	Overseas Development Institute
OECD	Organisation for Economic Co-operation and Development
PRC	People's Republic of China
PRGF	Poverty Reduction and Growth Facility
Proton	Preusahan Otomobil Nasional Berhad
SACU	Southern African Customs Union
SADC	Southern African Development Community
SADF	South African Defence Force
SANDF	South African National Defence Force
SAIIA	South African Institute of International Affairs
SAP	Structural Adjustment Programme
UK	United Kingdom
UMA	Union of the Arab Maghreb
UN	United Nations
UNCTAD	UN Conference on Trade and Development
UNDP	UN Development Programme
UNITA	National Union for the Total Independence of Angola
UNMO	United National Malay Organisation
US	United States
WEF	World Economic Forum
WSF	World Social Forum
WTO	World Trade Organisation

SELECT INDEX